D1601580

Constitutional Originalism

CONSTITUTIONAL ORIGINALISM

A Debate

ROBERT W. BENNETT AND LAWRENCE B. SOLUM

CORNELL UNIVERSITY PRESS
ITHACA AND LONDON

First published 2011 by Cornell University Press
Printed in the United States of America

Library of Congress Cataloging-in-Publication Data

Bennett, Robert W. (Robert William), 1941–
  Constitutional originalism : a debate / Robert W. Bennett and
Lawrence B. Solum.
    p. cm.
  Includes bibliographical references and index.
  ISBN 978-0-8014-4793-8 (cloth : alk. paper)
 1. Constitutional law—United States.   I. Solum, Lawrence B.
II. Title.
  KF4550.B377   2011
  342.73—dc22   2011001824

Cornell University Press strives to use environmentally responsible suppliers and materials to the fullest extent possible in the publishing of its books. Such materials include vegetable-based, low-VOC inks and acid-free papers that are recycled, totally chlorine-free, or partly composed of nonwood fibers. For further information, visit our website at www.cornellpress.cornell.edu.

Cloth printing   10 9 8 7 6 5 4 3 2 1

CONTENTS

PREFACE

Debates about constitutional originalism and its rival, living constitutionalism, are old. Originalists insist that the meaning of the United States Constitution is fixed. The words and phrases of the constitutional text have the same meaning today as they did when the Constitution was ratified by the requisite nine states in 1788 (or when each amendment was ratified). Living constitutionalists believe that the meaning of the Constitution must adapt to changes in values and circumstances. The two authors of the essays that follow clearly have different attitudes toward what is called originalism in constitutional interpretation. Lawrence Solum advocates a form of constitutional originalism; Robert Bennett's views align with a version of living constitutionalism. But the essays reveal that this contrast shrouds a host of complexities, both in the definitions of the concepts and in approaches to interpretation. Together the essays provide an introduction to the contemporary debates about the role of original understanding in constitutional interpretation.

Though the term *originalism* is of fairly recent origin, tensions between an originalist approach and living constitutionalism have been evident for a long time. For example, in *Home Building & Loan Ass'n v. Blaisdell*, Justice George Sutherland dissented on originalist grounds: "A provision of the Constitution, it is hardly necessary to say, does not admit of two distinctly opposite interpretations. It does not mean one thing at one time and an entirely different thing at another time."[1] And Charles Evans Hughes, the chief justice, authored a majority opinion that echoes living constitutionalist themes: "If, by the statement that what the Constitution meant at the time of its adoption it means today, it is intended to say that the great clauses of the Constitution must be confined to the interpretation which the framers, with the conditions and outlook of their time, would have placed upon them, the statement carries its own refutation. It was to guard against such a narrow conception that Chief Justice Marshall uttered the memorable warning—'We must never forget that it is a constitution we are expounding.'"[2]

Debates between originalists and living constitutionalists surface in ordinary judicial decisions but also in more structured debates among and between judges and commentators about judicial activism in constitutional decision making. There are many definitions of judicial activism, but a recurrent theme in much of the criticism of such activism is that activist judges are not really interpreting the Constitution. This was the launching pad for criticism of activism that Edwin Meese made in the 1980s when he was attorney general in the administration of Ronald Reagan. Meese did not use the word *originalism*—it had only recently been invented by Paul Brest, then on the Stanford Law School faculty—but both the idea and some of its ambiguities are evident in Meese's criticisms. And since Meese's foray, debates about originalism in constitutional interpretation have been a regular feature of both American politics and American academic discussion. The dueling essays of this book build on this flourishing literature.

The Reagan administration was, of course, identified with the conservative end of the contemporary American political spectrum. And in the years since Meese ignited (or reignited) debates about originalism and judicial activism, those who identify themselves as originalists have been predominantly conservative. As Solum's essay suggests, however, there is nothing inherent either in originalism or in positions on judicial activism that needs to be identified with positioning on the political spectrum. Both Bennett and Solum are convinced that this is so regardless of how one is aligned in the clash of their views on originalism.

This counsels a more general point about the growing body of literature on interpretation in the law. The literature reflects many more than two positions. This exchange introduces the subject and explores a wide range of the salient issues. We hope that it prepares the serious student for exploration more broadly, with both basic understanding of what is at stake and sophistication about many of the intriguing questions along the way.

Constitutional Originalism

We Are All Originalists Now

Lawrence B. Solum

What Is Originalism?

Debates about originalism are often full of sound and fury. Originalists rail against judicial activism. Living constitutionalists claim that originalism is nothing more than a political ideology that wraps itself in a constitutional flag. Originalists claim that respect for popular sovereignty requires contemporary courts to defer to the opinions of the framers. Living constitutionalists retort that the founding generation knew nothing of contemporary circumstances like the global Internet or the modern administrative state. Originalists argue that living constitutionalism is a thin disguise for Supreme Court decisions that are based on naked politics. Living constitutionalists argue that constitutional adjudication inevitably involves value choices and that apolitical judging is a myth. And so it goes.

If we are going to make progress in the debates about originalism, we need to transcend political rhetoric and eschew straw-man arguments. Despite political paranoia from both the Left and the Right, there are good arguments to be made both for and against various forms of originalism and living constitutionalism. Despite the claims that originalism is bunk and living constitutionalism is empty, there are serious constitutional theories advanced on both sides of the debate. The first step we need to take is to clear the ground of the thickets of misunderstanding that crowd the field of constitutional disputation. In other words, we must begin by answering the question, What is originalism?[1]

So let us begin with the question, What is the content of originalism as a constitutional theory? It turns out that there is no good answer to that question that also has the virtue of being short. The word *originalism* means different things to different people. What we call *originalism* has evolved over time into a family of related theories. But we have to start somewhere, and it may be useful to take a first look at the state of the art in contemporary originalist constitutional theory before we dig into historical evolution and contemporary variation. We can start with four core ideas that define one version of what is sometimes called the *"new originalism."*

First, at its core, originalism claims that the meaning of each provision of the Constitution becomes *fixed* when that provision is framed and ratified. But we need to be careful about the nature of that claim. When originalists claim that the meaning of the Constitution is fixed, their claim is about meaning in the linguistic sense. For example, the phrase *domestic violence* was used in the Constitution of 1789. Today, that phrase means violence within a family or spousal abuse, but that usage was unknown in 1789. At that time, domestic violence meant something like violence within the boundaries of a state, including riots and insurrections. Originalists claim that we should interpret the Constitution on the basis of the meanings that the words and phrases had back then: the fixed meaning of the Constitution cannot be altered by accidental changes in linguistic practice. Thomas Cooley, as famously quoted by Justice George Sutherland, put it this way: "The meaning of the constitution is fixed when it is adopted, and it is not different at any subsequent time when a court has occasion to pass upon it."[2]

The second idea that forms part of the core of contemporary originalism is that sound interpretation of the Constitution requires the recovery of its *original public meaning*.[3] Although the first generation of originalists focused on the original intentions of the framers, contemporary originalists believe that the original meaning of the Constitution is the meaning that the words and phrases had (or would have had) to ordinary members of the public. So when we read the Constitution of 1789, our question should be, How would an ordinary American citizen fluent in English as spoken in the late eighteenth century have understood the words and phrases that make up its clauses? To the extent that grammar and syntax are relevant, we should consult evidence of linguistic practice during that era. Our concern is not directly with the mental states of the framers. Rather, our quest is for the linguistic meaning that the words and phrases of the text had for the public (including farmers, seamstresses, shopkeepers, and even lawyers) in the 1780s.

A third notion at the core of contemporary originalism is the claim the original public meaning has the *force of law*. Originalists believe that courts and officials are bound by the text of the Constitution. To be more precise: the linguistic meaning of the text (as fixed at the time each provision was framed and ratified) is the supreme law of the land. This claim may strike some readers as obvious, but some opponents of originalism do not agree. Originalists reject the claim that the text of the Constitution is just a starting point for judges who are free to depart from the letter of the Constitution so long as they have good reasons. They reject the idea that the text of the Constitution of 1789 and its amendments is a mere symbol of the aspirations of the American people. To put things more directly, originalists believe that the text (and therefore the meaning of the text) should have binding or constraining force.

There is a fourth idea that many contemporary originalists embrace but that is more controversial than the three ideas we have just discussed. Many originalists believe that it is important to distinguish between two distinct aspects of constitutional practice: *constitutional interpretation* and *constitutional construction*.[4] The distinction between interpretation and construction is an old one made in many areas of the law. The basic idea is that there are two different steps in the process of understanding and applying a legal text. The first is interpretation. When we *interpret* a legal text, we look for its linguistic meaning. The second step is *construction*. When we *construe* a constitutional provision, we determine the legal effect of the text: in other words, *construction* enables officials to apply the text. Such application can occur in a variety of different contexts. When an appellate court engages in constitutional construction, it may fashion doctrines or rules of constitutional law. But construction can also occur when Congress or the president acts in ways that require implementation of the Constitution.

Many contemporary originalists believe that constitutional interpretation (the determination of original public meaning) must be supplemented by constitutional construction because our Constitution contains provisions that are abstract and vague. The original linguistic meaning of the phrase *legislative power* in Article I does not provide us with bright-line rules, but courts may need such rules to decide particular cases. Many originalists believe that the original meanings yielded by constitutional interpretation should constrain the doctrines produced by constitutional construction.

One last point about the interpretation-construction distinction: although this idea is controversial, some of the controversy may be a function of the kinds of misunderstandings that are almost inevitable when a new idea is introduced into theoretical discourse. In this essay, I shall claim that the distinction between interpretation and construction marks a real difference that can be ignored but cannot be denied.

In sum, our first look at originalism yields four basic ideas:

- *The fixation thesis*: The linguistic meaning of the constitutional text was fixed at the time each provision was framed and ratified.
- *The public meaning thesis*: Constitutional meaning is fixed by the understandings of the words and phrases and the grammar and syntax that characterized the linguistic practices of the public and not by the intentions of the framers.
- *The textual constraint thesis*: The original meaning of the text of the Constitution has legal force: the text is law and not a mere symbol.
- *The interpretation-construction distinction*: Constitutional practice includes two distinct activities: (1) constitutional interpretation, which discerns the linguistic meaning of the text, and (2) constitutional construction, which determines the legal effect of the text.

As we shall learn, this is not the only version of originalism. Two of these ideas—the fixation thesis and the textual constraint thesis—are accepted by almost every originalist thinker. The second idea (the public meaning thesis) and the fourth idea (the interpretation-construction distinction) characterize an important (and perhaps the dominant) strand of contemporary originalist theory. That strand is sometimes called the *new originalism*.

Politics and Constitutional Theory

Debates about originalism and living constitutionalism have been raging since the 1970s and have their intellectual roots deep in our nation's constitutional history. Should judges abide by the original meaning of the United States Constitution or look to the original intentions of the framers? Or should we prefer a living constitution that grows in response to new circumstances and changing values? Have the justices of the United States Supreme Court engaged in judicial activism or legislated from the bench? Is originalism merely political rhetoric or perhaps a kind of code for judicial conservatism? Would originalism lead to the tyranny of the dead hand, insulating the most fundamental decisions regarding our self-identity as a polity from democratic processes? Or is originalism a necessary corrective for a government by judiciary?

These are important questions, but before we can debate the merits of originalism, we need to know what we are debating about. Words like *originalism* and *originalist* and phrases like the *original intentions of the framers, original public meaning*, and *living constitutionalism* have different meanings in different contexts. Originalism may mean one thing to the proponents of originalist theory and something quite different to the advocates of living constitutionalism. Debates about originalism among politicians and pundits may have only a loose connection with discussions among constitutional theorists. Misunderstandings and confusions abound.

We want to understand originalism and its rival, living constitutionalism, in their best light—in their most sophisticated and defensible versions. In this essay, we will be looking for the best and most defensible version of originalism. And we will do the same when we examine its rival. Our focus will be on the ideas and arguments rather than the politics and rhetoric.

It turns out that it takes considerable work to extract the best version of originalism from the tangled history of debates about constitutional theory that have occupied many of our best legal minds—both in the academy and on the bench—for several decades. Contemporary American constitutional theory has been preoccupied (or even obsessed) with the Supreme Court, and especially by the changes in the Court's constitutional jurisprudence that began with the New Deal and extended through the Warren Court and its landmark decisions in *Brown v. Board of Education* (segregated schools violate the Equal Protection Clause),[5] *Griswold v. Connecticut* (laws against the use of contraception by married couples violate an unenumerated constitutional right to privacy),[6] and *Miranda v. Arizona* (requiring criminal suspects to be informed of their right to remain silent and to assistance of counsel):[7] these three decisions are really just important examples of a transformation of American constitutional law. One of the most important and controversial decisions was *Roe v. Wade*, rendered by the Court in 1972, after Warren Berger had replaced Earl Warren as the chief justice.[8] New Dealers had been sharply critical of the "nine old men" who had struck down important legislation proposed by President Franklin D. Roosevelt. Roosevelt appointed justices like Hugo Black, William Douglas, Felix Frankfurter, and Robert Jackson with the expectation that they would restrain an activist Court and reverse cases that had struck down progressive legislation. Perhaps the most controversial of these was *Lochner v. New York*, which invalidated a state statute that regulated the hours worked by bakers on the basis of the due process clause of the Fourteenth Amendment.[9] Justice Oliver Wendell Holmes, Jr., dissented in *Lochner*, famously opining, "This case is decided upon an economic theory which a large part of the country does not entertain.... The Fourteenth Amendment does not enact Mr. Herbert Spencer's Social Statics."[10]

One of the great conundrums of contemporary constitutional theory has been the tension between these two strands of twentieth-century constitutional jurisprudence. On the one hand, the lesson of *Lochner* is judicial restraint. The Supreme Court should not abuse its power by elevating the moral and political views of the justices to the status of constitutional law. On the other hand, the lesson of *Brown* and *Griswold* is that action by the Supreme Court may be required to avoid grave injustice and the infringement of fundamental human rights. The tension between these two lessons is a version of what is sometimes called the "countermajoritarian difficulty"—the institution of judicial review frequently disregards the will of democratic majorities when it safeguards the liberty, privacy, and equality of individuals.[11]

There may be no perfect solution to the countermajoritarian difficulty. Political scientists have observed that in many cases, the exercise of the power of judicial review is supported by the ruling coalition and hence by majoritarian politics.[12] Legal theorists have argued that the Supreme Court is a forum of principle and that its function is to articulate the fundamental requirements of justice that properly limit the powers of even the most democratic political process. Other theorists have joined Justice Hugo Black, who emphasized the constraining force of the constitutional text. Still others have suggested that the role of the Court should be limited to "representation reinforcement," or support of democratic institutions: the Court should use the freedoms of speech and press and equal protection clause doctrines like the one-person, one-vote rule to help democracy work but should defer to elected officials on matters of substance like contraception or abortion.[13]

Although the Warren Court rendered many decisions that have come to be almost universally admired, many of its decisions were controversial both then and now. President Richard Nixon promised to appoint judges who would be strict constructionists, and President Ronald Reagan expressed a related concern with the perils of judicial activism. During the 1970s, originalism began to emerge as an alternative solution to the countermajoritarian difficulty. The Supreme Court should restrain itself by following the original intentions of the framers of the Constitution.

So when we ask, What is originalism? we will be asking a question of constitutional theory. Our aim will be to recover the best and strongest version of originalism and then to test that theory, paying close attention to objections, criticisms, and questions. Originalism (like most strong theories) is a work in progress.

Everyone who engages in constitutional practice (judges, lawyers, officials, and citizens) or constitutional theory (students and scholars of the law) must judge originalism for himself or herself. In a constitutional democracy, every citizen can make decisions that will affect constitutional practice. For example, presidents frequently campaign on their philosophy for the selection of Supreme Court justices. Every federal official takes an oath of loyalty to the Constitution. The best thinking about originalism (from both advocates and critics) seeks to discover the truth about constitutional meaning.

The Evolution of Originalism

Originalism has evolved. One of the best ways to understand contemporary originalism is via its history. In a sense, the history of originalism goes back to the great constitutional controversies of the late eighteenth and early nineteenth centuries, but we can make sense of contemporary debates if we begin with the 1970s and early 1980s. The precursors of contemporary originalism include the law professor and later judge Robert Bork,[14] the justice department lawyer and later chief justice William Rehnquist,[15] the Reagan administration attorney general Ed Meese,[16] and the legal historian Raoul Berger.[17] These men shared a skeptical attitude toward the jurisprudence of the Warren Court; each of them was concerned with the original intentions of the framers to some degree.

Putting aside the amendments for a moment, we can focus on the Constitution as drafted in the Philadelphia Convention in 1787 and subsequently ratified by the states. The simple idea shared by the early precursors of contemporary originalism is that the meaning of the text of the Constitution is a function of the intentions of those who wrote it. As a practical matter, we could look to the records of the Philadelphia Convention; James Madison, who played a prominent role in drafting the Constitution, took notes on its proceedings. We could also look to the Federalist Papers, a compilation of what we would think of as newspaper opinion pieces that were authored primarily by James Madison and Alexander Hamilton under the pseudonym Publius. Crudely put, the idea was that the Supreme Court should approach a constitutional case by asking, What would the framers have thought about this case?

The evolution of theories is frequently driven by criticism, and this has certainly been true of originalism. One of the most important critics of original-intentions originalism was Paul Brest, who wrote "The Misconceived Quest for the Original Understanding."[18] But there were many other such critics in the 1980s. Rather than repeat the criticisms, we can get a flavor of the problems that Brest identified simply by asking several questions. (1) What mental states constituted the intentions of the framers? (2) What was the original intent if the mental states of the framers differed? (3) How do we know what the intentions of the framers were? (4) What if the framers did not form an intention with respect to a contemporary constitutional issue? These questions all address the same fundamental problem. In the case of a single speaker in face-to-face communication, the intentions of the speaker may be the meaning of what is said. But when there are multiple authors of a text that must function across decades and centuries, it is not clear that there is such a thing as the intention of the framers that could guide the application of the text to future cases. Instead, we find ourselves with fragmentary evidence of multiple and inconsistent intentions that fail to answer many of our constitutional questions.

H. Jefferson Powell identified another problem with original-intentions originalism in his famous article, "The Original Understanding of Original Intent."[19] Powell argued that the framers themselves believed that their intentions should not be regarded as binding sources of constitutional meaning. For example, James Madison withheld his notes of the Philadelphia Convention for decades after the Constitution was ratified. If Powell was right, then it might even be argued that original-intentions originalism is self-defeating. In any event, his historical findings were an embarrassment for an intentionalist understanding of original meaning.

At about the same time as these criticisms were being developed, originalist theory turned in a different direction, embracing what is sometimes called "the original understandings of the ratifiers."[20] This in turn was motivated by one of the normative arguments sometimes made for originalism: the original meaning has democratic legitimacy *because* it (and not a living constitution) was ratified by "We the People" or at least by democratically constituted ratifying conventions (in the case of the Constitution of 1789) or a supermajority of state legislatures (in the case of the amendments). Moreover, ratification was a public process, whereas the deliberations of the Philadelphia Convention were mostly secret.

But the move from intentions of the framers to understandings of the ratifiers was not successful. Much depends on what is meant by the ambiguous phrase *understandings of the ratifiers*. If this phrase refers to the psychological states of the individuals who attended the ratifying conventions held in the several states, then all the problems with original intentions reappear. There were many more ratifiers than framers. Their understandings were incomplete and often contradictory. And in the overwhelming majority of cases, we know almost nothing specific about their individual mental states.

Suppose, however, that by understandings of the ratifiers we mean their understanding of the linguistic meaning of the text of the Constitution put before them; we might call that the original public meaning. That brings us to the next phase in the evolution of originalism. It is at this point that Justice Antonin Scalia makes his first major appearance in the story. Justice Scalia has suggested that originalism would be stronger if the focus were on the original public meaning of the constitutional text and not the original intentions of the framers. Of course, the writings of the framers would still be relevant—but now as evidence of the public meaning.

The public meaning of words and phrases to ordinary readers is a function of general linguistic practice; words acquire meanings through consistent patterns of usage—or conventions. That means that the linguistic meaning of a legal text like the Constitution is a function of (1) the conventional semantic meanings of the words and phrases that make up the text and (2) the rules of syntax and grammar that combine the words and phrases. The version of originalism that focuses on these public meanings can be called *original-public-meaning originalism.*

This form of originalism focuses our attention on a wide range of sources. If we want to know what the word *commerce* meant, we could look at newspapers and diaries that used that word—even if the subject at hand was not the Constitution. Because we are looking for patterns of usage that reveal conventional semantic meanings, the best evidence would be the outcome of large-scale empirical investigation of the ways that words and phrases were used in ordinary written and spoken English.

Although there are still originalists who believe that the intentions of the framers or ratifiers are decisive, the public-meaning view is now the mainstream of originalist theory. This theoretical shift had a number of consequences, and some of these may not have been anticipated or fully appreciated by originalists themselves. Theories take on a life of their own, and this has happened in the case of originalism.

Originalists frequently rely on evidence about expectations regarding applications. We want to know what the privileges or immunities clause of the Fourteenth Amendment meant during the Reconstruction era. We find evidence of a newspaper report indicating that some group believed that adoption of this clause would result in the application of the Bill of Rights to the states—a result that we now call *incorporation.* It seems natural to say that this evidence proves that the original meaning of the Fourteenth Amendment included incorporation, but that would be a mistake. Expectations and linguistic meanings are two different things.

Unfortunately, the word *meaning* is ambiguous. When we discuss the meaning of a legal text, we can refer to any one of at least three different things. The first sense of *meaning* is linguistic meaning, the kind that dictionary definitions try (but usually fail) to capture. The second sense is purpose or teleological meaning. The third refers to implications or applicative meaning. When we ask, What does the Fourteenth Amendment mean for the question of incorporation? we are using *meaning* in the applicative sense. Original-meaning-originalism is committed to the idea that it is the public meaning of the text (the linguistic meaning) that provides binding law. Expectations about the application of the text to particular cases or general types of cases provide relevant evidence of linguistic meaning, but it is only evidence. As anyone who has ever tried to draft a statute or constitution knows, it is all too easy to be mistaken in one's assumptions and beliefs about future applications—even of a legal text that you yourself drafted.

It might be thought that evidence of original expected applications provides decisive and reliable evidence of original meaning, but the theoretical move from original-intentions originalism to original-public-meaning originalism undercuts the basis for that belief. Originalists were forced to reconsider their arguments on a variety of issues. In particular, an argument that goes directly from expected applications to a conclusion about original meaning is no longer sound. Originalist arguments must now focus directly on the linguistic meaning of particular words and phrases and on the grammar and syntax of particular clauses of the Constitution. Expected applications may still have a role to play because they provide evidence of the linguistic meaning, but they are no longer decisive.

Normative and Semantic Originalism

At a more abstract level, the shift in focus from intentions to public meaning has prompted a reconsideration of the foundations of originalist constitutional theory. Critics of originalism long contended that many of the arguments for originalism seemed to beg the question. That criticism began with a premise that appeared sound. Constitutional theory in general is a normative enterprise. If originalists want judges to adhere to the original meaning, then they need to provide arguments of political morality that answer the question, Why should I regard the original meaning as binding? Originalists have accepted this challenge and produced normative arguments (like the argument from popular sovereignty that we will examine in the next section), but in doing so, they have sometimes fallen victim to a conceptual mistake and tried to provide normative reasons for factual conclusions. The Scottish philosopher David Hume is sometimes said to have argued that you cannot derive an *ought* from an *is*; the other side of Hume's coin is that you cannot derive an *is* (a fact about the world) from an *ought* (a premise about how the world should be).[21]

It turns out that two of originalism's most important claims are not normative; rather, they are claims about linguistic facts and theories of meaning. The *fixation thesis* claims that the linguistic meaning of a text is fixed when the text is written. The *public meaning thesis* claims that the linguistic meaning of the constitutional text is provided by its meaning to ordinary speakers as determined by patterns of usage. If these claims are true, it is because they correspond to the way that language works. Arguments about the linguistic meaning of the Constitution are arguments about the way the world is: they are *not* arguments about how the world should be or how the world must be in order to satisfy the requirements of law. Arguments that seek to derive facts about linguistic meaning from normative premises commit a grave conceptual error—something we call a *category mistake*.

Of course, originalists do not limit themselves to claims about the linguistic meaning of the Constitution. They also claim that the linguistic meaning of the text is legally binding and that constitutional actors, including the Supreme Court, should respect and adhere to the legally binding linguistic meaning of the text. These claims are normative claims, and they can only be established by normative arguments. The claim that the text is legally binding is a legal claim; the proper warrant for a legal claim is a legal argument. The claim that constitutional actors should respect and adhere to the law is a claim of political morality; the proper warrant for that kind of claim would be an argument of political morality. But these are not claims about what the linguistic meaning of the constitution *is*; they are claims about what we should do *with* the linguistic meaning after we have found it.

It turns out that contemporary originalism has two parts. The semantic component rests on claims in linguistic theory and the philosophy of language. We can call that part of the theory *semantic originalism*. The normative component rests on claims of legal theory and political morality: we can call that part of the theory *normative originalism*. A fully developed originalist theory will be a union of semantic and normative originalism. A complete version will include a theory of the meaning of the constitutional text and a theory of the binding legal and moral force of that meaning.

Public Meaning

What is original public meaning and why do contemporary originalists believe that this concept is the key to the linguistic meaning of the Constitution? Answering those questions requires us to take a brief excursion into the philosophy of language.

Let's start by putting law and the Constitution to the side and asking a simpler question: How does meaning work in the case of an ordinary conversation? Suppose you and I are together in a room, and I want to communicate with you. How does that work? How do you figure out what I mean by something I say? Most of the time, meaning happens so easily and transparently that we don't take any notice of the ways we do things with words. I say, "Would you please bring me the chalk?" You see some chalk in a box and bring it to me. Voila! Successful communication. You speak English; I speak English. You know the meaning of *chalk, bring, me*, and *please*, and from my use of those terms and the context, you infer that my understanding of the terms is the same as yours. I want you to do something based on your recognition of my intention, you recognize my intention, and I know that you recognize it. You and I have *common knowledge* of my intentions.

But suppose things go a little differently. We are in a room with a whiteboard and markers. At the beginning of my lecture, I say, "I can never get used to these newfangled boards. In fact, I keep saying *chalk* when I mean *marker*. Isn't that silly?" Then, a few minutes later, I say, "Could you please bring me the chalk?" You see the markers and bring them to me: you know that when I say *chalk* in this context, I mean *marker*. You get that what I meant is not quite the same as what I literally said. In face-to-face communication, common knowledge of communicative intentions does not require that we use words in their ordinary sense. Conventional semantic meanings help, but they are not essential.

In situations like these, the meaning of words can be understood as *speaker's meaning* or in the case of a written text, *author's meaning*.[22] Intentions are the key to meaning in such cases. Communication relies on the listener's or the reader's successfully recognizing the speaker's or author's intentions. For such communication to work reliably, both the speaker and the listener must grasp the speaker's intention. That process works well in one-on-one communications, where listeners can reliably grasp the speaker's intention and the speaker can count on that fact. But it can also work in group communication as long as the context in which communication occurs includes information about the speaker's intentions that is sufficiently rich to satisfy the common knowledge conditions for the conveyance of the speaker's meaning. The key is that the speaker must be able to know that the audience will grasp the speaker's intention.

But legal texts, especially constitutions, are different. Why? Because constitutions are written by multiple authors (sometimes over an extended period of time), and they are written for multiple audiences (dispersed in space and time over vast nation-states and many generations). That means that there is no such thing as *the* intentions of the author; multiple authors are likely to have multiple and even conflicting intentions. And the readers of a constitution (who may be reading the text dozens or even hundreds of years after it was written) are unlikely to have reliable information about the intentions that do exist. In other words, the *success conditions* for speaker's meaning (which we can now call *framers' meaning*) are not met. These are the very problems that Paul Brest identified in his "Misconceived Quest for the Original Understanding."

So the idea of speaker's meaning cannot provide a general theory of the way in which communication occurs. We need an idea of meaning to account for successful communication in cases where there is no single intention or the author knows that the speaker will lack sufficient knowledge of that intention. This is where the idea of *expression meaning* (or *sentence meaning*) comes in. We use this label to express the idea that a text (an expression) can have a meaning that does not depend on common knowledge of the particular author's intention on the particular occasion upon which the text was written. Texts can have a *conventional semantic meaning* or what constitutional theorists call a *public meaning*. We can use the label *clause meaning* to refer to the expression meaning of the Constitution.

Suppose, for example, you wanted to send a message in a bottle and thereby successfully communicate with an unknown reader, perhaps in a distant land generations from now. You couldn't rely on the reader's knowing anything about you, your intentions, or the context in which you wrote the message. You would have to rely on the plain meaning of the words you used and the rules of English syntax and grammar. Of course, those meanings and rules might change over time, so it would be a good idea for you to date your message: if the reader were interested enough, he or she could check his or her assumptions about the plain meaning of your text against historical evidence of linguistic practices. Under these conditions, communication might not be perfect (or as good as a one-on-one conversation), but it is nonetheless possible. If your message is found and your reader understands the implications of the circumstances, your reader will interpret accordingly, focusing on the public meaning of the words you used at the time they were uttered and combining those meanings by the rules of syntax and grammar that prevailed as of the date of the message.

We get "messages in a bottle" all the time. Almost every day, we read scraps of texts that are detached from their authors. You see a flyer on the bulletin board of a coffeehouse. You read a memo from someone you don't know who does a job you've never heard of. You read a quotation from a post on a blog that you've never read before. When you read texts like these, your ability to comprehend their meaning depends on the conventional semantic meanings (the public meanings) of the words and phrases (the units of meaning) and the regularities of usage that we describe as the rules of syntax and grammar of English. Most of the time, you have intuitive (but imperfect) knowledge that permits you to grasp the public meaning of a text without difficulty. Sometimes, even with a conventional text, you may come up against a word or phrase you don't know. You might look it up in a dictionary, but sometimes even that will not suffice—new usages come into being every day, and some of these grow and spread and enter the public language. In the Internet age it is relatively easy to decipher the meaning of new usages because you can use a search engine such as Google to quickly survey patterns of usage. When you do this, you are engaging in the same kind of task as would be required to decipher the archaic language of a message in a bottle that was written one hundred years ago.

Writing a constitution is like putting a message in a bottle. To communicate successfully, you must rely on the public meaning of the words and phrases you employ and the standard rules of grammar and syntax. To understand what a constitution means, the reader must understand the circumstances of constitutional communication. If both the framers and the interpreters of a constitution share this understanding, then communication is possible.

Of course, the full version of the argument for the public meaning thesis will be more elaborate, employing the technical vocabulary of linguistics and the philosophy of language. But lawyers, judges, and citizens do not need to familiarize themselves with elaborate arguments or technical jargon to grasp the fundamental reason for affirming the idea that the linguistic meaning of the Constitution is the public meaning of the words and phrases as combined into larger units of meaning (phrases and sentences) by the rules of syntax and grammar. Every competent speaker of a natural language such as English already has intuitive knowledge of this point. Every one of us could figure out how to read a message in a bottle that was dated 1789—if we were willing to do the work required.

The Fixation of Meaning

What about the fixation thesis? Why is the linguistic meaning of a text fixed? Can't meanings change over time? Isn't it the case that different readers can assign different meanings to the same text? Answering these questions and others will enable us to both grasp the point of the fixation thesis and see why the thesis should not be controversial.

But before we begin, it is important to avoid a possible misunderstanding of the idea that the linguistic meaning of a constitutional provision is fixed at the time the provision is framed and ratified. The fixation thesis is a claim about linguistic meaning and not about constitutional doctrine. Many provisions of the Constitution are very general, abstract, and vague: even if their linguistic meaning is fixed, the rules of constitutional law that implement them may change over time. That is one of the implications of the distinction between constitutional interpretation and constitutional construction. A good *interpretation* aims at the fixed, original, linguistic meaning of the text. But *constructions* may and do change over time.

Why is the linguistic meaning of a text fixed at the time the text was written? If this does not seem obvious to you, consider an example that has nothing to do with the Constitution. Suppose you were reading a letter from the twelfth century that used the word *deer*. You might assume that the letter referred to the animals that we now call *deer*—a member of the family Cervidae. But if you were aware of the etymology of the word *deer*, you would know that in the twelfth century, any four-legged mammal was a deer, including the animals that we now call sheep, pigs, and horses. If you were after the linguistic meaning of the letter, you would take this fact into account. And you certainly wouldn't think to yourself, Well, the meaning of the word *deer* has changed, so the meaning of this twelfth-century letter must have changed as well. That thought would be very peculiar indeed. The meaning of the letter was fixed when it was written by the linguistic practices of the twelfth century.

Of course, the meanings of words and phrases do change, but the linguistic meanings of particular texts or utterances do not. This fact is not altered by another obvious truth: a reader's beliefs about the linguistic meaning of an utterance can change. I can believe that a text means one thing, get some new evidence, and then believe it means something else. We could call reader's beliefs about the meaning of a text *reader's meaning*. But what has changed is not the meaning of the text—what has changed is the reader's beliefs about that meaning. In the legal context, that means that courts can change their minds about the linguistic meaning or the legal significance of a constitutional provision, but those changes are not changes in the linguistic meaning of the text itself.

One final point about the fixity of the linguistic meaning of the Constitution is this. Suppose you were to reject the fixation thesis and instead embrace the view that the linguistic meaning of the text is the contemporary linguistic meaning and not the original meaning. What odd consequences your theory would have. You would be committed to the idea that accidental changes in linguistic practice would change the meaning of the Constitution. Suppose all the sick dudes started using the phrase *freedom of speech* to mean forced confession. Then in movies and on television, we might hear dialogue like the following:

JACK: That pig was really heavy on Duane—he freedom of speeched him.

JIM: I know, man. He didn't even Mirandize him before he gave him the full freedom of speech treatment.

Gradually, this new meaning might become the only contemporary meaning of the phrase *freedom of speech*, but does anyone really think that this shift in linguistic practice would change the meaning of the First Amendment to "Congress shall pass no law infringing the power of police to extract forced confessions"? Of course, some high school students might think exactly that if they read the First Amendment without any information about the change in linguistic practice. But they would be making a mistake.

A Written Constitution

Up to this point, we have focused on the linguistic meaning of the Constitution. But what about the law? Is the linguistic meaning of the Constitution binding on judges? Or are judges legally empowered to alter it? One of the core ideas of contemporary originalism is the claim that the linguistic meaning of the text has binding legal force. We call this the *textual constraint thesis.*

Notice that the claim is that judges are legally bound. That is not the same as the claim that judges always respect this legal constraint. Judges make mistakes all the time. And sometimes some judges deliberately ignore the law and make decisions that are legally incorrect. Originalists do not claim that the Supreme Court has always respected the original meaning of the Constitution, but they do claim when the Court departs from the original meaning, it is either mistaken or acting unlawfully.

Many nonoriginalists are ambivalent about the question of whether the constitutional text is legally binding. Thus they may say something like, "Well, if the meaning of the Constitution were clear, then judges and other officials would be obligated to respect it. And maybe there are some cases where it is clear; for example, the provision that gives each state two and only two senators seems pretty clear." On the other hand, some nonoriginalists seem to believe the text does not bind us in any substantial sense. For example, they might say, "If the text were binding, then the First Amendment freedoms of speech and press would apply only to Congress, because the text says 'Congress shall make no law. . . .' But the Supreme Court has applied the First Amendment to judicial action, so the text of the Constitution is not legally binding."

Why might we think the text of the Constitution is legally binding? One reason is obvious: What other point could there be to having a written constitution that declares itself the "supreme law of the land"? The supremacy clause states:

> This Constitution, and the laws of the United States which shall be made in pursuance thereof; and all treaties made, or which shall be made, under the authority of the United States, shall be the supreme law of the land; and the judges in every state shall be bound thereby, anything in the Constitution or laws of any State to the contrary notwithstanding.[23]

By its reference to "this Constitution" the supremacy clause refers unequivocally to the text of the Constitution of 1789. By stating that "this Constitution" "shall be the supreme law of the land" and limiting the authority of statutes to those that are made "in pursuance thereof," the clause places the Constitution at the top of the hierarchy of legal authority. Of course, this is all familiar to everyone who has had high school civics. The Constitution is the top dog of American legal texts.

But the fact that the Constitution says it is the supreme law of the land is not decisive, because a text cannot make itself legally binding simply by saying so. The role of the Constitution as fundamental law depends on the practices of legal officials and ordinary citizens. It might be argued that something other than the Constitution is at the top of the hierarchy, and in particular, that it is the decisions of the Supreme Court (and not the Constitution) that are (in legal practice as recognized by officials and citizens) the true "supreme law of the land." It might even be argued that the Supreme Court has the power to amend the Constitution by judicial fiat. Moreover, there is a certain sense in which this seemingly implausible and certainly radical claim is true. Even those who believe that the Supreme Court is bound by the Constitution will acknowledge that except in an extraordinary case, the Court is responsible for correcting its own mistakes. The Senate could impeach a group of justices who went beyond the limits of their constitutional authority and attempted to stage a coup d'état by judicial fiat. This surely would happen if the Supreme Court went so far off the tracks that we all began to call it crazy or tyrannical. But absent such far-fetched scenarios, the responsibility for correcting the Court's constitutional errors belongs to the Court itself.

Does our current legal practice recognize a general power of the Supreme Court to amend the constitution by judicial construction? A full and complete answer to that question would involve detailed consideration of the whole constitutional history of the United States. But some facts are telling. The Supreme Court has never claimed the authority to render decisions that are inconsistent with the constitutional text. The Court does go beyond the text in various ways. It constructs constitutional doctrines that provide specificity where the text is abstract: think of the "clear and present danger" test that implements the freedom of speech. The Court articulates principles that elaborate the structure of the Constitution when individual provisions interact: think of the separation-of-powers doctrine that constructs a relationship among the judicial power, legislative power, and executive power conferred by the first three articles of the Constitution. But implementation and supplementation are not the same as alteration and amendment.

Would a Supreme Court opinion that purported to overrule or amend a provision of the Constitution be legally valid? Originalists believe that the answer is no. If living constitutionalists believe that the Supreme Court does have this power, they surely owe us an explanation for that belief. What is the evidence for the legal validity of amendment by judicial fiat? Why is that power legitimate? And why has the Supreme Court failed to claim this power explicitly?

The Fact of Constitutional Underdeterminacy

Some critics of originalist constitutionalist theory complain that the so-called new originalism with its emphasis on original public meaning is old wine in a new bottle. These critics have a point: the shift from intentions to public meaning left two of the core commitments of originalism in place. Old originalists and new originalists agree on the fixation thesis and the textual constraint thesis: almost all originalists believe that the original meaning of the Constitution binds us today. But there are two substantial disagreements between old and new originalists. We have already discussed the first one: most old originalists emphasized the intentions of the framers and ratifiers, whereas new originalists focus on public meaning. But there is a second and perhaps more fundamental difference between old and new originalists. The new originalism embraces a distinction between constitutional interpretation and constitutional construction, whereas the old originalists do not seem to have been aware of either the distinction or its significance.

The interpretation-construction distinction marks a seismic shift in originalist thought. The old originalists believed that the original intentions of the framers provided a sort of universal solvent that dissolved every problem of constitutional interpretation. Faced with a concrete problem in a constitutional case, they operated on the assumption that the solution could be found by asking how the framers and ratifiers would have answered that question. Of course, old originalists were no fools; they understood that divining the intent of the framers and the ratifiers could be a tricky business. If opinion among the framers would have been divided, then we would need to determine the majority view. If the evidence of the framers' intentions is scanty, contradictory, or inconclusive, then we would need to determine which view is supported by the weight of the evidence—a task that often may be daunting. But after they had acknowledged these difficulties, many old originalists clung to the belief that every constitutional issue could, at least in principle, be resolved on the basis of our best estimation of the original intentions of the framers. In practice, they believed that the job of judges is to give their best estimate of the original intentions of the framers, even if the best estimate involves considerable guesswork.

In other words, the old originalists were implicitly committed to what we might call the *fact of constitutional determinacy*, which we might state as follows: the resolution of every issue of constitutional law is determined (in principle) by the meaning of the constitutional text.

The fact of constitutional determinacy has its attractions. If the original meaning of the constitutional text did resolve every constitutional issue, then originalism would provide (in principle) a perfect constraint on judicial power. Of course, that constraint would be perfect in principle but imperfect in fact because willful or lawless judges might disregard the meaning of the Constitution. And even judges who attempted to find original meaning in good faith would make mistakes. After all, the evidence of original intentions is fragmentary and inconclusive in many cases. But no theory of constitutional interpretation can be perfect in practice. If originalism provided a target at which lawful judges could aim and a standard for criticizing the decisions of lawless judges, it would have done all the work we can expect a constitutional theory to do.

One of the great weaknesses of the old originalism is the implausibility of the claim that original meaning provides a uniquely correct answer for every constitutional question. The claim seemed plausible to old originalists because they were focused on the idea that original meaning was in the heads of the founders, but once we focus on the original public meaning, things begin to look quite different. It is true that some provisions of the Constitution have a determinate original meaning, providing us with bright lines and sharp distinctions. The president must be thirty-five years of age. Each state gets two senators. We have a president but no prime minister. Congress has a constitutional obligation to establish a Supreme

Court. But many of the most important provisions of the Constitution are general, abstract, and vague: think of phrases like *legislative power, due process, freedom of speech*, and *privileges or immunities*.

The new originalism recognizes what we might call *the fact of constitutional underdeterminacy*: many of the most important questions of constitutional law are underdetermined by the linguistic meaning of the constitutional text. The original meaning of many of the general, abstract, and vague provisions of the Constitution underdetermines the outcome of a wide range of constitutional controversies. An outcome is underdetermined if the meaning is inconsistent with some outcomes but would be consistent with two or more resolutions of the case. That is, new originalists reject the radical claim that the meaning of the Constitution is indeterminate (provides no constraint), but they do not embrace the implausible claim that the original meaning provides a fully determinate answer to every constitutional question.

The idea that the Constitution underdetermines outcomes is consistent with H. L. A. Hart's famous notion of the core and penumbra. Hart's idea was that legal rules have a hard core: a zone where the meaning of the legal text clearly applies (or does not apply) to particular cases. In this respect, Hart disagreed with the American legal realists (and their heirs in the critical legal studies movement), who claimed that all law is indeterminate and that therefore judicial decisions are always a function of politics or policy preferences. But Hart also understood that some legal rules are vague or open-textured. As a result, the core of the rule is surrounded by a penumbra—a shadowy zone in which Hart thought judges have discretion to decide whether the rule does (or does not) apply. New originalists agree with Hart about the existence of the penumbra, but they may disagree about the notion that *discretion* is the right word to describe the power of judges to engage in constitutional construction in the zone of constitutional underdeterminacy.

Interpretation and Construction

Once we recognize the fact of constitutional underdeterminacy, it becomes apparent that the phrase *constitutional interpretation* is misleading if we try to use it to describe the two distinct activities that are involved in constitutional decision making. Originalist judges use a two-step process to resolve constitutional controversies. (To be more precise, we should say that the deliberations of originalist judges can be reconstructed as a two-step process, because actual deliberations frequently omit obvious steps.) The first step involves the identification of the core of the constitutional rule. Originalists believe that the core is determined by the original public meaning of the words and phrases as combined by the rules of grammar and syntax and fixed by linguistic practice at the time each provision was framed and ratified. The second step involves the determination of the applicable rules of constitutional doctrine. In some cases, the second step is trivial. If the case is in the core of original meaning or the constitutional text provides a bright-line rule, then the decision follows directly. We might say that in such cases, the construction follows automatically from the linguistic meaning of the constitutional text. But if the case falls in the penumbra— what we can call *the construction zone*—then a second activity is required. New originalists call this second activity *constitutional construction*.

The distinction between constitutional interpretation and constitutional construction is an old one. It has been traced back to the nineteenth century, and it may be older. Moreover, this distinction is quite general. Common-law judges have employed it in contract law, the law of trusts and wills, patent law, and the law of statutory interpretation and construction. The general form of the distinction relies on the simple idea that legal decision making involves both an inquiry into the meaning of legal texts and a determination of the legal effect. Thus, in the law of contracts, we ask what the contract means (interpretation) and what legal effect will be given to its terms (construction).

The relationship between interpretation and construction is different in different areas of law. In contract law, interpretation yields the terms of the contract. Construction supplements those terms with default rules: where the contract is silent, the law may provide the terms. Mandatory rules of contract law can override the linguistic meaning of the terms. Given the hierarchy of legal authority, construction of contracts, wills, and even statutes may yield legal effects that are inconsistent with the linguistic meaning of the text. Courts will construe a contract to yield terms that the parties did not contemplate but that are required by a mandatory rule of contract law. Courts will construe a statute in order to avoid a constitutional question (the avoidance canon)—even if the ambiguity would ordinarily be resolved another way. When it comes to the United States Constitution, the conventional view is that there is no "higher law" that authorizes a Court to adopt amending constructions.

The distinction between interpretation and construction marks a real difference between linguistic meaning and legal effect. The new originalists are right to insist on this distinction. Those who do not observe it are always in danger of conceptual confusion, category mistakes, and invalid arguments. But it is the distinction and not the terminology that is important. If nonoriginalists wish to distinguish between *linguistic interpretation* and *legal interpretation* or *semantic construction* and *doctrinal construction* or to use some other set of words to mark the distinction, they are free to do so. But if they insist that there is no difference between the discovery of linguistic meaning and the determination of legal doctrine, they are simply asserting something that is quite obviously false.

New originalists have been accused of introducing the interpretation-construction distinction as a rhetorical ploy: trying to steal the rhetorical high ground of interpretation and relegating nonoriginalist constitutional decision making to the low ground of construction.[24] That isn't the point of the distinction, but the discomfort of nonoriginalists may reflect a weakness in their own theory. If nonoriginalism depends on a conflation of linguistic meaning with legal doctrine, then it rests on a conceptual mistake. Nonoriginalists will want to formulate their theories in a way that takes the distinction into account if they want their positions to be defensible. But the point of the interpretation-construction distinction is not to make the absurd claim that only originalists can properly use the word *"interpretation"*: nonoriginalists are free to use the word in the broad sense that encompasses both interpretation in the narrow sense and construction.

Vagueness and Ambiguity

The distinction between interpretation and construction is closely related to another distinction that is important to originalism—the distinction between *vagueness* and *ambiguity*. This distinction is familiar to anyone who tries to be careful about his or her use of language, but the two words are sometimes used interchangeably in informal discourse. A legal text is ambiguous if it has two or more distinct senses. A legal text is vague if it admits of borderline cases. The difference can be illustrated by examples. The word *tall* is vague because there is no bright line that distinguishes a tall man (or woman) from a short one. Seven feet is definitely tall: four feet is definitely short. But an adult male who is five feet eleven in the United States is a borderline case. The word *cool* is ambiguous because it has several distinct senses: one referring to low temperature, another referring to hipness, and a third referring to not losing one's temper. The same word can be both ambiguous and vague in one or more of its senses. *Cool* is ambiguous, and the temperature-related sense of *cool* is vague.

In most cases—perhaps almost all—problems of constitutional ambiguity can be resolved by reference to context. Consider the sentence "He was a cool cat and he kept his cool despite the fact that John ignored his request to make the room cool by turning on the air conditioning." In that sentence, the ambiguous term *cool* appears three times, but fluent speakers of English will have little trouble in determining that the first occurrence involves cool in the sense of hipness, the second in the sense of holding one's temper, and the third in the sense of temperature. The sentence itself provides sufficient context to disambiguate each of the three occurrences.

When the Constitution includes ambiguous words, phrases, syntax, or grammar, we can usually disambiguate by reference to context. First, the context of any provision in the Constitution includes the surrounding words and phrases of the particular clause at issue. Second, we can resort to the relationship of a clause to the structure of the Constitution as a whole. This is the method of intratextuality (advocated by the constitutional theorist Akhil Amar), or structural interpretation.[25] In the third instance, we can resort to those aspects of the framing and ratification of a given constitutional provision that would have been available to the general public: we can call the conjunction of these three dimensions of context the *publicly available context of constitutional utterance.*

Constitutional construction is required when the meaning of a constitutional text is vague. Once we understand the original linguistic meaning of the phrase *legislative power*, we learn that the phrase is vague—with no bright lines between ordinary statutes and executive orders. After we learn that a constitutional provision is vague and that the case at hand falls into the zone of underdetermination, constitutional interpretation must make its exit and constitutional construction enters the stage.

Theories of Constitutional Construction

Originalism is a theory of constitutional interpretation. Originalists are united by their beliefs about the meaning of the Constitution. But once we move from interpretation to construction, different originalists will have different views. Nonetheless, most or almost all of them will agree that the practice of constitutional construction should be constrained by the results of constitutional interpretation. In other words, they agree on the contours of the construction zone—the space of constitutional issues where legal doctrine is underdetermined by the original meaning.

The question upon which originalists may disagree is, What are the proper methods of constitutional construction inside the construction zone? Some originalists have suggested that courts should defer to elected officials when those officials act within the zone of constitutional under-determinacy. Others have suggested that constitutional construction must preserve the legitimacy of the Constitution by construing vague provi-sions so as to preserve the basic justice of the constitutional scheme. And yet other originalists have suggested that methods of constitutional con-struction should preserve the rule of law; in a common-law system this means that construction should be constrained by precedent and by custom (widely shared and deeply held social norms) when precedent is unavail-able. Finally, some originalists believe that something like original pur-poses or original principles should guide constitutional construction.

Originalism insists that constitutional construction should be con-strained by the original meaning of the Constitution. Beyond that, the topic of constitutional construction raises questions for which originalism does not provide the answers. The original meaning of the Constitution goes only as far as linguistic meaning will take it. Whereof originalism cannot speak, thereof it must be silent.

Originalism in Practice: *District of Columbia v. Heller*

A thorough exploration of the pros and cons of originalist constitutional theory would involve extensive investigation of the application of original-ist ideas to the major problems of constitutional practice. Ideally, we would like to know how originalists would handle the constitutional rights to pri-vacy, freedom of speech and religion, and due process, as well as the ques-tions arising from the prohibition on cruel and unusual punishment, the separation of powers, federalism, and all the rest. We cannot achieve this ideal in the compass allowed by this short introduction to originalism, but we can explore the application of originalist ideas to the right to keep and bear arms, an important constitutional question upon which the Supreme Court pronounced in originalist terms.

On June 26, 2008, the United States Supreme Court handed down its five-to-four decision in *District of Columbia v. Heller*, striking down a District of Columbia statute that prohibited the possession of usable handguns in the home on the ground that it violated the Second Amendment.[26] Justice Antonin Scalia's majority opinion drew dissents from Justice John Paul Stevens and Justice Stephen Breyer. Collectively, the opinions in *Heller* represent the most important and extensive debate on the role of original meaning in constitutional interpretation among the members of the contemporary Supreme Court.

Prior to *Heller*, the Court had squarely addressed the substantive meaning of the Second Amendment on only one prior occasion. The 1939 decision of *United States v. Miller* considered the meaning of the "right to keep and bear arms."[27] The *Miller* Court held that "federal convictions for transporting an unregistered short-barreled shotgun in interstate commerce" were not invalidated by the Second Amendment absent a demonstration on the record that possession of this type of weapon "has some reasonable relationship to the preservation or efficiency of a well regulated militia." There are instances in which the Court has resolved issues regarding the Second Amendment without interpreting the meaning of the key phrase *the right to keep and bear arms*. In 1876 the Court had held that the Second Amendment applied only to action by Congress and hence did not apply to the states; subsequent decisions in 1886 and in 1894 reaffirmed that holding.[28] Given the sparse precedent, *Heller* offered an opportunity that is rare in contemporary constitutional jurisprudence: the justices were asked to write on a slate that was almost clean.

In a typical constitutional case in the twenty-first century, the Court must deal with a plethora of probative precedent. In deciding *Heller*, however, the Court was guided by only a single case that addressed the substantive meaning of the Second Amendment, and the holding of that case was clearly distinguishable in the eyes of the majority. Given the absence of constraining precedent, *Heller* has exemplary significance for investigations of the relationship between constitutional theory and constitutional practice by squarely posing the following question: How should courts determine the meaning of the Constitution when they address a novel question of constitutional meaning?

Writing for the *Heller* majority, Justice Scalia addressed the issue of constitutional method as follows:

> The Second Amendment provides: "A well regulated Militia, being necessary to the security of a free State, the right of the people to keep and bear Arms, shall not be infringed." In interpreting this text, we are guided by the principle that "[t]he Constitution was written to be understood by the voters; its words and phrases were used in their normal and ordinary as distinguished from technical meaning." United States v. Sprague, 282 U.S. 716, 731, 51 S. Ct. 220, 75 L. Ed. 640 (1931); see also Gibbons v. Ogden, 9 Wheat. 1, 188, 6 L. Ed. 23 (1824). Normal meaning may of course include an idiomatic meaning, but it excludes secret or technical meanings that would not have been known to ordinary citizens in the founding generation.[29]

The Supreme Court rarely embraces a particular theory of constitutional interpretation, but this passage in *Heller* does exactly that. Of course, it is no accident that an opinion by Justice Scalia would embrace original-public-meaning originalism. Scalia played an important role in the evolution of the public meaning version of originalist constitutional theory. Moreover, the *Heller* majority implicitly endorses the fixation thesis. The opinion consistently relies on usage and meaning at the time of the adoption of the Second Amendment as evidence of original meaning. The opinion refers to "founding era," "18th century meaning," "the founding period," "the time of the founding," "in the 18th century," "in the 18th century or the first two decades of the 19th," and "historical usage." In addition, the Court does not cite evidence of usage from other periods, such as the early twenty-first century or the fifteenth century. This strongly suggests that the majority opinion is premised on the notion that the linguistic meaning of the Second Amendment was fixed by linguistic facts—patterns of usage—at the time of utterance, not before and not after.

While Justice Scalia inquired into the semantic content of the operative clause, Justice Stevens focused on the purpose or teleological meaning of the Second Amendment. In a rough way, this disagreement corresponds to the difference between original-intentions originalism and original-meaning originalism. There is extensive evidence of an emphasis on intentions in Justice Stevens's dissent, including the following passages:

The opinion the Court announces today fails to identify any new evidence supporting the view that the Amendment was intended to limit the power of Congress to regulate civilian uses of weapons.

[T]he ultimate purpose of the Amendment was to protect the States' share of the divided sovereignty created by the Constitution.

The history of the adoption of the Amendment thus describes an over-riding concern about the potential threat to state sovereignty that a federal standing army would pose, and a desire to protect the States' militias as the means by which to guard against that danger.

The evidence plainly refutes the claim that the Amendment was moti-vated by the Framers' fears that Congress might act to regulate any civilian uses of weapons.[30]

A similar concern with purpose is mentioned (but does not play a prom-inent role) in Justice Breyer's separate dissent:

[T]he Second Amendment protects militia-related, not self-defense-related, interests. These two interests are sometimes intertwined. To assure 18th-century citizens that they could keep arms for militia purposes would necessarily have allowed them to keep arms that they could have used for self-defense as well. But self-defense alone, detached from any militia-related objective, is not the Amendment's concern.[31]

In both dissents, the clear implication is that if the purpose of the Sec-ond Amendment is militia-related, it follows that the amendment does not create a legal rule that protects an individual right to possess and carry fire-arms outside the context of service in a state militia. The majority approach is different—the primary question is the linguistic meaning of the phrase *the right to keep and bear arms*. For Justice Scalia, if the conventional seman-tic meaning of this phrase would encompass an individual right outside militia service, then the purpose for which it was adopted does not limit either that linguistic meaning or the resultant rule of constitutional law.

The *Heller* case also provides an illustration of the importance of the distinction between interpretation and construction. To see why, consider the following passage in the opinion:

Although we do not undertake an exhaustive historical analysis today of the full scope of the Second Amendment, nothing in our opinion should be taken to cast doubt on longstanding prohibitions on the possession of fire-arms by felons and the mentally ill, or laws forbidding the carrying of fire-arms in sensitive places such as schools and government buildings, or laws imposing conditions and qualifications on the commercial sale of arms.[32]

This passage is puzzling, and many critics of *Heller* question the Court's failure to justify its dicta on originalist grounds. Of course, the critics might be on to something. But there is a straightforward reading of this passage that is consistent with the new originalism's interpretation-construction distinction. Let us assume that Justice Scalia's interpretation of the opera-tive clause in *Heller* was correct and hence that the Second Amendment forbids "infringement" of a right "to keep and bear arms" that is vested in individual persons. Is that a sufficient basis for the *Heller* decision? This question is crucial, and it is not quite as easy to answer as it might seem on the surface. On the one hand, it might be argued that a ban on handgun ownership is an obvious violation of an individual right to keep and possess weapons. On the other hand, it might be argued that both infringement and the right to keep and bear arms are vague and hence that construction is required.

Let us assume that the verb *to infringe* had at the time of the framing a sense that seems identical or nearly identical to the modern sense, to commit a breach or infraction of (a law, obligation, or right). *Infringe* in this sense is vague because there will be borderline cases in which the rule or regulation may or may not be an infringement of the right. One ex-ample of such a case is gun registration requirements. A simple registra-tion requirement for which all citizens can easily apply with minimal cost seems like a clear example of a noninfringing regulation of the right to keep and possess weapons. One can imagine, however, many registra-tion requirements that would be invalid, like a registration scheme that requires the payment of a $10,000 administrative processing fee. Be-tween these points on the spectrum of burden, there will necessarily be borderline cases.

Consider next the phrase *right to keep and bear arms*. Each of the op-erative components of this phrase may have been vague, at least in some contexts. "To keep" involves questions about the borderlines of posses-sion. "To...bear" involves issues at the boundary of carrying, and "arms" involves disputed cases of weapon. Last, there is the further question of

what constitutes the operative concept of "right." Application of each of
these terms to particular circumstances may reveal the existence of borderline cases, and if there are borderline cases, then by definition these terms
are vague.

New originalists can handle the problem of vagueness by invoking
H. L. A. Hart's metaphor of the core and penumbra. One way of reading
Justice Scalia's opinion in *Heller* might be summarized as follows:

> The portion of the District of Columbia ordinance that bans possession and
> carrying of handguns is a core case of infringement of the right to keep and
> bear arms. It is infringement because a ban is the most extreme form of reg-
> ulation and therefore is within the core meaning of infringement. It reg-
> ulates arms because handguns are within the core meaning of weapon, as
> confirmed by usage at the time the Second Amendment was adopted. It
> regulates keeping and bearing because it prohibits all or almost all posses-
> sion and carrying.

On this reading of Justice Scalia's opinion, the work in *Heller* was done
by interpretation of the Second Amendment. The actual words of his
opinion come very close to our reconstruction: "We know of no other enu-
merated constitutional right whose *core* protection has been subjected to a
freestanding 'interest-balancing' approach."[33] In other words, the District
of Columbia ordinance was a core case of infringement of the individual
right to keep and carry weapons. But many other cases will be outside the
core. The puzzling dicta in *Heller* can be read as simply making the point
that the holding in *Heller* does not reach these questions of constitutional
construction—because issues of construction simply did not arise on the
facts of *Heller*.

The Supreme Court's decision in *Heller* provides a marvelous example
of the general structure of originalist thought. Justice Scalia's opinion illustrates the methodology of original-public-meaning originalism; Justice
Stevens adopts an original-intentions approach. Whatever you think of
the merits of the particular arguments made by the justices, their opinions
provide us with a model of the general methods by which originalist jurisprudence can proceed in practice.

One final word about *Heller*: all three of the opinions are controversial. Thoughtful critics of Justice Scalia's opinion believe that the Second
Amendment was intended to apply *only* to weapons used in connection

with service in a state militia. Thoughtful critics of Justice Stevens's opinion believe that he failed to offer a plausible theory of the linguistic meaning of the Second Amendment. The way to resolve the debates over the merits of the *Heller* opinions is through a close and careful examination of the evidence: appeals to the authority of eminent lawyers and historians will not do the trick. And when we examine the merits, we must be very careful about the theoretical assumptions that are frequently implicit rather than explicit in the arguments advanced by the justices and their critics and supporters. The assertion that the purpose of the Second Amendment was to protect state militias is not necessarily inconsistent with the assertion that the linguistic meaning of the text of the Second Amendment protects a general right to possess and carry weapons. This is not the right occasion for a full review of the arguments and evidence—many books and articles will be written that do exactly that. For our purposes, *Heller* is important as an example of the way that different versions of originalism can operate in practice.

An Initial Word about Precedent

What about precedent (or the doctrine of stare decisis)? Are originalists committed to the idea that decisions of the Supreme Court should no longer be afforded precedential force? Must the Supreme Court revisit the question of original meaning de novo (as if it were new) every time it interprets the constitutional text?

First things first. Originalists disagree about the relationship between precedent and original meaning. Some are deeply skeptical of precedent; others believe that the doctrine of stare decisis is an important component of the rule of law and for this reason is fundamentally compatible with originalist theory. Here are some of the views articulated by contemporary originalist thinkers:

- The Supreme Court may not follow precedents that are inconsistent with the original meaning of the Constitution, but they may give weight to precedents on matters of constitutional construction.
- The Supreme Court may not follow precedents that are inconsistent with original meaning if those precedents restrict the political rights of democratic majorities.

- The Supreme Court is bound to follow the original methods of constitutional interpretation and construction: those methods authorize the Court's reliance on precedent.
- The Supreme Court should consider itself bound by precedents so long as the precedent is lawful (in the sense that it relies on legal grounds and does not explicitly or implicitly disavow the authority of the constitutional text).

Almost everyone agrees that Supreme Court decisions can bind lower courts (the doctrine of vertical stare decisis) even though there is a range of opinion on the question of whether the Court can or should consider itself bound by its own prior opinions (the doctrine of horizontal stare decisis). As a practical matter, no originalist theorist advocates what we might call a constitutional big bang—where the Court would restore the original meaning of the whole Constitution in a single "superterm" in which hundreds of precedents that are inconsistent with original meaning would be overruled willy-nilly. As a practical matter, almost every originalist will accept the proposition that nonoriginalist precedents should continue to govern the lower courts for many years—even if the majority of Supreme Court justices were to be originalists.

Originalists who believe the Court can and should rely on precedents that are erroneous usually endorse a gradual transition to original meaning. When open constitutional questions occur, original meaning should prevail. As more originalist precedents accumulate, the foundations of erroneous precedents will gradually be eroded. At some point, precedents that cannot be sustained by originalist arguments will be so isolated that they can be contained to their own facts or even overruled. For example, if the original meaning of the interstate commerce clause were inconsistent with pervasive federal regulation of intrastate activity (e.g., consumer product safety), the transition to original meaning might begin by decisions that struck down statutes that expanded federal power by regulating areas currently governed by state law. After these decisions accumulated, an originalist Supreme Court might then gradually begin to exempt purely intrastate activity from existing legislation. Over a period of many decades, this process might result in the restoration of the original meaning of the interstate commerce clause. Eventually, Supreme Court decisions that authorized the regulation of intrastate activity might be overruled or their force might be limited to the particular statutes to which they had already been applied.

Qualifications and Clarifications

At this point, one version of originalism, original-public-meaning originalism, has been developed in broad outline. Before we proceed further, some qualifications and clarifications require our attention. The first qualification concerns the role of context in constitutional interpretation. When we investigated the difference between framers' meaning and clause meaning, we emphasized the idea that the clause meaning of the Constitution is the conventional semantic meanings of the words and phrases, combined with the rules of syntax and grammar, as they existed at the time each provision of the Constitution was framed and ratified. And we even analogized the Constitution to a message in a bottle in order to bring out the role of public meaning in constitutional interpretation. But the Constitution was not literally a message in a bottle. The framers and ratifiers knew that some facts about the context in which they acted would be available to anyone who would engage legally significant interpretation of the text. For example, the Constitution replaced the Articles of Confederation. There were states before the Constitution was adopted. They had been colonies of Great Britain, which had a monarchy and a parliamentary system. These facts and many others are part of what we can call the *publicly available context of constitutional utterance*. That context can be used in constitutional interpretation to resolve ambiguities that would persist in its absence.

The second qualification is connected to the idea that the linguistic meaning of the Constitution must be its public meaning. For the most part, that seems absolutely correct, but there are some words and phrases in the Constitution that seem to have technical meanings. For example, it might be the case that the phrase *letters of marque and reprisal* would have been familiar to seamen, officials, and admiralty lawyers but almost unknown to the general public. If this is the case, it might seem that this provision lacks public meaning. To solve this problem, we can borrow an idea from the philosophy of language, which recognizes that the meaning of some words and phrases is conveyed via the *division of linguistic labor*. Thus a Massachusetts farmer who encountered the phrase *letters of marque and reprisal* might say, "That sounds like a term of art. I'd better consult a lawyer or judge if I want to know what it means."

The third qualification is also connected to the idea that the linguistic meaning of the Constitution must be public. Some of the words and phrases in the Constitution acquired their meaning when it was adopted. Consider the phrase *House of Representatives*: taken out of context, it is ambiguous—it might to refer to a structure where representatives lived. But that is a silly interpretation because in context it is clear that the phrase refers to a new institution, the House of Representatives created by adoption of the Constitution. This meaning is stipulative: the Constitution could have used any of a number of suitable names for this body (e.g., House of Legislators). This phrase and others like it acquire their meaning via what we can call *constitutional stipulation*.

Finally, there is an important way in which the discussion of originalism needs to be clarified. Originalism might claim that original meaning must prevail come hell or high water, under all circumstances and despite the existence of an emergency or other extraordinary circumstances. There is no need for originalists to make such an extreme claim. The binding force of the original meaning of the Constitution can be defeasible, just as other binding obligations can be overridden for special or extraordinary reasons. Originalists might or might not embrace a national emergency exception to the general rule that the original meaning is legally binding. Similarly, an originalist might accept that a long-standing historical practice that has generated substantial reliance might be lawful, even though it turns out to be contrary to original meaning. Originalism must claim that the original meaning acts as a substantial constraint on constitutional doctrine, but it need not claim that the constraint is absolute and indefeasible.

A Family of Theories

We are now in a position to return to our original question: What is originalism? The best answer to that question is that originalism is a family of constitutional theories. Although originalists disagree among themselves (as do living constitutionalists), they are united by their agreement on two core ideas. First, the linguistic meaning of the Constitution was fixed when each provision was framed and ratified. Second, the original meaning of the constitutional text should be regarded as legally binding.

In other words, originalists agree that the original meaning of the constitutional text is the supreme law of the land. The family of originalist theories is organized around these two core ideas.

Originalists disagree about many other important questions. One source of their disagreement concerns the question as to how original meaning is fixed. Original-intentions originalists (the old originalists) believed that the meaning of the Constitution was fixed by the original intentions of the framers and ratifiers. Original-meaning originalists disagree, maintaining that the linguistic meaning of the constitutional text is its original public meaning, determined by the conventional semantic meanings of the words and phrases that make up the text, as they are combined by the rules of syntax and grammar that prevailed at the time each provision of the Constitution was framed and ratified. Although the debate between intentionalist and public-meaning theorists continues to this day, the weight of scholarly opinion has shifted to original-public-meaning originalism, and we have examined some of the reasons for this shift.

Originalists also disagree among themselves about the distinction between interpretation and construction. Once again, there has been a movement of originalist thought. Those who embrace public meaning have very good reasons to affirm the distinction between interpretation of the linguistic meaning of the constitutional text and construction of legal doctrines that allow the courts to apply the general, abstract, and vague provisions of the Constitution to particular cases.

Should We Be Originalists?

Our next task is to examine the foundations of originalist constitutional theory in normative legal theory and political morality. But before we begin that enterprise, we need to ask a more fundamental question: What kind of justification does originalism require? Viewed from the perspective of legal practitioners (judges, lawyers, and others who take up what H. L. A. Hart called "the internal point of view" toward the law),[34] originalism is supported by good and sufficient reasons if two things are true: (1) the linguistic meaning of the constitutional text is its original public meaning; (2) the text of the Constitution has the force of law.

From the external perspective, we can ask questions such as the following. (1) Should we regard the constitutional text as legally authoritative?

(2) Should we change our fundamental rules of constitutional law so as to give the Supreme Court the power to override or amend the Constitution by judicial fiat? (3) Should we recognize constitutional principles (or principles of natural law) that are superior to those expressed in the written Constitution? Those are important questions, but normal constitutional practice puts those questions to the side. Our constitutional practice assumes that the written Constitution has the force of law, that the Supreme Court may not amend it, and that natural law principles do not authorize judges or officials to depart from it.

From the internal point of view, originalism does not require justifications that come from outside the law. When originalists take up this perspective, their argument is that the original meaning of the Constitution is the law, and thus all those who take themselves to be bound by the law should heed the original meaning. But the internal validity of originalism as a theory of the law does not answer the question, Should we be originalists? That question is relevant to every citizen (and to legal officials in their capacity as citizens and lawmakers), as is the more general question, Should our Constitution be amended or is it good enough as it stands?

What kinds of justifications could be offered for originalism as a matter of political morality? That question is simply a variation of a much more general question: How can we justify our political institutions (or the basic structure of our society)? These questions will immediately lead to others. What is political legitimacy? What makes a society just? And those questions in turn raise others. Is democratic participation or acceptance by a majority necessary for political legitimacy? Under what circumstances do considerations of justice trump the democratic will of the majority? Indeed, our quest for the normative foundations of originalism can lead us to the deepest questions of morality. What is the nature of the good? What are our obligations to one another? What kind of people (and what kinds of citizens) do we want to be?

It may well be that these deep questions must be answered for us to determine whether we should affirm originalism as a theory of constitutional interpretation, but if that is the case, we ought to put the search for normative justifications for originalism (or living constitutionalism) aside and turn to the study of moral and political philosophy. Is there some other way to proceed? We might focus our discussion on principles, reasons, and arguments that reasonable citizens can accept despite their disagreements about the deep premises of morality and religion. Let us use the term *public reasons* to designate the premises upon which reasonable citizens might be asked to agree.[35] Of course, not every citizen will agree with every premise: our strategy is to focus on facts about social and political life that are not deeply contested and on values that are drawn from the public political culture and that are accessible to our fellow citizens who acknowledge the need for a shared basis of political discussion.

With those thoughts in mind, we can reformulate our question: Can originalism be justified by public reasons? In answering this question, we will rely on values like the rule of law, democracy, and the core elements of political justice that are already the subject of wide agreement. We will avoid reliance on deep theories of morality or particular religious doctrines. We will aim for an overlapping consensus among the disparate groups that make up our pluralist society in the early twenty-first century. Ideally, the justification for originalism should speak to liberals and conservatives, progressives and libertarians. The hope is that fundamental constitutional practices can serve as the basis for agreement. If agreement is not possible, then we should aim to narrow the range of disagreement.

The first and perhaps the fundamental justification for originalism is rooted in the idea of the rule of law.[36] The value of the rule of law is widely accepted in contemporary democracies. The associated values of certainty, predictability, and stability of law are widely endorsed as among the most important values in a well-functioning constitutional order. It is not difficult to discern the mechanism by which originalism contributes to the rule of law: treating the original public meaning of the Constitution as the supreme law of the land is the means by which the core principles of constitutional law can be fixed and thereby insulated from ideological and political struggle. Of course, the rule-of-law argument is, by its very nature, comparative. Originalism is not the only method for securing the rule of law: the same task could be accomplished by other means. When originalists claim that originalism enhances the rule of law, they implicitly compare it with some versions of living constitutionalism that explicitly or implicitly endorse the politicization of constitutional law.

The argument for originalism from its contribution to the rule of law can proceed by answering four questions: (1) What is the rule of law? (2) Why is the rule of law valuable? (3) How does originalism safeguard the rule of law? (4) How can some nonoriginalist modes of constitutional practice damage the rule of law?

What is the rule of law? A. V. Dicey's historically influential formulation of the rule of law incorporated three ideas: (1) the supremacy of regular law as opposed to arbitrary power; (2) equality before the law of all persons and classes, including government officials; and (3) the incorporation of constitutional law as a binding part of the ordinary law of the land.[37] We might add the following to Dicey's list: (4) the law should be public, and its meaning should be clearly defined.

Why is the rule of law valuable? Democratic societies embrace it for many reasons. The rule of law constrains arbitrary power and acts as a check against the abuse of power, which can take many forms, from high tyranny to petty corruption. The rule of law, when combined with reasonably just legal norms, can secure a zone of individual liberty or autonomy. It may be instrumentally valuable for the effective functioning of markets and public institutions. It can serve these ends because it functions to create predictability, certainty, and stability. It enables us to predict the legal consequences of our actions, to have epistemic confidence in our beliefs about the content of the law, and to rely on the continuity of legal norms.

How does originalism safeguard the rule of law? The answer to this question goes to the underlying rationale for a written constitution. It is possible to have an unwritten constitution: Great Britain has one, and it functions well. Nonetheless, having a written constitution serves several of the functions identified as constitutive of the rule of law. A written constitution serves as an explicit limit on arbitrary power by providing a public standard by which the legality of actions by high government officials can be judged. It serves as the vehicle for making constitutional norms a binding part of the ordinary law of the land. The United States Constitution does this explicitly via the supremacy clause, which explicitly establishes "[t]his Constitution" as "the supreme law of the land." A written constitution also serves the function of publicity—precisely because it is written, widely distributed, and hence easily consulted by any citizen.[38]

At this point, the opponents of originalism will surely object. Yes, they might say, a written constitution does serve the rule of law, but that writtenness does not entail originalism—and they are right, for the relationship is not one of entailment or logical necessity. The point about originalism is that it creates a fixed connection between the linguistic meaning of the written text and the legal rules that implement that meaning. Originalism takes the meaning of the text (a meaning that is fixed by linguistic practice at the time the text is written) and then uses that meaning to constrain the content of legal doctrine. Linguistic meaning is the tool that originalist constitutional practice can use to create legal rules with a stable core of fixed meaning.

All the alternatives to originalism advocated by nonoriginalists lack the capacity to generate constitutional rules with a stable core of fixed meaning. When it comes to the expression of legal rules, the only tool we have is language. What enables us to fix the content of legal rules by writing them down is the fact that our writings are not mere marks but convey publicly accessible meanings. Any theory of constitutional interpretation that says that the legal meaning of the Constitution is not constrained by the linguistic meaning of the text is, by its own terms, a theory that denies that there is a stable core of fixed meaning. There is no alternative to the linguistic meaning of the text to do the necessary work. If you deny that the original public meaning constrains constitutional interpretation, the necessary implication is that interpretation lacks a stable core of fixed meaning.

Many critics of originalism will concede this point. After all, they are criticizing originalism precisely because originalism fixes meaning and creates stability, predictability, and certainty. Complaints about the dead hand of the past and the unsuitability of eighteenth-century practice to modern conditions are premised on the fact that originalism produces stability by fixing the core content of constitutional doctrine.

In the next section, we will investigate the relationship between originalism and living constitutionalism. We will learn that living constitutionalism, like originalism, is a family of theories. Some members of that family are consistent with originalism, but other versions of living constitutionalism are true rivals of original-public-meaning originalism. Imagine a living constitutionalist who believes that the content of constitutional doctrine should not be strongly constrained by the original public meaning of the text—although original meanings and purposes might be one of several factors that can legitimately be considered in the process of constitutional decision making, along with precedent, public opinion, the views of the political branches, and the judge's own values. This version of living constitutionalism is not utterly lawless: indeed, consideration of the effect of a doctrinal shift on the predictability, certainty, and stability of the law could be one of the considerations brought to bear by a living constitutionalist judge. For the sake of convenience, let us call this version of living constitutionalism *pragmatic living constitutionalism.*

How do originalism and pragmatic living constitutionalism compare with respect to the rule of law? Both theories are capable of sustaining the rule of law to some degree. Adherence to originalism guarantees a stable core of fixed constitutional meaning. Pragmatic living constitutionalism cannot provide such a guarantee—because it explicitly endorses the power of judges to override the original meaning of the text for pragmatic reasons. Such a power would not exist in a political vacuum. Presidents and senators would have powerful incentives to appoint Supreme Court justices who would use this power to entrench their policy preferences as rules of constitutional law. Likewise, if the president and Congress had policy preferences that would require violation of the stable core of fixed constitutional meaning, the appointment of pragmatic judges who shared those preferences might enable circumvention of the Constitution— although history teaches us that it might not. Politicization of the Supreme Court would tend to undermine central components of the rule of law—and especially the ability of the Constitution to constrain powerful political forces. One thing is certain: measured against the rule of law, originalism bests pragmatic living constitutionalism as a strategy for maximizing the predictability, certainty, and stability of legal rules.

Critics of originalism may argue that originalism is unnecessary for maintenance of the rule of law. One variation of this argument begins with the premise that the current Supreme Court is not consistently originalist but that the rule of law prevails. More generally, it might be argued that the rule of law requires a minimum threshold level of predictability, certainty, and stability in the law—and that this threshold can be met by adherence to precedent and pragmatic case-by-case consideration of the value of the rule of law. Perhaps it can, but this argument goes awry to the extent that it assumes that the status quo already recognizes the power of the Supreme Court to nullify or amend the Constitution on the basis of pragmatic considerations. No opinion of the Court asserts that power, and no nominee to the Court has ever affirmed the existence of such a power. It is possible that a majority of the Court has, on rare occasions, made a decision with full knowledge that it was effectively amending the Constitution, but the effective ability of the Court to engage in lawless behavior may well depend on the Court's public affirmation of a duty to obey the Constitution and its conformity to that duty in the overwhelming majority of cases. There is no good reason to believe that the Court could remain insulated from naked partisan politics of the worst kind were the justices to openly affirm the amending power implied by pragmatic living constitutionalism.

Critics frequently claim that the rule of law can be preserved without adherence to the stable core of constitutional doctrine guaranteed by adherence to originalism. But we do not have to take them at their word. We can ask for explanations. Which particular nonoriginalist theories guarantee the rule of law? How do they provide that guarantee? Would that mechanism work given the incentives it would create for political actors? These are serious questions, and anyone who contends that there is a rule-of-law-preserving alternative to originalism should give them serious answers.

Popular Sovereignty and Democratic Legitimacy

If there are any values that are widely shared in contemporary America, popular sovereignty and democratic legitimacy are surely among them. Lincoln declaimed, "[G]overnment of the people, by the people, for the people, shall not perish from the earth." The preamble of the Constitution begins, "We the People of the United States, in order to form a more perfect union, establish justice, insure domestic tranquility, provide for the common defence, promote the general welfare, and secure the blessings of liberty to ourselves and our posterity, do ordain and establish this Constitution for the United States of America." If "We the People" established "this Constitution," then judicial amendment or nullification might be thought to thwart popular sovereignty and undermine democratic legitimacy.

Of course, it is not as simple as that. When courts enforce the original meaning of the Constitution, the result may be contrary to the will of the majority as expressed by their elected representatives (or, in the case of direct referenda, as expressed by the people themselves). Although there are cases where the original meaning of the Constitution will support democratic decision making, there will be many cases where enforcing the commands of "We the People" (circa 1789) will frustrate the desires of "We the People" (circa today).

Nonetheless, there is an important sense in which the original meaning of the Constitution expresses the will of the people but ordinary legislation does not. In a representative democracy such as ours, political institutions are (at best) an imperfect reflection of the true preferences of the citizenry.

The majority of citizens do not vote. Those who do vote are frequently unaware of the likely consequences of their ballots. Special interests dominate ordinary politics through lobbying, campaign donations, and the weak institutional structures of many legislative and executive institutions. The political branches are truly *political*, but that does not imply that they are deeply *democratic*.

By contrast, the Constitution was adopted through an intensely democratic process. Of course, that process was imperfect, even by the standards of the day; by contemporary standards, the ratification process was woefully inadequate because of the exclusion of women, slaves, and white males who did not meet the property qualification. Despite these imperfections, the creation of the Constitution represented the most democratic process for establishing the basic institutions of government that had occurred up to that time. If democratic legitimacy is measured by the limits of the possible (and not by the dreams of the ideal), then the ratification of the United States Constitution must count as one of the most profoundly democratic moments in human history.

The connection between democratic legitimacy and original public meaning is so close and the argument for that connection so obvious that very little needs to be said about it.[39] The original public meaning is the meaning that was ratified. The notion that the people could ratify constitutional meanings that had not yet come into being when the ratification conventions were held is difficult to formulate as a coherent claim. If a democratic majority wants to establish rules that will bind their agents in the legislative, executive, and judicial branches, the only tool with which they can accomplish that goal is language. The meaning of the language that the people use is the original public meaning—not meanings that arise decades or centuries later because of changes in linguistic practice, not meanings that are invented by judges, and not the meanings that that can be produced by complex argumentative practices.

Constitutional amendment is difficult, perhaps too difficult, but that difficulty does serve popular sovereignty in one profoundly important respect. The requirement that constitutional amendments be proposed by two-thirds of both houses of Congress and be ratified by three-quarters of the legislatures of the several states ensures that there will be multiple opportunities for democratic participation and popular input before ratification. If the opportunity to participate is the key to democratic legitimacy, then the notion of public meaning is the key to meaningful participation. The people can participate in the making of their Constitution only if they have access to the meaning of the text: fixing the original public meaning enables that access.

The relationship between original public meaning, popular sovereignty, and democratic legitimacy is frequently misunderstood. The advocates of originalism sometimes advance a naive picture of the Constitution as the product of a fully engaged democratic majority. Opponents of originalism sometimes rely on an equally naive conception of ordinary legislation and its implementation in the modern bureaucratic state. Once we clear the brush, a more subtle view of the relationship emerges. Original public meaning is the enabling condition for democratic participation in constitutional politics given the institution of a written constitution.

Supermajorities and the Difficulty of Amendment

Article V of the Constitution establishes procedures for amendment:

> The Congress, whenever two thirds of both Houses shall deem it necessary, shall propose amendments to this Constitution, or, on the application of the Legislatures of two thirds of the several states, shall call a convention for proposing amendments, which, in either case, shall be valid to all intents and purposes, as part of this Constitution, when ratified by the legislatures of three fourths of the several states, or by conventions in three fourths thereof, as the one or the other mode of ratification may be proposed by the Congress; provided that no amendment which may be made prior to the year one thousand eight hundred and eight shall in any manner affect the first and fourth clauses in the ninth section of the first article; and that no state, without its consent, shall be deprived of its equal suffrage in the Senate.[40]

There are two procedures here. The first requires proposal by two-thirds of both the House and the Senate and ratification by three-quarters of the state legislatures. The second procedure begins with an application from two-thirds of the state legislatures, followed by a constitutional convention that proposes amendments, again followed by ratification upon the concurrence of three-quarters of the legislatures of the several states. Although it might be technically possible for a constitutional amendment to become law with votes from the representatives of a minority of the American people, all the likely scenarios require a substantial supermajority that persists over time. The Article V process has resulted in twenty-seven amendments—all of them proposed by Congress and ratified by the states.

Article V makes amendment difficult, and as a result there have been very few truly transformative amendments to the Constitution. The first ten are now seen as profound, although their chief architect, James Madison, believed they were largely redundant. The Reconstruction amendments (the Thirteenth, Fourteenth, and Fifteenth) substantially changed the constitutional structure. The Seventeenth Amendment, which provided for the direct election of senators, consolidated populist practice and ended direct representation of the states in the national government. The remaining amendments involve changes that vary in importance and impact. The enfranchisement of women was profoundly important; the rules of succession to the presidency, although significant, are of little systematic import in constitutional practice.

One argument against originalism is that the Article V amendment process is so cumbersome that it created a need for an alternative mechanism of constitutional change. In the absence of a reasonable procedure for formal amendment of the Constitution, an informal mechanism was created—amendment by Supreme Court decision. One version of this story, told by Bruce Ackerman, focuses on "transformative appointments" to the Supreme Court, supposedly made by President Franklin D. Roosevelt.[41] Another version of the story emphasizes the role of political movements who mobilize around proposals to give the Constitution "new meaning."[42] The participants in these movements may not fully realize that they are advocating constitutional change rather than constitutional restoration, but popular mobilization can, in time, create pressures for the nomination and confirmation of justices that the political branches will find hard to resist (or so the story goes).

Does the difficulty of amendment justify the Supreme Court's assuming a power to amend the Constitution outside the formalities of Article V? If you put the question like that, the popular answer to the question is surely no. But if you ask individual Americans about the desirability of particular decisions that may be the functional equivalent of constitutional amendments, the answer might be yes. This leads to a side dispute between originalists and nonoriginalists about who gets to claim the sacred cows, the most revered decisions of the Supreme Court of constitutional jurisprudence for their own. Living constitutionalists have argued that *Brown v. Board of Education*[43] is a nonoriginalist decision,[44] but many of the most prominent originalists have produced powerful (and to this author's mind convincing) arguments that the outcome (but not the reasoning) in *Brown* was entirely consistent with the Fourteenth Amendment.[45] Let us put *Brown* aside for now and consider the more general question: Should the power to amend the Constitution be limited to the procedures of Article V?

No one should doubt that there are substantial advantages to supermajoritarian procedures for constitutional change. James Madison famously warned of the dangers of "faction" (we would say "special interest groups") in the Federalist Papers.[46] He hoped that the creation of a national republic would disarm special interest groups—that the large scale of national politics and local nature of special interests would combine to prevent a coalition of factions from logrolling special interest legislation (including what we call pork barrel spending or just plain pork) through Congress. Madison was wrong. Indeed, there is an entire subdiscipline of economics (public choice theory) that takes as its field of study the various ways that factions capture and control the institutions of government to extract private benefits (which economists charmingly call "rents") from their fellow citizens.

Supermajoritarian procedures tend to defeat special interest groups. It is a notable fact about the United States Constitution that it is almost entirely free of provisions that are designed to benefit a combination of special interest groups at the expense of the public interest. But if a simple majority of the Supreme Court could amend the Constitution, the task of special interests would be much simplified. Five votes could be obtained with greater ease than could the votes of 66 senators, 291 representatives, and thousands of state legislators. Putting the problem of faction aside, it does seem reasonable to believe that a horrendous constitutional error (an amendment of passion or a well-intentioned proposal with disastrous unintended consequences) would be more likely to slip past five justices than to make it through the cumbersome, difficult, and time-consuming process prescribed by Article V.

In short, there are costs and benefits of the Article V process. It makes amendments difficult but not impossible. On balance, most Americans seem to think this is a good thing. The calls for amending Article V itself—to permit a simpler, more majoritarian process of constitutional amendment—have never gotten very far, and there is no evidence that such proposals enjoy much popular support. Political scientists and economists may debate the question whether supermajoritarian procedures for amendment produce better constitutional law (or prevent the adoption of truly awful amendments). But so far as I know, there is no substantial body of systematic research that argues that vesting the amendment power in a simple majority on a council of constitutional revision with nine members appointed for life is the best institutional design. Indeed, it seems rather unlikely that anyone would get on board for such a proposal if it were required to fly under its true flag.

The Question of Justice

We come now to the most serious objection to originalism—an argument that lurks beneath the surface of constitutional theory but poses a profound challenge for originalists. Is the original meaning of the Constitution so fundamentally contrary to justice that the Supreme Court must be given authority to amend it? This question has special urgency because most constitutional scholars believe that the Constitution as it existed before the Thirteenth Amendment sanctioned and protected the institution of slavery—an injustice of the very highest order. The famous abolitionist William Lloyd Garrison called the United States Constitution "a covenant with death, an agreement with hell."[47] Virtuous citizens and officials in an evil society have a moral obligation to end the evil; if that requires Supreme Court justices to amend the Constitution and dissemble while they do it, then so be it. No one should think that any theory of constitutional interpretation can solve the problem of a fundamentally evil regime—that problem requires action of a kind that is outside the scope of theories of constitutional interpretation.

Before we leave the topic of slavery, we ought to note that the constitutionality of slavery was hotly contested. The brilliant antebellum abolitionist and constitutional theorist Lysander Spooner argued that the Constitution not only did not sanction slavery but, on the contrary, effectively forbade the enslavement of human persons.[48] The key to Spooner's argument was original public meaning: the framers did not dare to use the words *slave* or *slavery* in the Constitution. The question whether slavery was ultimately compatible with the Constitution of 1789 is hotly contested even today, but for our purposes the interesting point is that the case against its constitutionality had to rest on public meaning, given the obvious fact that no one expected slavery to be declared unconstitutional by the Supreme Court in the early years of the republic.

Our Constitution no longer sanctions slavery: the Thirteenth Amendment forbids slavery and gives Congress the power to outlaw its badges and incidents. The worst evil of the post-Reconstruction era was Jim Crow: segregation was the American apartheid, an evil regime of oppression. Most originalists believe that *Plessy v. Ferguson*[49] was contrary to the original public meaning of the Constitution and that *Brown v. Board of Education*[50] reached the right result but for the wrong reason. But even if we suppose that originalists are wrong and that the Reconstruction amendments allowed state-sanctioned segregation, that fact would not settle the originalism debate. Constitutional theorists of every stripe must confront the possibility that their preferred method of constitutional interpretation will sanction horrendous evil. On those occasions, it is the law that must give way—and not our theories of constitutional meaning. If *Brown* could not be justified on originalist grounds, and if a unanimous Supreme Court decision was the best or only means to end the evil of segregation, then the justices were right to adopt what amounts to an unlawful judicial amendment to the Constitution. But that does not suggest that an amending power should then become the norm and adherence to constitutional meaning the exception.

But what about the general question: Should the Supreme Court have the power to adopt amending constructions of the Constitution on the grounds that the justices believe that the cause of justice will be served thereby? If the Supreme Court were truly composed of Platonic guardians, each with both the right view of justice and the wisdom to know when judicial action would effectively achieve justice in a complex world, granting them this power would have a powerful attraction. Comparing the imperfect institutions of the actual world with the perfection of ideal theory will always favor the latter. But that would be comparing apples and oranges—or more to the point, perfectly ripe and juicy pears with moldy desiccated peaches. The question we face is whether we should give the actual Supreme Court, composed of imperfect individuals selected by an imperfect political process, the general power to override the original public meaning of the Constitution on the basis of the individual justices' beliefs about justice.

Should we give the actual Supreme Court that power? The power to enact Mr. Herbert Spencer's social statics[51] if that is their view of justice? The power to enact Mr. John Rawls's difference principle[52] if that is their view of justice? The power to limit the powers of government to those of Mr. Robert Nozick's night-watchman state[53] if that is their view of justice? The power to amend the Constitution on the basis of the views of Rousseau or Hobbes, Marx or Hegel, Obama or Bush, Henry Wallace or George Wallace, Al Franken or Rush Limbaugh? Of course, the advocates of the Supreme Court as a forum of principle will insist that the power they would grant the Court is the power to do justice—real and true—and not the power to impose their political ideology on the rest of us. But that is no answer. There is no direct line between the Platonic Ideal of Justice in the Heaven of Legal Concepts and the chambers located at One First Street N.E. in Washington, DC. The power to do justice is the power to do what one believes is just. And beliefs about the nature of justice vary widely, especially in early twenty-first-century America.

This brings us to the crux of the matter. Arguments about the power of the justices to override the Constitution on the basis of their beliefs about justice have an unnerving quality. Participants in these debates seem to switch sides, depending on the chances that their views will gain ascendancy on the Court. When our political enemies control the Court, we are in favor of judicial restraint and strict construction. When our friends are in the ascendancy, our hearts warm to the prospect of an activist court and dynamic interpretation. We should be fair. Those who stand on principle can be found on both sides of the aisle—literally in Congress and figuratively in newsrooms and ivory towers. Likewise, hypocrisy is a vice that respects no ideological boundaries.

The real point of our ambivalence at the prospect of a Supreme Court that is explicitly empowered to do justice is what that ambivalence says about the question whether we have sound reasons to endorse such a power in theory. If you were behind a veil of ignorance that deprived you of information about the current and likely future makeup of the Supreme Court and the institutions that appoint it, would you choose to populate the Court with justices who affirmed the view that their own beliefs about the requirements of justice could override the constitutional text? If your answer to this question is no, then you do not believe in the justice-trumps-text view as a normative theory of constitutional interpretation. Whether you would endorse that view as a matter of political expediency when the veil of ignorance was lifted is a different matter.

The value of the rule of law is very great, and under a wide range of political circumstances the rule of law and justice go hand in hand. But not in all circumstances. If the history of the United States in the nineteenth and twentieth centuries teaches us anything, it is that great evil can happen here. When the law is on the side of evil, then we must be against the law. If you believe that the words and phrases that make up the operative text of the Constitution of the United States are on the side of evil, then you should not be an originalist. But if you believe that the Constitution we have is imperfect but reasonably just and that the rule of law is of very great value in those circumstances, then the idea of the Supreme Court unbound by law should give you pause.

Political Realities and Legal Realism

Even if originalism is a good idea in theory, can it work in practice? Are the judges and officials who interpret the Constitution capable of setting aside their preferences and political ideologies when faithful adherence to the constitutional text would require them to do so? Can presidents and senators overcome the temptation to appoint political judges who will advance their ideological agendas?

These questions about the practicality of originalism are important ones. In 1920s and 1930s, the American legal realists mounted a critique of what they called "mechanical jurisprudence" or "formalism."[54] They argued that considerations of policy and social interest were the driving forces of legal decision making. At their most radical, the realists and their contemporary heirs in the critical legal studies movement argued for the indeterminacy thesis—the claim that almost any decision one might imagine could be justified on the basis of perfectly respectable legal arguments. Political scientists have reinforced these claims with both empirical research and rational-choice modeling. The attitudinalist school contends that the best predictor of the outcomes of Supreme Court cases is the political ideology of the justices. Positive political theory constructs game theoretical models of the Court and the process of judicial selection that predict that political ideology will drive the selection of justices and the decisions they make. If this were all true, then normative constitutional theory would be more or less irrelevant and inexorable political forces would determine the decisions of the Supreme Court.

This dismal view of "judicial politics" (as political scientists are wont to call the study of legal institutions) appeals to the cynic in all of us. But is this one-dimensional and mechanistic view of the legal process true to the complex realities of real-world legal systems? There are good reasons to doubt that it is. In the grand sweep of human history and in the light of judicial practice across the globe, the theories advanced by the American legal realists and their heirs are aberrational. For most of human history and in most of the legal systems of the developed world, the ability of judges to follow the law has been accepted in theory and demonstrated in practice. Outside the halls of the legal academy, the proposition that there is no such thing as following a rule rings hollow—because ordinary people successfully understand and follow written rules all the time.

The fact that written texts that communicate rules can function to regulate human behavior does not depend on the absurd notion of a mechanical jurisprudence that was the favorite whipping boy of the American legal realists. No one thinks that rules apply themselves or that the application of general legal rules to particular facts works like a fantastically complicated Rube Goldberg machine. Originalists do not deny the role of judgment and perception in mediating between the language of the constitutional text and the complex factual settings of particular constitutional cases. In some cases, constitutional commands are straightforward and the relevant facts are clear-cut. In other cases, discovering the meaning of the Constitution may require the resolution of thorny questions of interpretation. The factual record may be contested and complex as well. Some cases are easy; others are hard. Judges are human, and in hard cases even the most careful judges may be unable to completely escape the biasing effects of their politics. But the inescapability of bias at the margins should not obscure the fact that judges (like ordinary people) have the capacity to follow the law in a wide range of circumstances.

But even if most judges have the ability to follow the law and many judges are disposed to do so, it might nonetheless be the case that the judicial selection process will populate the Supreme Court with justices who are reliably disposed to vote their politics and ignore the Constitution.

Perhaps the judicial selection process is a prisoner's dilemma. Here is how it might go. Suppose that conservatives select ideological judges when they control the presidency and liberals select neutral judges who adhere to the Constitution—in the long run, the Court will tend to make ideological decisions with a conservative bias. Liberals know this, and they know that conservatives can see this as well. So liberals will appoint liberal ideologues to the Court. But conservatives know that liberals will do this, and therefore conservatives will appoint conservative ideologues. The result: a Court populated by ideological extremists who vote their ideology and ignore the Constitution.

But this picture is too simple. The judicial selection process is not a game played solely by extremists of the Right and Left. The first-past-the-post system of elections tends to produce presidents and senators who (on average over the long run) approach the political valence of the median voter. (In the Senate, this will be true of the "median senator," i.e., the senator whose political ideology is at the midpoint of the hundred members of that body.) Nomination and confirmation of a Supreme Court justice require the concurrence of the president, the majority of senators (whose votes are required for confirmation), and the tacit concurrence of at least sixty senators (the number required to end a filibuster). This means that when there are forty-one senators who are not aligned with the president, nominees who will move the Court toward the political extremes will not be confirmed. Perhaps the justices will be ideologues, but at least they will be moderate ideologues.

But wait! Once again, this picture is too simple. There are two ways to produce moderation. Decisions can be moderate and ideological: this occurs when a judge from the ideological center votes her politics. But there is another way of producing moderate decisions. Judges who follow the law will tend to produce moderate decisions because their decisions will tend, on average, to reproduce the mean political valence of the law as a whole—the average political effect of all the constitutional, statutory, and precedential rules. Given the ebb and flow of politics and the institutional structure of American government, the average political effect of adhering to the law is moderate. Of course, the two effects interact synergistically; the best way to guarantee judicial moderation is to select judges who are willing to follow the law and whose political ideology is centrist. The two tendencies reinforce each other: political centrists are likely, on average but not in every individual case, to find their political beliefs aligned with the formal legal rules. This means that moderate justices will find that following the law rather than making it is comfortable over the long run of cases.

Presidents know that their nominees must be confirmed by the Senate. From time to time, both the president and sixty members of the Senate will be significantly to the left or right of the historical center of American politics. But Supreme Court justices serve life terms, and there are nine members of the Court. This means that moving the Court substantially away from the historic center will require control of the presidency and a sustained supermajority of the Senate over a course of many years.

What does this mean for originalism? Much depends on what you think about the political valence of the original public meaning of the Constitution. If you believe that the original meaning is close to the historic center of American politics, then originalist judges with centrist political views could come to constitute a stable majority of the Court. If you believe that the original meaning is outside the mainstream, then an originalist Court would be unlikely—unless senators and presidents could be persuaded that originalist judging was better than the alternative despite its political valence.

What is the political valence of the original meaning of the United States Constitution? Talk about big questions! The Constitution is a complex document filled with political tensions. Most Americans believe that it is well within the mainstream of American politics, in part because it is an important part of the self-identity of the American people as a nation. If you believe the original meaning of the Constitution is within the mainstream of American politics, then you should believe that an originalist Supreme Court is a practical possibility and not a utopian ideal. If you believe that the Constitution itself represents an extreme ideology, then you should believe that originalism would face substantial and perhaps insurmountable political obstacles.

Debates about originalism have been fiercely ideological, but we need to be very careful when we identify the reasons for that phenomenon. It has become clear that originalism is a family of theories that has evolved over time. The originalism that sparked partisan fervor was the old originalism. The new originalism shares two core commitments with the old—(1) to the truism that the linguistic meaning of the constitutional text was fixed at the time each provision was framed and ratified and (2) to the mundane legal fact that the text of the Constitution is a binding source of the supreme law of the land. Those core commitments were not the source of political discomfort with the old originalism. That discomfort stemmed from the old originalist belief that the original expectations and intentions of the framers and ratifiers could and should be understood as freezing the entirety of constitutional doctrine for all time. The new originalism insists on a stable core of fixed constitutional meaning, but it acknowledges the existence of the construction zone—where the stable meaning of the text must be supplemented by other modes of constitutional decision making.

History versus Originalism

Critics of originalism are fond of accusing originalists of the sin of "law office history," reflecting the concern of many historians that an adversary system with generalist judges is an inappropriate method for the discovery of historical truth.[55] This criticism raises many interesting and complex issues—the relationship between law and history is not as simple as the criticism suggests. But there is an aspect of this criticism that should be embraced by originalists. There will be times when the discovery of public meaning will require careful research—involving the laborious assessment of legal materials and large-scale evidence of linguistic practices. Lawyers are trained to do legal research that focuses on legal texts: they are not trained to investigate eighteenth- or nineteenth-century linguistic practice. Although one can imagine a team of law-firm associates being trained in the appropriate methodologies and doing large-scale empirical research on eighteenth-century texts, this would be an enormously expensive and likely an unreliable method for producing the inputs that good originalist analysis would require. In such cases, lawyers and judges will turn to scholars.

Before we investigate the practices and institutions that can produce good originalist scholarship, however, we need to interrogate the law-office-history criticism more carefully. Why are historians critical of law office history? One reason for the criticism might be the protection of academic turf, but it seems more likely that historians become concerned when legal texts (judicial opinions and briefs) contain serious historical errors. Such errors are likely to occur because the lawyers who write the briefs and the judges who write the opinions are not trained as historians. Nor are judges and lawyers immersed in either the primary materials or the full range of secondary sources. Indeed, it is common practice for the supporting citation for a point of history to be a case—with the consequence that a single error can be repeated or that the findings of new historical research can be ignored. Moreover, the adversarial process focuses on the disputes that make a difference. If the appellant's brief makes a historical mistake but the outcome of the dispute is not affected by the accuracy of the history, it is unlikely that either the appellee or the judge will invest resources in investigating the historical point. Legal resources are scarce and costly; the regrettable fact of historical mistakes is an inevitable consequence of the decisions made by legal actors to allocate these resources to the issues that will make a legal difference.

The concern over law office history has translated into a criticism of originalist constitutional theory and practice. This criticism was particularly salient to a particular form of the old originalism, which emphasized the purposes, goals, and expectations of those who participated in the drafting and ratification of legal texts. For some historians, that is a familiar enterprise. One of the standard approaches to intellectual history emphasizes the need to understand the purposes for which ideas are produced and the uses to which texts (for example, John Locke's *Second Treatise of Government* or Thomas Hobbes's *Leviathan*) are put. Some historians have applied this method to the study of the pamphlets, books, articles, and speeches that were produced in connection with debates over the adoption of the Constitution. Good historians do not limit their research to the easily available primary sources: *The Federalist Papers* are supplemented by obscure pamphlets, unpublished letters and diaries, and so forth. It is not surprising that this kind of research reveals a myriad of purposes, goals, and expectations, leading historians to the conclusion that the original intentions of the framers were multitudinous, contradictory, fluid, partial, and incomplete.

In this respect, some historians and the new originalists have a common cause. If we are looking for an unambiguous agreement on the purposes and goals that motivated those who produced arguments for (or against) the Constitution of 1789 (or all but a very few of the subsequent amendments), we are likely to be disappointed. We are likely to discover that there were many groups and that they varied by cultural affiliation, economic status, and region. South Carolinians who supported the Constitution may have had different motives than Rhode Islanders had; rural South Carolinians from the interior might have seen things differently than Charleston merchants did. In the face of a rich historical understanding of the motivations of various individuals and groups, the notion of a single intention or purpose seems to dissolve.

It is for precisely this reason that new originalists came to realize that the linguistic meaning of a legal text like the Constitution (with multiple authors and audiences extended over time) cannot be understood as the sum of the mental states of those who participated in group processes of framing and ratification. This realization reflects a much more general point about the success conditions for communication in a whole range of circumstances in which authors of written texts cannot rely on the reader's knowledge of the author's intentions. Communication through legal texts cannot succeed if the meaning to be communicated is the intentions (mental states) of the authors. The meaning of legal texts is, for this reason, a function of the conventional semantic meanings and patterns of usage that prevailed among competent speakers of the natural language at the time the texts were written.

The method applied by some legal and intellectual historians supports the criticism of the old originalism by new originalists, but what does it have to say about original-public-meaning originalism? It is precisely at this point that we need to be very careful about our use of the word *meaning*— because that word is radically ambiguous. Imagine a historian who hears a constitutional theorist say, "The meaning of the Constitution is the original public meaning." The historian might reply, "That view of meaning is historically naive. The meaning of the Constitution is a complex function of the purposes and intentions of the framers, ratifiers, and others who participated in the debates and processes that started long before the Philadelphia Convention and continued long after ratification was legally complete."

On the surface, it might seem that there is a disagreement here, but that is not necessarily the case. When new originalists use the word *meaning*, they refer to the linguistic meaning or semantic content of the text of the Constitution. When some historians use the word *meaning*, they refer to uses to which the whole constellation of texts (arguing for and against the Constitution) were put and the purposes that motivated the deployment of these texts.

In other words, new originalists and some historians are talking about two different things: (1) meaning in the linguistic sense and (2) meaning in the intellectual-history sense. The historians' objection to original-public-meaning originalism—that it is historically naive because it fails to recognize that original purposes and uses are multitudinous—is based on a simple logical fallacy, albeit one that is perfectly understandable given the gap between the training and competences of historians and legal theorists. Historians may not understand what lawyers mean by *meaning* and vice versa.

It is possible that some historians will object to my demonstration of the ambiguity of the word *meaning*. They might insist that the historian's understanding of *meaning* is the one true and correct theory and deny the existence of conventional semantic meaning (or any other account of meaning that does not reduce it to uses and purposes). Once historians make this move, they are no longer doing history or historiography; they are entering instead into debates in the philosophy of language and linguistic theory. Like the discipline of history, theorizing about language (semantics and pragmatics) is a specialized field of inquiry. As it happens, the kind of intellectual history that we have been discussing was influenced by the philosophy of language via the work of the influential intellectual historian Quentin Skinner.[56] Although Skinner's views of historiography may have a great deal of merit for the practice of intellectual history, his understanding of the philosophy of language can fairly be characterized as dodgy. Many historians assume that his reports about the implications of the views of Ludwig Wittgenstein and J. L. Austin for the study of meaning are philosophically respectable, but they would do well to read the original sources and surrounding literature before they draw that conclusion. Just as history advances, so does the philosophy of language and linguistic theory: even if Skinner's views had been accurate in the 1960s (they were not), theories of meaning have changed considerably since then. So far as I know, no historian has attempted to make the argument that the intellectual historian's conception of meaning is the one true account of the meaning of legal texts. It would be a very difficult argument to make.

Just as we should be wary of law office history, we should be suspicious of "history common-room philosophy of language" and "history department legal theory." Some historians are trained as lawyers; some lawyers are trained as historians. Much can and should be learned by collaborations between the two disciplines. But contemporary originalists are not aiming at the same target as are some historians, and the methods and assumptions of intellectual history of a certain kind do not provide the appropriate methodology for the recovery of the linguistic meaning of legal texts. If we want to grasp the linguistic meaning of a word like *commerce* or a phrase like *natural born citizen* in the late eighteenth century, the most rigorous method involves the systematic sampling and evaluation of usage as revealed in a wide variety of sources. Arguments for and against the adoption of the Constitution (e.g., the Federalist Papers, the records of the Philadelphia Convention, diaries, reports of speeches, pamphlets, etc.) are relevant, but they hardly constitute an adequate basis for establishing the linguistic practices that form the basis of conventional semantic meaning and the usages that constitute the rules of syntax and grammar. The historian's search for purposes of (and uses to which) the texts were put is simply beside the point. Historians who use the method of intellectual history that we have been discussing are not aiming at recovering the conventional semantic meaning of legal texts.

Although the historian's complaints against law office history and the old originalism completely miss the mark as applied to contemporary originalist theory, there is still a lesson to be learned. The new originalism has methodological implications. Sound originalist research requires investigation into patterns of usage at particular times. There is much to learn from the discipline of historical linguistics about how such research might be conducted in a neutral, systematic, and replicable manner. Because the new originalism is "new," it is still developing in important ways, both theoretically and methodologically. One of the most encouraging developments in contemporary constitutional scholarship is the recognition of the issues by originalist scholars, but (in my opinion) there is still much work to be done on all fronts: originalist methodology is an especially urgent concern.

Multiple Modalities and the Burden of Persuasion

Legal theorists usually have legal training, and lawyers are fond of making arguments about the burden of persuasion. Who has the burden of proof, originalists or living constitutionalists? Originalists are no better or worse than living constitutionalists in this regard: they believe that living

constitutionalists have the burden of persuasion, and living constitutionalists would have it vice versa.

One of the living constitutionalist strategies for shifting the burden of
persuasion invokes the idea of multiple modalities of constitutional argument (or pluralist constitutional practice).[57] The argument begins with
an observation about current practices of constitutional argument. When
judges and lawyers engage in constitutional practice, they do not limit
themselves to a single type or (modality) of argument. The practice of
constitutional argument and deliberation includes appeals to the original
meaning of the text; the purposes, policies, and principles that animate particular constitutional provisions; the structure of the Constitution and its
parts; considerations of justice, precedent, and historical practice; and so
forth. From this fact, living constitutionalists draw the conclusion that plu-
ralism is the status quo and that originalists are calling for a radical change
in constitutional practice. This implies that the burden of persuasion is on
the originalists to give us compelling arguments of political morality in
support of their radical proposal.

This argument sounds quite plausible, but it is based on a fundamental
conceptual error or perhaps on a linguistic misunderstanding. Contemporary
originalists and living constitutionalists use the phrase *constitutional interpretation* differently. For new originalists who embrace the interpretation-
construction distinction, this phrase refers to the discovery of the linguistic
meaning of the constitutional text. Originalists don't argue that the linguistic
meaning *should be* the original public meaning; they argue that the original
public meaning *is* the linguistic meaning—the use of the word *should* in this
context would be misleading or wrong.

The new originalist picture is that constitutional interpretation is a moment or step in constitutional practice. We begin with the linguistic meaning of the constitutional text. If that meaning is neither ambiguous nor
vague, then (unless there are very unusual circumstances) we proceed to
apply the rule of constitutional doctrine that corresponds to the linguistic meaning to the issue that is before us. If the text is ambiguous, then
we attempt to revolve the ambiguity on the basis of the publicly available
context (the facts that everyone could know) of constitutional utterance
(framing and ratification). Information about constitutional structure or
purposes might be relevant in this process of interpretation (determining linguistic meaning). If the text is vague, then we need to determine

whether we have a borderline case. If we don't, then we can simply ignore the vagueness—its resolution is not required for the decision at hand. If we do have a borderline case, then constitutional construction is required. Originalism itself does not have a theory of constitutional construction, but originalists can and should agree that constitutional construction (as currently practiced) involves a plurality of methods—purposes, structure, precedent, and all the rest.

In other words, originalists can agree with living constitutionalists that there is a plurality of methods that are employed in constitutional practice but simultaneously assert that constitutional interpretation is concerned with one and only one end—the discovery of the original public meaning (the linguistic meaning) of the constitutional text. Once that meaning is determined, these methods are properly brought to bear on the task of constitutional construction. Most originalists believe that the linguistic meaning of the text should *constrain* constitutional construction, but only a few would go so far as to argue that the original meaning should *completely determine* the answer to every constitutional question.

Living constitutionalists may be of two minds about this originalist reply to their point about multiple modalities and pluralist practices. They might embrace the substance of the originalist reply but reject the use of the phrases *constitutional interpretation* and *constitutional construction*. They might say that there are two distinct moments in the process of constitutional interpretation—the linguistic moment and the doctrinal moment. Or they could use a variety of alternative locutions. If a living constitutionalist accepts that the linguistic meaning of the Constitution constrains constitutional practice (in all but exceptional circumstances), then there is no contradiction between multiple modalities and pluralist constitutional practice on the one hand and the originalism on the other.

But some living constitutionalists reject the idea that the linguistic meaning of the Constitution acts as a constraint on constitutional practice. They believe that the Supreme Court or officials in the political branches have the power to adopt what amount to "amending constructions" of the Constitution. Of course, living constitutionalists of this stripe will not want to admit that they are advocating an amending power—it sounds bad. But if they want to be honest and accurate, they must admit that they are advocating a power to change constitutional doctrine in ways that are inconsistent with the linguistic meaning of the text—even if those changes are not called amendments or amending constructions.

We can now return to the burden of persuasion. If living constitutionalists want to claim that our current practices of constitutional argument and deliberation sanction constructions that contradict the linguistic meaning of the text as legitimate and legally correct, then they must be careful about the evidence they use. In particular, their arguments will be fallacious if they rely on the plurality of methods used in constitutional construction as evidence that the same methods are used in the same way in constitutional interpretation. (Once again, the vocabulary is not important, but the underlying distinctions are.) As far as I can tell, living constitutionalists have yet to make the necessary demonstration. This is understandable. The interpretation-construction distinction is relatively recent, and most living constitutionalists are unaware of its existence. Of those who are, many believe that it is a mere rhetorical ploy because they have yet to grasp the real difference the distinction marks. Of those who know the distinction and grasp the difference, many have not yet seen the connection between the interpretation-construction distinction and their argument that multiple modalities or pluralist constitutional practices are the status quo. The end of this chapter in the debate is still to be written. Living constitutionalists should be given an opportunity to marshal their evidence.

A Restatement of the Case for Originalism

Should we be originalists? Of course, the answer to that question depends on what one means by *originalism*. There are good reasons and sound arguments that favor a certain kind of originalism—one that embraces original public meaning and the distinction between constitutional interpretation and constitutional construction.

The core of the case for original-public-meaning originalism is based on a two-step argument. The first step is the claim that the linguistic meaning of the constitutional text is the conventional semantic meaning of the words and phrases as combined by the rules of syntax and grammar found in linguistic practice at the time each provision of the constitution was framed and ratified. This step of the argument conjoins the fixation thesis and the public meaning thesis. The second step of the argument is the claim that the linguistic meaning of the Constitution is legally binding in the sense that it constrains legal practice outside very exceptional circumstances. This step of the argument expresses the textual constraint thesis. The two-step argument is sufficient to give anyone who takes up the internal point of view toward American law good reason to affirm originalism.

Originalist theorists also believe that there are good reasons to affirm originalism from an external point of view and that there are good and sufficient reasons for maintaining our current practices. Whereas the two-step argument provides decisive reasons for those who take up the internal point of view, the persuasiveness of originalist arguments for those who take an external view of the law are contingent and must be weighed in light of a variety of considerations, including comprehensive moral and political doctrines and beliefs about the feasibility of alternative forms of constitutional practice. The external case for originalism is always comparative—we are comparing originalism with a range of possible alternatives.

Originalists have offered two fundamental arguments for originalism from the external point of view. The first focuses on the fundamental value of the rule of law. It argues that originalism is superior to a variation on our current constitutional practice that explicitly endorses the power of the Supreme Court to offer amending constructions of the Constitution. It argues that such an amending power is inconsistent with the values of predictability, certainty, and stability that the rule of law serves. This rule-of-law argument also claims that an amending power is likely to foster the politicization of constitutional law and that politicization would further undermine the rule of law.

The second argument for originalism from the external point of view draws on democratic theory and the idea of popular sovereignty. The fundamental premise of this argument is that the constraining force of original meaning is a prerequisite for a constitutional order that enables "We the People" to lay down constitutional rules that will bind our agents— officials in the legislative, executive, and judicial branches. If the people's agents have the power to amend the people's instructions, then the agents (and not the people) are the true sovereigns.

The two fundamental arguments for originalism from the external point of view are powerful, but they are not decisive (in the same sense that the two-step argument is decisive from the internal point of view). They aim to provide public reasons—reasons that could be accepted by reasonable citizens who affirm the public values of the rule of law and popular sovereignty. It may well be the case that there are reasonable citizens who believe that other public values are simply more important than lawfulness and democracy. The most plausible candidate for such a value is political justice.

Anyone who believes that the original public meaning of the United States Constitution is fundamentally evil will have good reason to reject originalism—and is likely to have good reason to engage in struggle against the existing legal order by whatever means are likely to overturn that order. He or she may acknowledge that the rule of law and popular sovereignty are public values but believe that those values are outweighed by the need to overcome a fundamental evil. Citizens on both the extreme Left and the extreme Right of the political spectrum hold such beliefs.

Those who believe that our existing constitutional order falls short of fundamental evil but still involves serious, substantial, and intolerable injustice are likely to believe that the appeal of originalism depends on prevailing political circumstances. If living constitutionalism would favor injustice, then originalism might be the way to go. Under other circumstances, judicial manipulation of constitutional meaning might be the only feasible strategy for alleviating intolerable serious injustice.

Those who believe that our existing constitutional order and the original meaning of the constitutional text are reasonably just are likely to have good reason to conclude that the two fundamental arguments (from the rule of law and from popular sovereignty) provide good and sufficient reasons to affirm original-public-meaning originalism from the external point of view. This does not mean that we should view our existing constitutional arrangements as ideal. Each of us can imagine possible worlds with constitutions that would improve upon the United States Constitution in various ways. The two fundamental arguments from the external point of view are directed at the alternative conceptions of constitutional practice that are available in the here and now. One can believe that the status quo falls far short of the ideally just society but also affirm the values of the rule of law or popular sovereignty—given the likely effects of subordinating those values under existing circumstances.

One last word about the case for originalism. The arguments that we have explored are neither partisan nor political (in the narrow sense of that word). Although originalist theory has developed in tandem with a set of political arguments, it has lost much (but not all) of its political valence. Originalist ideas are embraced by legal theorists of both the Right and the Left. The first occurrence of the term *originalism* in the legal litera-ture seems to be in Paul Brest's "The Misconceived Quest for the Original Understanding."[58] Since then, originalism as a constitutional theory has taken on a life of its own, perhaps to the consternation of its early champi-ons and opponents. Many readers may have approached this statement of the case for originalism with the assumption that it would begin and end with a conservative critique of a liberal Supreme Court: that assumption might have been correct twenty years ago, but it is no longer true today. That is not to say that originalists are not critical of the Supreme Court—they are. But the new originalism that we have been discussing is not a political ideology. It is a constitutional theory.

Originalism and Living Constitutionalism

What Is Living Constitutionalism?

The case for originalism is necessarily comparative, but so far we have said more about originalism than about its rival, living constitutionalism. Just as originalism is a family of theories, there are disagreements among scholars about the meaning of living constitutionalism. Its roots might be found in Chief Justice Hughes's opinion in *Home Building & Loan Ass'n v. Blaisdell*:[59]

> It is no answer to say that this public need was not apprehended a century ago, or to insist that what the provision of the Constitution meant to the vi-sion of that day it must mean to the vision of our time. If by the statement that what the Constitution meant at the time of its adoption it means to-day, it is intended to say that the great clauses of the Constitution must be con-fined to the interpretation which the framers, with the conditions and out-look of their time, would have placed upon them, the statement carries its own refutation. It was to guard against such a narrow conception that Chief Justice Marshall uttered the memorable warning—"We must never forget that it is a constitution we are expounding—a constitution intended to en-dure for ages to come, and consequently, to be adapted to the various crises of human affairs."[60]

Hughes doesn't use the phrase *living constitution*, and because of the am-biguities in the word *interpretation* it isn't clear whether he means to claim that the Court can override the linguistic meaning of the constitutional text or whether he is instead arguing for flexible constructions within meaning that is fixed.

Charles Reich provided another important formulation in his 1963 article "Mr. Justice Black and the Living Constitution":

> [I]n a dynamic society the Bill of Rights must keep changing in its application or lose even its original meaning. There is no such thing as a constitutional provision with a static meaning. If it stays the same while other provisions of the Constitution change and society itself changes, the provision will atrophy. That, indeed, is what has happened to some of the safeguards of the Bill of Rights. A constitutional provision can maintain its integrity only by moving in the same direction and at the same rate as the rest of society. In constitutions, constancy requires change.[61]

It is apparent that the meaning of the word *meaning* in this definition of living constitutionalism is ambiguous. Recall that the word has multiple meanings: it can refer to linguistic meaning, to purposes, or to legal implications and applications. Reich could be asserting, "The application meaning of the Constitution must change in order for the linguistic meaning to remain the same." Or he might be asserting, "The linguistic meaning of the Constitution must change in order for the purposes to remain the same."

Justice William Brennan offered a third influential formulation of living constitutionalism:

> To remain faithful to the content of the Constitution, therefore, an approach to interpreting the text must account for the existence of the substantive value choices and must accept the ambiguity inherent in the effort to apply them to modern circumstances. The Framers discerned fundamental principles through struggles against particular malefactions of the Crown: the struggle shapes the particular contours of the articulated principles. But our acceptance of the fundamental principles has not and should not bind us to those precise, at times anachronistic, contours.[62]

Brennan's formulation could be glossed in a variety of ways. One natural reading is the following:

> In order to remain faithful to the linguistic meaning of the constitutional text, we must rely on principles (understood as animating purposes or

values) to guide the application of vague constitutional provisions to contemporary circumstances. The precise formulations of constitutional purposes by the framers were made in the context of specific disputes. When we apply the purposes to contemporary circumstances, we should not be bound by those precise formulations.

But this passage could be read differently, because "articulated principles" could refer to the constitutional text (the text could be the articulation of the principles). On that reading, Brennan is suggesting that the semantic content of the Constitution may need to be altered in order to be faithful to purposes for which that content was articulated.

Not only are Brennan's and Reich's formulations ambiguous, but there are other ways we could formulate the idea of living constitutionalism. Some of the possibilities include the following:

- Living constitutionalism is the view that constitutional law evolves to adapt to changing circumstances and values.
- Living constitutionalism is a political theory that aims to justify a national bureaucratic welfare state as initiated by the New Deal.
- Living constitutionalism is the view that the linguistic meaning of the constitutional text changes to adapt to changing circumstances and values.
- Living constitutionalism is the view that constitutional constructions change to adapt to changing circumstances and values.
- Living constitutionalism is the view that functions or purposes attributed to constitutional provisions change to adapt to contemporary values, and these purposes should guide constitutional construction.

And so forth. And these possibilities do not exhaust the field, because the broad family of living constitutionalist theories may embrace the fully elaborated views of particular constitutional theorists (for example, Ronald Dworkin) that have a complex internal structure consistent with the idea that constitutional law is like a living organism as it grows and changes in response to its own internal logic (i.e., "the law works itself pure") and adapts to changes in external circumstances.[63]

What we need is a working definition of living constitutionalism that embraces a variety of views but also provides a focal point for comparison with originalism. I propose that we adopt the following definition (for our purposes and not as our understanding of the ways that living constitutionalists would characterize their own views): Living constitutionalism is the view that the rules of constitutional doctrine are not fixed at the time that particular constitutional provisions are framed and ratified. This definition is neutral among several different versions of the theory of living constitutionalism, but it affirms the fluidity of constitutional doctrine all living constitutionalists embrace.

What Is the Relationship between Living Constitutionalism and Originalism?

Are originalism and living constitutionalism truly rivals or might there be a sense in which they are compatible? In the days of the old originalism, this question seemed to have an obvious answer. Old originalists seemed to deny that constitutional doctrine should ever depart from the expectations and intentions of the framers and ratifiers; in response, living constitutionalists insisted the constitutional doctrine must change. There were several variations on this story. Today, some living constitutionalists believe that the fundamental principles were fixed but the implementing doctrines changed to adapt to changing circumstances. Others emphasize changing values and believe that constitutional principles change over time.

We can get at the question of whether living constitutionalism and originalism can be reconciled or must remain antagonists via the distinction between constitutional interpretation and constitutional construction. "Compatibilism" could be the view that originalism and living constitutionalism have separate domains. Originalism has constitutional interpretation as its domain: the semantic content of the Constitution is its original public meaning. Living constitutionalism has constitutional construction as its domain: the vague provisions of the Constitution can be given constructions that change over time in order to adapt to changing values and circumstances. A fully specified living constitutionalism would have to provide a theory of constitutional construction that satisfies this description, and we can imagine that there could be a variety of such theories.

Here is another way of getting at the same point. If living constitutionalism accepts the fixation thesis, some theory of linguistic meaning, and some version of the textual-constraint thesis, then it is committed to the idea that the Constitution provides constitutional law a hard core. Metaphorically, the idea of a hard core might be expressed in terms of materials. Living constitutionalists might see the hard core as made of wood, hard enough to constrain and bind but capable of growth in response to the grafting of amendments and the new limbs grown by enduring constructions. Let us call this kind of living constitutionalism *hard-core living constitutionalism*.

But some living constitutionalist may deny that there is a hard core. They might believe that even the core of constitutional law is malleable and subject to manipulation. That is, they might assert that the living constitution has a soft core. Once again, we might express this idea through a metaphor. We can think of a soft core in terms of Silly Putty and not wood: Silly Putty can take on a shape in response to manipulation, but it offers only slight resistance, easily giving way to the warm hands of the justices. We can call this version of living constitutionalism *soft-core living constitutionalism*.

What then about "incompatibilism"? The incompatibilist story assumes that originalism and living constitutionalism compete for the same domain. In the case of original-public-meaning originalism, that domain must be limited to constitutional interpretation. There are, however, at least two different ways in which living constitutionalism could deny what originalism asserts about constitutional interpretation.

One possibility is that living constitutionalism is a theory of linguistic meaning. That is, living constitutionalists could be understood as denying the fixation thesis and asserting that the linguistic meaning of the constitutional text changes in response to changing circumstances. That version of living constitutionalism could be predicated on an implausible view of the way that meaning works, e.g., the theory that changes in linguistic practices have retroactive effect. Another possibility is the view that meaning changes on the basis of normative arguments; that view reflects a fundamental conceptual error—a category mistake. Although living constitutionalism might be understood as denying the fixation thesis, the principle of charity suggests that we try to understand living constitutionalism some other way.

There is a more charitable interpretation that would result in incompatibilism. This interpretation would view living constitutionalism as a theory that advocates judicial power to adopt amending constructions. Articulation of this version of soft-core living constitutionalism would require the articulation of a theory of the relationship between linguistic meaning and the legal content of constitutional doctrine. That is, living constitutionalists would then need a theory that justifies official or judicial override of the constitutional text. In other words, living constitutionalism might be understood as denying the textual constraint thesis.

There is yet hope for reconciliation between living constitutionalists and originalists. This would represent that rare thing—true progress in constitutional theory. Reconciliation could be accomplished so long as living constitutionalists embrace the idea that the constitution has a hard core.

The Construction Zone

Up to this point, I have studiously avoided an important question. What do originalists say about what we are calling the construction zone—the fields of constitutional doctrine that allow for the application of the general, abstract, and vague provisions of constitutional theory to particular cases? In a sense, originalism as a theory should be silent on this topic. It is a theory of constitutional interpretation, and when it offers an opinion on questions of constitutional construction (i.e., what should be done when the original meaning is underdeterminate), originalism exceeds its jurisdiction.

But even if originalism (in its pure theoretical form) has nothing to say about constitutional construction, individual originalists have offered theories of construction that complement their originalist theories of constitutional interpretation. All originalists should agree on one bedrock principle: absent extraordinary circumstances, constitutional constructions must operate inside the construction zone (the zone of underdeterminacy created by the general, abstract, and vague provisions of the constitutional text).

We can examine three theories of constitutional construction. The first theory, associated with Keith Whittington, adopts *the model of construction as politics*.[64] The second theory, associated with Jack Balkin, adopts the *model of construction as principle*.[65] The third theory, inspired by the work of John McGinnis and Michael Rappaport (but not their own view), adopts *the model of construction by original methods*.[66] These are not the only theories of constitutional construction that we can imagine, but they illustrate the range of originalist thought.

The model of construction as politics is naturally associated with popular sovereignty as a normative justification for originalism. The core idea of this model is simple: when judges leave the realm of constitutional interpretation and enter the construction zone, they defer to the decisions made by political processes. When judges interpret the Constitution, they execute the will of the people, but in the construction zone, by definition, the people have expressed no command. The respect for democracy that underlies popular sovereignty therefore requires that judges defer to democratic decision making in the construction zone. Democratic constitutional construction by the political branches is itself a political process, responding to the values appropriate for democratic deliberation and decision making.

The model of construction as principle begins with a different premise—that the Constitution itself embodies fundamental principles or political values. Thus, the First Amendment guarantee of freedom of speech embodies a principle regarding the value of freedom of expression, and the equal protection clause of the Fourteenth Amendment embodies a principle of the fundamental political and moral equality of persons. Constitutional construction should be guided by these fundamental principles. In the construction zone, judges should aim to create constitutional doctrines that comport with political ideals for which the general, abstract, and vague provisions of the Constitution aim. Construction on the basis of constitutional principle seeks a balance or reconciliation between the rule of law (constraint) and the notion of constitutional progress (justice).

The model of construction by original methods attempts to utilize the resources available to originalism (in the broadest sense) to guide work in the construction zone. The basic idea is simple. When the Constitution was adopted, the common law had developed techniques for the construction of legal texts (when they were vague or ambiguous). The Constitution was adopted with certain implicit and widely shared background assumptions in mind. One of those was that judicial construction of legal texts would proceed by the well-established methods of the common law. So when modern courts engage in constitutional construction, they should employ those methods and not others. Construction by original methods could be understood as emphasizing the rule-of-law function of originalism in constraining the discretion of judges.

Whole books could be written about each of these three methods of constitutional construction and about others as well. It may well be that the methods of construction that are advocated by theorists who self-identify as originalists will systematically differ from the methods offered by living constitutionalists who nonetheless share originalism's commitment to hard-core constitutionalism. Debates about constitutional construction are vitally important to constitutional theory, but they are not the same as debates about originalism as a theory of constitutional interpretation.

The Role of Precedent Revisited

Let us return to an important topic, the doctrine of stare decisis or precedent—which we discussed briefly above. The role of precedent in originalist theory is important and controversial. To the extent that originalism can embrace elements of common-law constitutional precedent, there will be a sense in which it will be compatible with some aspects of living constitutionalism. If originalism were utterly inconsistent with the role of stare decisis in constitutional adjudication, then the incompatibility of originalism and living constitutionalism would seem evident.

Some originalists believe that a relatively strong doctrine of constitutional stare decisis is consistent with originalism. Others would limit the force of precedent to the construction zone. And yet others might argue that precedent that operates contrary to popular sovereignty must give way, while precedents that reinforce popular sovereignty should be respected. An originalist who advocated original methods of constitutional construction might evaluate precedents on the basis of their adherence to original methods.[67]

We have already taken a quick look at the range of originalist opinion on this topic. As we revisit the role of precedent, we can focus on two fundamental points. The first concerns the compatibility of precedent and originalism in constitutional construction. Although particular originalists may oppose reliance on precedents in the construction zone for various reasons, originalism as a theory can have no objection to a vigorous doctrine of constitutional stare decisis so long as the original public meaning of the Constitution is respected. Precisely because originalism *is* a theory of constitutional interpretation, it is *not* a theory of constitutional construction in the zone of constitutional underdeterminacy. Some of the normative arguments for originalism from the external perspective may have implications for constitutional construction, but (for this purpose) we can distinguish between those arguments and originalism itself.

The second fundamental point concerns the compatibility of originalism and precedent on issues of constitutional interpretation. At first blush, it might seem that originalism must take the position that the only precedents that count are the ones that get the original meaning right. On this view, no precedents could have true authority on questions of constitutional interpretation, since the evaluation of the validity of the precedent would require evaluation of the underlying questions of constitutional interpretation on which the precedent was based. Some originalists may believe that this is the correct originalist view of precedent. That is, some originalists believe that the doctrine of stare decisis cannot apply to issues of constitutional interpretation.

But things are not as easy as that. One way to understand the complexities is to distinguish between the doctrines of vertical stare decisis and horizontal stare decisis. Vertical stare decisis applies when a decision of a higher court (e.g., the Supreme Court) binds a lower court (e.g., a United States district court). Horizontal stare decisis applies when a court gives precedential effect to its own prior decisions (e.g., when the Supreme Court considers itself bound by one of its prior decisions). Although there may be a few dissenters, almost all originalists will concede that the doctrine of vertical stare decisis is compatible with originalism: the alternative would be that every court and tribunal would approach every issue of constitutional interpretation de novo. This would not mean utter chaos because the related doctrine of the law of the case would prevent lower courts from flouting the decisions of higher courts in particular cases. But there are forms of disorder that are short of utter chaos, and if constitutional interpretation by the lower courts were not constrained by the doctrine of vertical stare decisis, the disorder would be substantial.

This point about vertical stare decisis can be generalized to the relationship of the courts to the political branches. Judges are simply one kind of political official; members of Congress and high executive officials (including the president) swear an oath to uphold the Constitution. Without an institutional mechanism for settling the original meaning of the Constitution, each public official would be a constitutional free agent. Of course, this would not pose a problem for the unambiguous provisions and for those where the evidence of original public meaning is unequivocal, but where there is room for reasonable disagreement, constitutional free agency would be a big fat mess.

So most originalists should endorse mechanisms for the institutional settlement of disputed questions about original public meaning. Higher courts can bind lower courts. Judicial decisions can establish precedents that bind the political branches. These facts establish an important distinction.

What does the Constitution mean? is one question. Who gets to decide? is another. Specifying the institutional structure of constitutional adjudication requires that we answer both the what-it-means question and the who-decides question.

And that brings us to horizontal stare decisis in the United States Supreme Court. Whether the Court should regard its own prior determinations about the original meaning of the Constitution as authoritative is *not* a what-does-it-mean question; it is a who-decides question. But in this case the "who" is a prior version of the Supreme Court itself. Originalism is an answer to the what-does-it mean question, but originalism itself cannot answer the who-decides question (unless there is something in the constitutional text that specifies the role of horizontal stare decisis).

Originalism is consistent with the Supreme Court's adopting a practice of horizontal stare decisis with respect to its own prior determinations of questions of original meaning. At some level, everyone recognizes that the Court must, as a practical matter, regard its own prior decisions as having institutional authority of some kind. Otherwise, every issue of constitutional law would be up for grabs every year. And if that were the case, it is unclear how vertical stare decisis could function effectively. (Why would lower courts consider themselves bound by Supreme Court precedent if the Court reconsidered constitutional questions de novo on every occasion where a lower court disregarded a prior decision?) If the Supreme Court is to function effectively as an institutional settlement mechanism for constitutional disputes, then it must afford its own prior decisions some weight in its decision-making processes.

In sum, originalism is consistent with a wide variety of views about the role of precedent. Almost all originalists embrace precedent on issues of constitutional construction and the doctrine of vertical stare decisis. Although some are suspicious of the doctrine of horizontal stare decisis in the Supreme Court, there is nothing in that doctrine that contradicts the core commitments of originalist constitutional theory—so long as the precedent to be respected is one that aimed at a faithful (even if mistaken) interpretation of the meaning of the constitutional text.

It Takes a Theory to Beat a Theory

Contemporary originalism offers a theory of constitutional interpretation. That theory does the job that we want a constitutional theory to do. It tells us how we can determine the meaning of the Constitution and what we should do with that meaning. The question whether originalism is the right theory or best theory cannot be answered in a vacuum. At some point, the opponents of originalism must answer the question, What is the alternative?[68]

Many of the alternatives to originalism are true rivals—providing enough detail and texture for side-by-side comparison. Other theories are more difficult to evaluate. How would one know whether one should prefer originalism to any of the following theories?

- Constitutional law is a complex argumentative practice that changes over time in response to the reasons advanced in constitutional cases.
- Constitutional law should be guided by pragmatism—which encompasses all the considerations that are salient in particular factual contexts and rejects any settled rules or principles of constitutional interpretation.
- Constitutional law is the narrative constructed by the American people that constitutes their identity as a polity.
- Constitutional law is a pluralistic practice constituted by several distinct modalities of constitutional arguments.
- Constitutional law is the institutional embodiment of the fundamental aspirations of the American people.

Each of the statements on this list is in some sense a theory of constitutional law, but none of them can do the work of guiding constitutional practice. Perhaps a shapeless, formless theory is the best that we can do, but one consequence of adopting any of these so-called theories is that it will be very difficult to determine whether any particular judge or judicial decision is complying with it.

Living constitutionalists may disagree with the originalist claims that the linguistic meaning of an utterance is fixed by linguistic practice at the time the utterance is made or the claim that fixation is determined by conventional semantic meaning and the rules of syntax and grammar. That is, they may have a theory of the living linguistic meaning of particular utterances. (Of course, everyone agrees that the meaning of language changes over time: that fact is one of the motives for originalism's fixation thesis.) It takes a theory to beat a theory. To the extent that living constitutionalists want to argue for an alternative theory of linguistic meaning, they must tell us what that theory is—or face the charge that they don't have one.

We have been comparing original-public-meaning originalism with various versions of living constitutionalism. The crucial comparisons involve a subset of living constitutionalist theories, soft-core versions that affirm the power of judges or officials to override the linguistic meaning of the constitutional text in the course of creating doctrines of constitutional law (or that claim that the linguistic meaning itself changes). But a full comparison requires that we know more—we need an account of the method or rules that will determine the content of constitutional law. Some rivals of originalism are real theories. Others are pale imitations, mere gestures and hints.

Do We Need a New Constitution?

There have been a number of proposals to replace or amend what could be called "Our Imperfect Constitution."[69] Suppose that the arguments for these proposals were correct, and that we should start over, tear up the existing Constitution, and write a new one. Would this undermine the case for originalism?

To answer that question, we can put ourselves in the shoes of the new framers. As we write a new constitution, we would see all the issues that arise in connection with originalism but from a new angle. We would immediately encounter the problems of ambiguity and vagueness. If we were writing a constitution that was intended to endure, we would be acutely aware of the perils of private meanings. We would attempt to use words and phrases with clear public meanings—and to avoid jargon that had specialized meanings to specialized linguistic communities. We would try to avoid ambiguity and minimize unnecessary vagueness. But if we wanted to confer broad rights and powers, it is likely that we would find the use of general, abstract, and vague language to be inescapable. We might be concerned with the possibility that our new constitution would be nullified by the institutions we created to interpret, construe, and implement it. (Of course, it is conceivable—barely—that we would want exactly that; if so, we would do well to say that explicitly.) Or it is possible that we would want to make it clear that the constitution we had written should serve as the supreme law of the land and bind the courts—if so, we would do well to say that explicitly. But whatever we wanted to accomplish, we would need to rely on the conventional semantic meanings and the rules of English syntax and grammar.

In the shoes of the framers of a new constitution, we would have no choice but to be originalists. The original public meaning of language would be the only tool we had. And the same considerations would apply if we were members of a Supreme Court that wanted to rewrite the Constitution by writing opinions that adopted amending constructions. For those opinions to communicate their messages, they would have to be written using words and phrases and the rules of syntax and grammar as they existed at the time our opinions were drafted (although courts can freely use terms of legal art). For those opinions to do their transformative work, the judges and officials who applied them would need to follow their original meaning. Even a justice who wanted to rewrite the Constitution by interpretation would have to rely on a version of originalism for the opinions that did the rewriting to have their intended effects.

Does It Matter Whether We Call It Originalism?

This brings us to one last question: Does it matter whether we call the theory we have been discussing *originalism?* Deep down, of course, it does not matter. The theory might have been given any number of names—it was an accident of history that the word *originalism* was coined for this purpose. We can imagine other names that would do equally well—textualism, historical interpretation, and even strict constructionism might have been used to describe the theory that we now call originalism.

But now that we have the word *originalism* and a history of its use, we would do well to use it carefully and clearly. Here is one danger that we should avoid. It would be possible to define terms so that the word *originalism* was reserved for a theory that is obviously false or obviously true. Opponents of originalism might define *it* as the theory that constitutional actors must rely exclusively on the original public meaning of the Constitution when they engage in constitutional practice: no other factor can have any weight under any circumstances. The advocates of originalism might try to define it quite differently, contending that it is the view that judges must consider original meaning as a factor when they evaluate constitutional issues. Either one of these stipulated definitions would mark the disputed territory in a way that predetermined the outcome of the debate. No one should think that original meaning is the only thing judges may consider in any circumstances or that it is completely irrelevant. We would do well to avoid any attempt to resolve the originalism debate on the basis of stipulated definitions that guarantee victory to one side or the other. Likewise, we should avoid defining living constitutionalism in a way that makes any version of that theory either implausible or trivial.

As a matter of practical politics, the terminology might be important for another reason. The debates over originalism are associated in the popular imagination with partisan politics. Originalism is understood as a conservative theory; living constitutionalism is associated with liberalism. For this reason, liberals might believe that they must be against originalism; conservatives may think that they must oppose a living constitution. In a sense, this is very odd—one might think that theories of constitutional interpretation should eschew partisan politics, but the politicization of constitutional theory may have been inevitable given the Supreme Court's intervention in the great issues of the day.

For this reason, there may be those who can embrace the principal theoretical ideas of the new originalism but who would prefer to call these ideas by some other name. As long as confusion is avoided, there is nothing deeply wrong with the acceptance of originalism's major claims combined with a rejection of the label originalism. It is the content of theories that matter and not the names we call them.

The core commitments of the theory we now call originalism are to four ideas: (1) the linguistic meaning of each constitutional provision is fixed at the time it is framed and ratified; (2) the original meaning of the Constitution is the original public meaning of the words and phrases as combined by the rules of syntax and grammar; (3) the linguistic meaning of the Constitution is part of the supreme law of the land; and (4) there is a real distinction between constitutional interpretation (which discovers linguistic meaning) and constitutional construction (which translates that meaning into legal effects). If you are convinced that these four ideas are fundamentally correct, then you agree with originalism, even if you do not call yourself an originalist.

Originalism and the Living American Constitution

Robert W. Bennett

Originalism and Living Constitutionalism

What has come to be known as *originalism* in constitutional interpretation
has shown remarkable resilience. The basic idea of originalism is that, as
written law, the Constitution must be understood today in the same "fixed,
unchanging" way it was understood at the time it was crafted and adopted.[1]
But there are basic ambiguities in this originalist notion, and time and
again skeptical commentators have exposed problems with one or another
version. The response by adherents—*originalists* as they have come to be
known—has typically been to come back with a different formulation. Indicative of this shifting ground is that some recent versions are now touted
as a new originalism.[2] But what, it might be asked, can sustain the apparent belief that stable constitutional truth lies in an approach that must be
repeatedly reworked?

It could be, of course, that recent versions are simply refinements or
perhaps that the latest originalist accounts are finally getting it right. Even

in originalist terms, I have my doubts about some features of more recent versions, and so do a number of self-styled originalists, but, be that as it may, the resilience of originalism is surely attributable, in part at least, to problems with the apparent alternative. That alternative is most typically referred to as a *living Constitution*.[3] Proponents of living constitutionalism insist that understanding of the document must keep up with a world that does not stand still. Constitutional amendment, by this account, is both too difficult and insufficiently supple to do the job, with the result that the judiciary has stepped into the breach, making the Constitution a living one in an ongoing process of interpretation in the adjudication of cases over time.[4] But if living constitutionalism simply strives to keep the Constitution in touch with the times, it might seem that legislative consideration of constitutional questions would do just fine.[5] Legislators must periodically stand for popular election, and that should keep them in closer touch than life-tenured federal judges with changing facts and evolving values. If instead we retain judicial review, in the sense of a large role for federal courts as interpreters of the Constitution, it would seem that contemporary judges will identify—and in that sense choose—the values that keep that Constitution a lively one. And there is no accepted approach for such a process of identification, no discernible theory of what guides living constitutionalism to compete with the theory of originalism, even taking into account the difficulty of pinning originalism down.[6] Insistence on a living constitution is thus easily depicted as judicial willfulness, decision at the whim of "nine lawyers."[7]

Contemporary debate in the public square about an originalist approach is often traced to speeches and articles by Edwin Meese in the mid-1980s, when he served as United States attorney general in the administration of President Reagan.[8] Perceived judicial activism has generated hostile reactions at a number of points in American history, and it was in that vein that Meese objected to "an activist jurisprudence," one that "anchors the Constitution only in the consciences of jurists."[9] Meese's criticism was no doubt prompted by a variety of specific decisions that roiled the political waters at the time. Many of those were associated with the Warren Court of the 1950s and 1960s. But when Meese entered the picture, the most controversial surely was—and remains—the Burger Court's 1973 decision in *Roe v. Wade*, extending constitutional protection to a woman's choice of whether or not to have an abortion.[10] One person's judicial activism can be another's principled constitutionalism, and Meese attempted to justify his concern on broader grounds than simply disapproval of specific decisions or of judicial activism in general.

Quite apart from the merits, originalist themes were an obvious candidate for that broader ground. Emphasis on an intention attached to one or another constitutional provision has been a recurrent theme in Supreme Court decisions since our constitutional beginnings. A separate opinion by Chief Justice John Marshall in the 1827 case of *Ogden v. Saunders* makes the point rather directly, even if Marshall's formulation is riddled with ambiguities that would later come into focus. In applying the Constitution, Marshall wrote that "the intention of the instrument must prevail; that this intention must be collected from its words; that its words are to be understood in that sense in which they are generally used by those for whom the instrument was intended; [and] that its provisions are neither to be restricted into insignificance, nor extended to objects not comprehended in them, nor contemplated by its framers."[11]

This last emphasis on what was "contemplated" by the framers, moreover, comfortably drew on the approach to statutory interpretation of William Blackstone, whose writing was well known in the American colonies.[12] Writing in the English context, where, of course, no constitutional commands can override legislative provisions, Blackstone said that "there is no court that has power to defeat the intent of the legislature when couched in such evident and express words as leave no doubt whether it was the intent of the legislature or no." At the same time, Blackstone insisted that as long as the words left some room, they *need not* be followed where they might most naturally seem to lead if doing so would produce an "unreasonable" result. For, according to Blackstone, unreasonable results were likely "not foreseen by the parliament."[13] Since both statutes and the American Constitution take the form of writings, this emphasis on legislative intention seemed readily transferable to the new American "super-statute."[14]

Early originalist themes were not peculiar to Marshall, nor to his time. Though there has been something of an ebb and flow over the years, identifiably originalist language has appeared repeatedly throughout our constitutional history.[15] At the same time, however, other themes have played important roles in judicial decision making in the name of the Constitution. Thus nothing is more common in constitutional decisions than citation and quotation of earlier court decisions. Prudential and structural reasoning also make frequent appearances.[16] Or the author of an opinion will ascribe to the Constitution some value thought relevant but without specifying the nature of the association. In each case, it is possible to elaborate a connection to originalist themes. But the connection is not always clear, and, at least until fairly recently, neither courts nor commentators felt any particular obligation to make the nature of any connection explicit.

The idea of a living Constitution has also made frequent appearance, sometimes in tandem with originalist language. Probably the Supreme Court opinion most associated with a living Constitution is that of Chief Justice Hughes for the Court in the 1934 case of *Home Building & Loan Ass'n v. Blaisdell.*[17] During the Great Depression of the 1930s, Minnesota enacted a mortgage moratorium statute providing temporary relief for hard-pressed homeowners. This was challenged as inconsistent with the contract clause of Article I, forbidding states from passing laws that impair "the obligation of contracts."[18] As a dissenting opinion in *Blaisdell* emphasized, the Minnesota statute resembled debt relief statutes that the contract clause had been originally designed to disapprove. But the Court upheld the Minnesota statute, making a bow to originalist themes but more clearly sounding those of living constitutionalism:

> It is no answer to say that...[the] public need [involved here] was not apprehended a century ago, or to insist that what the provision of the Constitution meant to the vision of that day it must mean to the vision of our time. If by the statement that what the Constitution meant at the time of its adoption it means today, it is intended to say that the great clauses of the Constitution must be confined to the interpretation which the framers, with the conditions and outlook of their time, would have placed upon them, the statement carries its own refutation. It was to guard against such a narrow conception that Chief Justice Marshall uttered the memorable warning— "We must never forget that it is a constitution we are expounding"—"a constitution intended to endure for ages to come, and consequently, to be adapted to the various crises of human affairs."...
>
> Nor is it helpful to attempt to draw a fine distinction between the intended meaning of the words of the Constitution and their intended application....[W]e find no warrant for the conclusion that the clause has been warped [over time]...from its proper significance or that the founders of our Government would have interpreted the clause differently had they had occasion to assume that responsibility in the conditions of the later day.[19]

Though identifiably originalist language has been around for a long time, the word *originalism* was coined by Paul Brest in a 1980 law review article.[20] And Brest brought a critical approach to the discussion of originalism that had not always been evident in prior academic discussions, where some form or another of the idea was frequently deployed as if both its meaning and appropriateness needed neither elaboration nor justification.[21] In the years since Brest wrote, this critical approach has flourished.

In this essay, I propose to cast a similarly critical eye on the clash between originalism and living constitutionalism. I will examine the maze of variants of originalism, highlighting unsolved problems and continuing disagreement. I will draw on lessons from the enterprises of contractual and legislative interpretation, lessons derived from both similarities to and differences from the constitutional setting. In each of the three contexts—contractual, legislative, and constitutional—language promulgated at one point in time must be applied at a later time. Quite frequently the application will be to problems that had not even been foreseen when the language was adopted. That is one reason why an occasional "unreasonable" result of which Blackstone wrote in the statutory context should not be surprising. The analysis will make it clear that, in any reasonably coherent form, originalism has limited capacity to stem a constant flow of contemporary values into the decision-making process. In the real world of constitutional adjudication, the result will often be that any contribution of original animating values is deeply subordinate. In this sense a living Constitution is, if not logically inevitable, effectively irresistible.

I will concentrate on judicial interpretation of the Constitution, dealing only in passing with interpretation by other actors—executive and legislative officials, and nongovernmental persons and entities—and with interactions between judicial interpretations and those of others. The dynamics of constitutional adjudications make reliance on contemporary values appealing in elaboration of the whole Constitution, but for a large subset of the most salient problems that make their way to court, there is no realistic hope of escaping that reliance. The Constitution contains sweeping generalities, and a large share of contentious constitutional questions that come to court are initially framed in terms of that general language. When courts are called upon to address many of those questions, there are simply no originalist materials from which they might obtain a large degree of guidance. Inevitably, then, the void will be filled by the judge's sense of values that matter in the here and now.

To be sure, living constitutionalism comes in different shadings. In a much-cited article written before Meese entered the fray, Supreme Court Justice William Rehnquist criticized the notion of living constitutionalism if it were understood to give judges a "roving commission to second guess" political actors "concerning what is best for the country."[22] But Rehnquist thought that "scarcely anyone would disagree" with a different version of living constitutionalism, Justice Holmes's likening of the document to an "organism," so that its "wisely" chosen "general language" would provide "latitude to those who would later interpret the instrument to make that language applicable to cases that the framers might not have foreseen."[23] Only a few paragraphs later, however, Rehnquist seemed, in the name of what we might now call *originalism*, to take back some of the liveliness suggested by this latter formulation. He told us that it is only "values…derived from the language and intent of the framers" that appropriately flesh out constitutional meaning.[24] And in discussing the generally worded Civil War amendments, Rehnquist saw the intent of some of those most active in pursuit of those amendments as the prevention of "abuses in which the states had engaged prior to that time."[25]

The liveliness I claim is effectively irresistible is, of course, a good deal more than would result from a focused concern with prior abuses but also much less than is suggested by talk of a "roving commission." Our Constitution is most obviously given life by the wide-ranging discretion that judges exercise in giving content to constitutional generalities. Judicial discretion is not, however, limited to the application of general constitutional language. Constitutional ambiguities must also be resolved, and, as we shall see, there are other inviting occasions for judicial introduction of contemporary values. I know of no way to quantify the discretion that judges exercise. But there is really no mistaking the fact of wide-ranging discretion, at least once it has become clear that originalism has insufficient resources to satisfactorily corral it.

This discussion will not deal fully with the point regarding judicial whim, perceived problems with judicial review as the enterprise for making the Constitution a living one. I will have some comments about that set of concerns, suggesting that the problem is at least softened if one has a clear-eyed vision of American democracy and of the place of the courts in it. But I have no present ambitions to explore in detail how judges might satisfactorily go about identifying the contemporary values they employ. Some systematization in the elaboration of living constitutional law may well be possible, but the guidance in any such enterprise would itself feed on contemporary values. Rooting around in some of our constitutional beginnings may help us think through those contemporary values, but it has little capacity to define them or keep them effectively in check.

Strictly speaking, then, mine is not a normative justification for living constitutionalism so much as it is a demonstration of its inevitability, at least once a far-ranging judicial review is in place. Nor do I completely dismiss constraints on judicial decision making that might be characterized as originalist. One might even think of my position as a reconciliation of originalism and living constitutionalism. To be sure, I do not think of myself as an originalist, but that is not because I am opposed to the restraining effect of constitutional language or even of an examination of the history behind its formulation. It is rather because I associate originalism with the claim that it brings a good measure of constraint on judicial review. In what follows I hope to show that any such claim is not only unrealized in the real world but also unattainable. Constraint on judicial decision making is both available and desirable. Indeed, constraint is encouraged by the judicial process. But the most robust forms of that constraint do not, and cannot, come from originalism. There is, one might say, much less to originalism than meets the eye.

Wrestling with the Troubles of Originalism

Meese sounded one theme that we saw Justice Rehnquist stress as well—the authoritativeness of the Constitution's language.[26] But just how far this gets one is an ongoing source of difficulty. For even originalists—most of them, most of the time—appreciate that all by itself the text is meaningless, just a scrawl on a page. As one originalist puts it, "The text is not inherently meaningful but requires active intelligence to breathe life into barren marks."[27] The text takes on meaning only when appreciated as social practice, as a vehicle of communication that humans employ to advance their aims and facilitate their interactions. But social practices are themselves often imprecise or ill defined. They may also be variable at any given time—by and among individuals—and they may change over time. The meaning that one person or another may associate with those barren marks is then often a function of differences among the persons involved or differing aspects of the context in which the meaning is being ascribed. And there may be misunderstanding.

The problem this creates is rather obvious for general—or as it is sometimes called "open-textured"—constitutional phraseology, like "due process of law," "equal protection of the laws," "unreasonable searches and seizures," and "cruel and unusual punishment," around which many contemporary constitutional controversies revolve.[28] It may seem clear, for example, that due process requires that in a criminal trial the defendant must be allowed to introduce evidence of his innocence, but that clarity is a function not of some pure language meaning of the phrase *due process* but rather of broadly shared assumptions among those who use or recognize the phrase as part of a constitutional command. And more will be required to give meaning to those barren marks where no such shared assumptions have yet jelled, such as whether in these early years of the twenty-first century persons classified as "enemy combatants" and held at the American facility at Guantanamo Bay, Cuba, are entitled to some sort of access to classified documentary evidence that might be useful in arguing for their release.

The necessity of bringing something more than those barren marks to the interpretive enterprise is often obscured by a seeming clarity in a good deal of constitutional language. When the Constitution states, for example (and then in an amendment repeats), that "[t]he Senate of the United States shall be composed of two Senators from each state," it seems obvious that four senators from a state is not permitted, anymore for California than for Wyoming, or anymore today than it was when the constitutional words were formulated.[29] Indeed, if this sort of stability were not present, we might wonder quite generally about the usefulness of language as a vehicle of human communication. For we do, in fact, understand words with great regularity without pausing to ask for details about the circumstances in which they were used. Two means two, seemingly no doubt about it.

Such apparent clarity can occasionally be misleading, however, for several reasons. First, seeming clarity may shroud an ambiguity. The Constitution requires that the president "have attained to the age of thirty-five years," a number seemingly as precise as the prescribed number of senators per state.[30] At present in our culture there is unlikely to be much ambiguity about whether a presidential candidate meets that requirement. But ambiguity can itself be a function of context. There are cultures that calculate age differently than we do, as the number of (lunar) calendar years in which one has been alive for any length of time rather than the number of calendar recurrences of the date of one's birth.[31] A person from one of those cultures—or perhaps even someone familiar with it— might then misconstrue the seemingly clear requirement. Or a conceptual framework that helps shape language usage may change. For example, if those who insist that human life begins at conception prove ascendant in the abortion controversy in the United States, it is possible that there will come a time when many people in the country will naturally think of one's age as calculated from conception—or perhaps from fetal "viability"— rather than from birth.

Another possibility is that seeming clarity might cause a draftsman to miss what others will see as ambiguity. In the case of the Constitution, of course, there were multiple draftsmen, and that increased the danger that problems might be glossed over in the drafting process. Consider the provision in Article I on the apportionment of the House of Representatives among the states. Aside from the now anachronistic treatment of slaves and Native Americans, that apportionment is to be based on population. The Constitution's phrase is "respective numbers." But the section then goes on to require that "the number of representatives shall not exceed one for every thirty thousand."[32] Quite early in our nation's history there arose controversy about whether that seemingly precise requirement was applicable within each state or only for the country as a whole.[33] The problem could easily have been foreseen and then might have been dealt with through different language, but it was not. The draftsmen may have fooled themselves by the seeming precision in the use of a number.

Or apparent clarity may unravel as one looks a little harder or a little more broadly. Article I also requires that

> Every Order, Resolution, or Vote to which the Concurrence of the Senate and House of Representatives may be necessary (except on a question of Adjournment) shall be presented to the President of the United States; and before the Same shall take Effect, shall be approved by him, or being disapproved by him, shall be repassed by two thirds of the Senate and House....[34]

This seems rather sweeping in requiring what is called *presentment* for consideration of a presidential veto of "every" matter where a vote was required by both House and Senate. If there were any doubt about its broad sweep, the one explicit exception for adjournment might seem to settle the matter. For why make a special point of one exception if others are possible?[35] But Article V of the Constitution deals with congressional action in proposing constitutional amendments, requiring a two-thirds vote of "both Houses" (the same vote necessary to override the president's veto!), and it says nothing about presidential involvement. This poses the question of whether for the amendment process Article V dissipates the seeming clarity in Article I about presidential involvement. To put the point another way, taken alone Article I seems clear about the amendment process, but when it is placed in a context that includes Article V, a different possibility comes into focus.[36]

To come to grips with at least some of these kinds of questions, Meese urged "a jurisprudence of original intention."[37] As we have seen, concern with the intention of legislation or of an enacting legislature had long played a central role in legislative interpretation, and it still does.[38] As we have also seen, concern with intention had early been imported into the constitutional setting. But the notion of intention had largely been accepted as if its meaning for a statute or the Constitution were clear,[39] and that was to change. There is now a growing literature, long overdue, on just what was meant by intention in the context of some written law.

The Summing Problem

The word *intention* is most commonly used to refer to mental states of individuals. The question then arises of just what might be meant by the intention of a multimember body that adopts a text through a process of voting. To be sure, the problem need not be seen as akin to ascribing a state of mind to a mountain. All the bodies, processes, and products to which intentions are attributed in the case of both legislation and the Constitution are suffused with individual human actors. There may be serious evidentiary problems in figuring out what was in the minds of individual participants. And these may be compounded by historiographical problems and questions about whether those trained in the law are suited for the historical digging that may be required.[40] Those are serious methodological problems, but if they could somehow be overcome, we would still have what I call a *summing problem*, whether and how we might appropriately move from states of mind for those individuals to a state of mind for the body as a whole, or to otherwise be associated with the words that the collection of individuals has adopted through a voting process.

In one sense the problem is more serious in the case of the United States Constitution than for the typical statute. In the statutory context, there is no real ambiguity (or at least not much, despite the present-ment requirement) about the body to which an intention is ascribed. It is the legislature. The relevant body to harbor the dispositive intention in the case of the Constitution is less clear. The document was crafted by members of the constitutional convention. (For purposes of simplification I will initially deal with the original Constitution, but we will return to the complication of amendments.) It was then sent on to the states by the Continental Congress, requiring the assent of at least nine states acting through ratifying conventions. At the very least, the constitutional fram-ers and the initial nine ratifying conventions might lay claim to harboring the relevant original intention. By one count, there were "roughly two thousand actors who served in the various conventions that framed and ratified the Constitution."[41]

One possibility for dealing with the summing problem is to treat the intention of the body as a whole as an amalgam of all the separate inten-tions of its individual members. But the rules for any such amalgamation are, to say the least, unclear. In votes that are taken on written laws, for example, each member of a voting body typically counts equally—one leg-islator in a given chamber, one vote—and a majority of each body must accede to any final formulation. No vote is ever taken on intentions, how-ever, and no showing of any degree of concurrence on them is required. If we attempted nonetheless to reconstruct intention votes—overcoming the formidable historiographical and evidentiary problems, and with each constituent member counting equally—we would risk producing an im-penetrable tangle. For different individuals might vote for identical lan-guage with different intentions in mind.[42] Some might, for example, have thought the "one for every thirty thousand" limitation applied to each state, while others thought it applied to the country as a whole. Still others might have given the question little or no thought.

There might well be some commonality among the views of those casting votes, of course. Assuming we could discover the commonalities, we would still have to ask what degree of commonality might suffice for attribution of an intention to the enacting collectivity, or to its words. At the extreme, if we could find unanimity, or, to use a more ambiguous word, a *consensus* intention behind the enactment, we might comfortably ascribe that intention to whatever was being interpreted.[43] But short of a consensus, what might be the right degree? Assuming that a majority of each voting body was required for enacting the language into law, would a similar majority be required for the governing intention? Or perhaps a majority of the majority that adopted the language, or a plurality of the adopting majority? There is no accepted answer to this question, and even if there were, there might well be no single intention that would satisfy it.[44]

In other contexts, we do ascribe states of mind to collections of individuals without agonizing over summing problems. For example, corporations and partnerships enter into contracts in which their intentions may be relevant to interpretation. They commit torts or crimes for which a culpable state of mind is required. This is usually accomplished by identifying a single individual who was the body's agent in the transaction and ascribing that individual's state of mind to the entity as a whole. In the legislative context, though courts still tend to avoid discussion of what is meant by legislative intention, it might similarly be possible to imagine some agency relationships. Thus a legislative chamber will frequently employ committees and subcommittees to consider legislation before it is submitted to a dispositive vote in the body as a whole. Those committees may then produce reports that ascribe certain aims to the legislation. Or committee members may reach a consensus. Those committees might then be considered agents of the chambers with regard to the legislation. If this is done, the summing problem is at least narrowed a bit. Or the sponsor of legislation or the chair of a committee that handled the legislation might take the lead in explaining it to the chamber and could be seen as the agent of the chamber. Almost all American legislatures are bicameral, and when each chamber has passed a different version of a piece of legislation, a conference committee of the two chambers may undertake the task of reconciling the versions. If that committee produces a report, that report might then be taken as the product of an agent of the entire legislature.

Courts do in fact treat committee reports and statements of legislative sponsors or of committee and subcommittee chairs as particularly good evidence of legislative intention.[45] Still, there may be more than one intimately involved individual who spoke up, or there may be dissents from committee reports or concurrences that offer different interpretations of statutory language. And even if there is only a report for the committee as a whole or just one individual who chose to speak up, there seems to be no agreed-upon norm in the legislative context through which any such individual is actually taken to be an agent for the whole. I know of no court discussion that makes an assumption of any such agency relationship explicit.[46] Indeed, the remarks of ordinary legislators without any special role regarding the legislation are sometimes cited by courts.[47] Backbenchers who speak, moreover, as well as those who remain silent, will have the same voting power in the eventual decision as those more visibly involved. And the vote, when it is taken, will ostensibly be on the words of a statute, not on what anybody thought or said about it. The backbencher can thus claim with great plausibility that his state of mind is just as important as that of the legislation's sponsor or what was expressed in some committee report. Justice Antonin Scalia argues, moreover, that an agency conception of legislative intention would be unconstitutional because the "legislative power . . . is nondelegable."[48] In the constitutional setting this summing problem is particularly acute if the ratifying conventions are taken as having harbored the dispositive intention, since they were numerous and their deliberations were largely disconnected (and in many cases undocumented to boot). And the idea that only the first nine ratifying conventions counted is somehow counterintuitive.

Short of finding a consensus intention, the only appealing way to cut through this summing problem for legislative or constitutional intention is to recognize the notion as a figure of speech. In this way one treats the legislature or the bodies responsible for the Constitution as a single hypothetical legislator or constitution maker who enacted the text.[49] It is that hypothetical individual whose intentions we might then seek to understand and project in an originalist interpretive process geared to intention. In the discussion that follows I will occasionally refer to this hypothetical construct as *Mr. Intender.*

We should be clear, however, that the invention of Mr. Intender does not dispel problems of amalgamation. Because the words were in fact produced by numerous individuals who may have sought to accomplish a variety of things and who have human frailties in the use and appreciation of language, the words adopted may cover up differences through ambiguity or vagueness, may not be farsighted, or may even be sloppy or otherwise confusing as applied to problems that arise. If we seek to understand Mr. Intender on the basis of what we learn about those individuals, we will still have to work out some sort of amalgamation; we will have to emphasize some actual influences and put others to the side. But even if the hypothetical construct does not dispel the summing difficulties, it does at least provide a suggestive framework that may better allow us to recognize the process of choice that is going on. We will return to that process of choice.

There need be no wrenching conflict between the consensus possibility on the one hand and the construct of Mr. Intender on the other. To be sure, one can conjure up possibilities suggestive of a tension between the two. Language might not be used carefully, so the words used would be susceptible to an interpretation different from that actually held by all the real participants. Recall the provision in Article I that seems to require presentment to the president of every item for which a vote was required in both houses of Congress.[50] It is conceivable that this provision was included without focused consideration of the constitutional amendment process of Article V. If that is so, then there might have been a consensus intention accompanying Article V that amendments need not be submitted to the president, even though the constitutional language in its entirety might comfortably be interpreted to the contrary.

But any inference of a consensus would have to be based in evidence, and that same evidence would presumably be available to inform our conclusions about the intentions of Mr. Intender. In any event, if there were a conflict between the consensus and hypothetical intender approaches, it seems clear that a consensus should be preferred, with the hypothetical construct deployed where a consensus could not reasonably be discerned. For it was actual legislators or constitution makers who had the authority to decide, and Mr. Intender was introduced to deal with the seemingly intractable summing problem. Where there is an actual consensus, there is no such summing problem and hence no reason to spurn the consensus.

No reason, that is, unless the concern with intention was misbegotten from the outset. We will turn shortly to other possibilities, but first we touch on yet another stumbling block in construing language in light of intentions. Even if we ascribe them to our hypothetical Mr. Intender, there is a problem of just how far those intentions should be taken to reach.

The Reach of Intentions

When I teach about interpretation of the United States Constitution, I introduce into class discussion a superhero called *Constitution Man,* who swoops down on the scene as the provision under scrutiny is being adopted. Constitution Man interrogates those promulgating the provision about its implications for some problem, typically a variant on the case we are discussing in class. If Constitution Man were to have posed questions about whether the limitation of one for every thirty thousand applies to each state or only nationwide or whether presidential involvement is required in the amendment proposal process, it is plausible to imagine that ready—and identical—answers would be given by all involved. Still, those answers might be generated in somewhat different ways. For example, the constitutional draftsmen might have thought consciously about the constitutional amendment question but not about the one-for-every thirty thousand question. Even in the latter case, however, a ready answer might be forthcoming because of assumptions about the matter, just below the level of conscious consideration.

The notion of intention as a way to answer interpretational questions is typically used to encompass both these possibilities, conscious intention and subconscious—but clear—assumption.[51] But that hardly exhausts the possibilities for the reactions Constitution Man might elicit. There may have been a quite conscious—or even subconscious—avoidance of some problems through the use of vague or ambiguous language. This may have been done to mollify constituencies, either by fooling them or by giving them more hope than would a resolution they would know they did not like. Controversy about the respective prerogatives of state and national governments, for example, arose soon after the Constitution was ratified and has been with us ever since. This may in part be attributable to the fact that the document itself is ambiguous about those trade-offs in various ways. And that ambiguity may have been quite deliberate, consciously introduced to make the tension less visible because of concern that controversy about the subject might get in the way of ratification. Or there may even have been a focused desire to pass the resolution of some kinds of problems to future generations.[52]

A second possibility is that there may have been confusion or a simple failure to think through problems, even though they were not at all hard to imagine at the time. As with inadvertent ambiguity, this latter possibility seems especially likely when multiple people are engaged in the drafting process. It is possible that the one-for-every thirty thousand question suffered this kind of neglect. An even more likely instance of carelessness is presented by the ambiguity in the now outdated provision of Article II that a person is eligible to be president of the country if he was "a citizen of the United States, at the time of adoption of this Constitution."[53] Sustained attention to the meaning of "the United States" in this formulation was prompted by the announcement in 1995 of a contest by the occasionally playful journal *Constitutional Commentary*. The editors explained that they were "shocked to discover that there are...grounds for questioning whether...[George Washington] was...constitutionally eligible for the Presidency."[54] The sparse offerings of contestants were also playful, but exploring Washington's eligibility can help expose layers of problems in ascribing meaning to the words of the Constitution.[55]

Washington's eligibility would seem to turn on whether the United States was an entity that preexisted the adoption of the Constitution or one that came into existence only with that adoption. Article VII of the Constitution says that "ratification...of nine states shall be sufficient for the establishment of this Constitution between the states so ratifying."[56] If adoption and establishment are the same thing, and the United States came into existence only upon that event, then Washington seems not to have been eligible because his home state of Virginia was not one of the first nine states to ratify the Constitution.[57] Because the assumption that Washington was to become the first president was very widespread at the time, any suggestion of ineligibility—at least if Virginia did eventually sign on—was almost surely not contemplated or subconsciously assumed by *any actors* in the process of making the Constitution law.

That decided awkwardness directs us to the possibility that the United States preexisted the Constitution, and there is ample material to support that interpretation. The nation's prior governing instrument, the Articles of Confederation, had referred to the "confederacy" to which it applied as "the United States of America," and several uses of the phrase in the Constitution seem to contemplate an entity that was already in existence. Members of the House and Senate, for example, must meet durational requirements of citizenship of the United States of seven and nine years, respectively, and that would have been impossible for the initial members if the United States had not had a preconstitutional existence.[58] And the supremacy clause refers to treaties "made, or which shall be made, under the authority of the United States."[59] Treaties that had already been made under that authority would similarly seem to have required a United States already in existence.

But that possibility also brings awkwardness, for what if Virginia had not signed up? Or what about the candidacy of a citizen of one of the other states that never came on board? (Rhode Island held out for an extended period of time.) The emphasis on citizenship in the presidential qualification provision suggests that the draftsmen would have been repelled by the possibility that such a "foreigner" would be eligible for the nation's presidency. If all this is right, then it seems that the draftsmen—individually and certainly as a group—had not thought through this set of problems. This is an example, in other words, of constitutional language that was rather carelessly drafted. Depending upon his formulation of the question, Constitution Man might then have gotten different answers about how to resolve the ambiguity. If he asked about Washington's eligibility, he would have gotten one answer. If he asked about the eligibility of a foreigner who was from a confederation state that never ratified the Constitution, he might well have gotten another.

A final possibility is that problems that arose would simply not have been salient at the time the language was devised. Problems might have been visible if one looked hard enough but were not of sufficient import to merit any piercing gaze. Even more likely, questions about the reach of constitutional provisions may have jelled over time, dependent upon subsequent developments. As we have noted, constitutional language, like that of contracts and legislation, is devised at one point in time and then applied later, most typically to problems generated by later events. To apply the constitutional language in the name of intention to many phenomena would then require, as Brest put it, an "imaginary act of projecting the adopters' concepts and attitudes into a future they probably could not have envisioned."[60] There would, in other words, have been no intention in either of the two senses distinguished above. We will return to this problem when we discuss the possibility for originalist reins on a living Constitution.

For a variety of reasons, then, there may have been no original intention to address a host of contemporary constitutional issues. In conjunction with the summing problem, the fact that intentions may "run out" in this way has raised questions as to whether the interpretive enterprise should really be focused on intentions.

The Move to Meanings

Problems with deploying original intentions to ascribe meaning to the barren marks of constitutional language caused many originalists to look elsewhere.[61] Several moved first to "original understanding" as the way to identify the meaning to be ascribed to constitutional language.[62] The term *understanding* had appeared on occasion over the years but usually in a context where it seemed synonymous with intention. In contrast, the more recent embrace of that formulation seemed to represent a shift from a focus on the promulgator or author of the constitutional language to its audience. And the shift may even have been facilitated by the ambiguity about whether some of those who made the Constitution law should be viewed as authors or audience.[63] Those who participated in the state ratifying conventions, in particular, were authors in the sense that they were an essential part of the formal processes that led to making the Constitution law but audience in the sense that the language had been formulated and then passed on to them by others acting earlier in the process. And ultimately, of course, the public at large, those who would be governed by the new law, were its audience. Regardless of how the audience is defined, a shift from author to audience would initially seem only to exacerbate the summing problem, there typically being more addressees of constitutional language than authors. But that dramatic increase in scale seemed instead to make it more comfortable to imagine—even if it was not typically put this way—a single hypothetical individual as an original understander.[64]

This focus on understanding rather than intention is familiar from the contractual context, where the reasonable understanding of the party to the contract who did not formulate the contractual words will often be preferred to a different but still reasonable understanding of the party who did. This rule of interpretation *contra proferentem* seems to be grounded in possible reliance by the nonformulating party and in some differential fault by the formulating party.[65] Justice Antonin Scalia may have some such argument in mind for lawmaking when he objects to having "the meaning of a law determined by what the lawgiver meant" as one step worse than the trick the emperor Nero was said to have engaged in: "posting edicts high up on the pillars, so that they could not easily be read." "Government by unexpressed intent," he tells us, "is similarly tyrannical."[66]

The contract context is not, however, terribly persuasive in this respect as a model for adjudication under a constitution or, for that matter, a statute. Most fundamentally, there is no baseline equality of status of intender and understander in these other contexts, as there is for the parties to a contract. The legislature has the authority to impose its will, as presumably do the makers of constitutions if that group is treated expansively as including the ratifying conventions.[67] And Justice Scalia's colorful rhetoric notwithstanding, reliance would seem to be much less of a concern in the legislative and constitutional contexts than in the contractual one. To be sure, in an extreme case where statutory or constitutional language seemed clearly to say one thing while it was intended to mean something quite different, reliance followed by hurtful consequences might occasionally justify the epithet of tyranny. But no such extreme scenario is likely in the real world of American legislating or constitution making. Many of those who seek to conform to statutory or constitutional formulations will know little about the precise language in question. We all know that traffic must stop for red lights, but I daresay there are precious few drivers who know the wording of the statute that imposes that requirement. And those who are alert to statutory or constitutional language will often be alerted as well to some uncertainty about just how it is to be understood. Often they will have been advised by lawyers who should warn of a range of possible interpretations. The problem will thus seldom if ever be some "unexpressed intent" that actually misleads people. If some understanders are misled, moreover, that will typically be on an individual basis, while it is usually assumed that statutory and constitutional interpretations cannot vary from person to person among those subject to its favors or strictures. An interpretation appropriate for the many would then likely be preferred to one advanced by the rare person who might have relied.

If the problems of reliance associated with the contractual context were thought to be serious, moreover, that would tend to call the originalist emphasis into question, at least as an antidote to the perceived problems of a living constitution. Occasionally in the case of statutes, but even more clearly in the constitutional context, those whose reliance might be cause for concern will consist of ongoing generations living under the dictates of the document. Changing language usage and, indeed, changing values will sometimes affect the ways in which language is understood. The contemporary audience may then well have relied on a different meaning than any original one. If the interpreter were to accede to the relied-upon meaning, he would then diverge from any original one he might be able to identify.

More recently, many originalists have abandoned talk of understanding as well and moved instead to *original meaning* as the proper object of inquiry.[68] Gary Lawson tells us, for example, that "the Constitution's meaning is its original public meaning. Other approaches to interpretation are simply wrong."[69] Michael Paulsen argues that the constitutional text instructs us to give it "the objective, original meaning of ... [its] language."[70] This move to original meaning may have been propelled by continued concern about the summing problem. And it surely does not help that intentions can run out while constitutional language might still seem applicable. These problems fed a sense that, like intention, the construct of understanding was inappropriately subjective.[71]

In the seemingly parallel context of legislation, very little use of understanding or meaning is found as an alternative to the intention of the legislature.[72] And the contemporary law of contract interpretation similarly focuses on intention. Suppose, I ask my contracts class each year (joining, I imagine, generations of contracts teachers before me with variants on the question), that two parties intend to enter into a contract for the purchase and sale of a horse, but they mistakenly use the word *cow*. Do they have a contract for a horse or for a cow (or perhaps for neither)? The classic contracts scholar Samuel Williston thought that there would be a contract for a cow: "If a written contract is entered into, the meaning and effect of the contract depends on the construction given the written language by the court, and the court will give that language its natural and appropriate meaning; and, if it is unambiguous, will not even admit evidence of what the parties may have thought the meaning to be."[73]

Williston's answer would, however, be decisively rejected today. As the *Restatement of Contracts* puts it, "Where the parties have attached the same meaning to a promise or agreement or a term thereof, it is interpreted in accordance with that meaning."[74]

Regardless of the appeal in these other contexts, we have already taken note of the most basic problem with this move to meaning. Meanings do not exist in the ether. Meaning is always meaning to a person or persons, whether existing out there or constructed in our imaginations. Thus while Justice Scalia is insistent that his originalism draws only on the meaning of enacted language because the language is all that is ever voted upon, he does recognize the inevitable relevance at least of "broad...social purposes" that statutes are "designed" to serve.[75] In a particularly revealing discussion, Scalia will have nothing of limiting First Amendment speech and press protections to speeches and the press. Rather, it is obvious to him that the protection extends to "the full range of communicative expression" because the words are used figuratively as, in his words, "a sort of synecdoche for the whole."[76] This he tells us is "reasonable construction." That it may well be but only because one can comfortably ascribe human aims to the use of those expressions.[77]

Scalia's willingness to extend First Amendment protections beyond the seeming reach of the amendment's language is suggestive of a broader problem that has received relatively little attention in the literature on constitutional interpretation—the implications of constitutional silence.[78] It is common to find that the Constitution implies something even though it does not say that thing directly. The indirection may have a variety of causes, some of which we have glimpsed earlier. Explicitness may be avoided because of concern that it will raise the hackles of some constituencies. Glossing over a question might then increase the chances of agreement. Or there may be a desire to defer problems, perhaps in the hope that they may never arise. Or silence may result from failure to think through a problem. Or it may be used for fear of implying more by words than seems desirable. (This is a frequent explanation of the failure to include very many explicit restraints on the federal government in the Constitution that was produced by the convention.)[79] And silence may even be the product of the clarity with which something is perceived; something is not said directly because it goes without saying.

Silences and their meanings also come in shadings. Sometimes the appropriate inference from silence is rather clear. Under the Constitution the president of the United States is selected by presidential "electors" who are allocated on a state-by-state basis according to a formula set out in the text. Those electors are to be appointed "in such manner as" each state legislature determines, but nothing is said explicitly about whether the legislature or anyone else can instruct those electors to cast their ballots for one candidate or another.[80] The Constitution's silence on the question of whether electors were entitled to exercise discretion in their voting was pretty clearly a result of the obviousness of the answer. Of course they could exercise discretion, for otherwise it is hard to see what the point was of creating the office.[81]

Perhaps less compelling are the Constitution's implications about the ability of the president's advisers to avoid legislative interrogation concerning their advice. There is nothing explicit in the Constitution about any such "executive privilege," but it is now broadly assumed to be implied in various provisions separating powers under the new government.[82] Whether that conclusion could find some justification in the name of real original intentions, even of the sort just below the level of conscious consideration, is not at all clear.

For yet a different kind of silence, consider what the Constitution does not say about selection of the chief justice of the Supreme Court. That there was to be such an officer is made clear by the provision of Article I that the chief justice was to preside at any Senate impeachment trial of the president of the United States.[83] But nothing is said about how the office is to be filled. The closest that constitutional language comes to the matter is the provision in Article II that the president "shall nominate, and by and with the advice and consent of the Senate, shall appoint...judges of the Supreme Court, and all other officers of the United States, whose appointments are not herein otherwise provided for, and which shall be established by law."[84] Perhaps the chief justice is "[an]other officer[] of the United States," to "be established by law," but that is far from clear, since "judges of the Supreme Court" are specifically mentioned. Being a chief might simply be descriptive of certain duties to be carried out by one of those judges. State supreme courts at the time had chief justices, but the manner of designation of those officers varied from state to state. So what are we to infer from the Constitution's silence? Perhaps it was assumed that the president would nominate a specific judge as chief justice. That is in fact what George Washington did the first time around, and that has been the practice ever since. But that is not the only possibility nor perhaps even the most likely candidate for what was intended. It may have been assumed that the judges of the Supreme Court would themselves pick a presiding officer. Or perhaps the matter was to be left to legislation.[85]

The strength of an implication certainly does not depend solely on how much is said explicitly in and around the subject. An extreme example of constitutional silence is the failure to include a single word about a role for political parties. But silence on that subject is rather easy to understand. At the outset, political parties were viewed as mischievous by many of the most influential figures in producing the Constitution. Politics was conceived as a high-minded search for the public good rather than as a struggle among factions. Thus it appears never to have entered George Washington's mind that he might actually campaign for the presidency, enlist organized movements to get him elected, and make promises in the process. Representative government was valued in part because it would allow for a good degree of detachment from organized pressures so that enlightened legislators could debate and resolve "the true interest of their country."[86] As Richard Hofstadter put it, "[T]he Founding Fathers...did not believe in political parties as such, scorned those that they were conscious of as historical models, [and] had a keen terror of party spirit and its evil consequences."[87] To be sure, some factional pressures might be inevitable, including those from organized political parties, but they were not going to be encouraged by acknowledging any formal role for those parties. The complete constitutional silence about political parties would then reflect the clarity with which disdain for them was felt. Such disdain could also be the meaning conveyed by the silence.

Despite the ascendancy among originalists of the construct of original meaning, there is a stubborn contingent that clings to original intention. Some of these insist that interpretation is *necessarily* about fathoming the intentions of authors.[88] Even Keith Whittington, often taken to be at the forefront of the new originalism, sometimes seems to take this position. He writes, for example, that "the text is ontologically equivalent to the intentions of the founders."[89] It seems fair to ask, however, whether a choice has to be made in such stark terms. We have seen that intentions can quickly run out in the real world of constitutional questions, and that is so even if we assign the task of intending to our hypothetical construct. But if that makes an emphasis on original meaning attractive, it does not necessarily follow that interpretation must also ignore intentions when they are clear.

In the context of interpretation of relatively precise statutory language, courts have used two doctrines that might be thought to mediate between meaning and intention. They will correct *scrivener's error*—clear error that has made its way into enacted language—and abjure *absurd results*. We caught a glimpse of the absurd-results doctrine in Blackstone's discussion of legislative interpretation, though in the passage we examined he used the word *unreasonable* rather than *absurd*. The most likely rationale for both doctrines is that the legislature could not plausibly be thought to have intended an absurd result or some clear error. Blackstone made that rationale explicit. But those doctrines cover only extreme cases, and that could leave room for allowing the conventional meaning of language to govern when the question of legislative intention is not so clear. This might be done in the name of intention by treating clear conventional meaning as evidence of what was intended. It is only evidence, however, for meaning can extend to things not intended, even well short of absurdity. As long as that meaning does not flout something that was intended, there is no direct clash between the two.

Many originalists embrace both these mediating doctrines for the constitutional context. Justice Scalia gives as an example of a scrivener's error the use of the word *defendant* in a statute where *criminal defendant* was the seemingly appropriate phrase.[90] This was not an instance where the language had no meaning at all. It was just that the meaning then became quite awkward and hence implausible for any real or imagined person, for there was no apparent reason in the context to distinguish a defendant from a plaintiff, while there was reason to distinguish a criminal defendant from a criminal prosecutor. This shows, I think, that the line between absurd results and scrivener's errors may also be unclear, and in his opinion in the case from which he took the example, Scalia actually used language of absurdity rather than of error.[91] Regardless of the doctrinal heading, however, Scalia's discussion illustrates how difficult it is to insist on meaning to the exclusion of intention.

In an explanatory essay, Scalia characterized the use of *defendant* rather than *criminal defendant* as an instance where "the legislature obviously misspoke," but earlier in the same essay he had insisted that "when the text of the statute is clear, that is the end of the matter." We are not permitted to look instead for the legislature's intention, he stated, even though "the legislature might have misspoken."[92] Although it seems clear that Scalia himself miswrote, my best explanation for the distinction he makes is that when intention is clear enough, he allows it to trump even clear meaning.[93]

There is a lot to be said for allowing intention to be invoked in clear cases. Recall the ambiguity we discussed earlier about "the United States" in Article II's provisions for presidential eligibility. If we decided not to consider how that phrase might affect the eligibility of someone from a state that never signed on to the Constitution, we might easily find that the best interpretation was that the United States was an entity already in existence. That is, after all, the interpretation suggested by the use of the phrase in the Articles of Confederation and by some uses in the Constitution itself. And that interpretation avoids the problem of Washington's having been ineligible. At the same time, however, the eligibility of a foreigner is decidedly awkward and would likely have been rejected by consensus among those who crafted and ratified the Constitution. In such a circumstance, it would seem appropriate—even perhaps imperative—to accede to that multitude. For if we reject a consensus among those responsible for the language in favor of what we conclude is a more reasonable meaning of the words lifted out of the real-world context in which they were formulated, we subject constitutional interpretation to the vagaries of careless drafting or lack of foresight. If the draftsmen were still around, we might want to scold them for their sloppiness, but it is hard to see what the point is now of giving their words an interpretation of which they would clearly not have approved (and one that, I assume, we would not approve of today either).

This would not deal with Washington's eligibility, but Justice Scalia's discussion might be mined for a way to corral that problem as well. If the constitutional provisions were read as extending eligibility to any citizen of a state governed by the Articles of Confederation that eventually signed on to the Constitution—and only to them—Washington's eligibility would be secured, but eventual foreigners would be excluded. The obvious problem with this interpretation is that there is no single comfortable reading of the language that yields that combination of results. But it is also true that the language does not comfortably accommodate the appropriate outcomes in cases of scrivener's errors or absurdity. To be sure, in the case of the presidential eligibility requirements, no simple rearrangement of the constitutional language—or even addition or subtraction of a word or two—would produce the set of meanings that was likely intended. In the statutory context, Justice Scalia seemed to think it important to do the "least violence to the text."[94] But there is no particular reason that the clearest of errors can typically be corrected by some simple rearrangement of a word or two. Nor is it apparent why less textual violence is preferable to more if more is required to align the results with clear intention. Constitutional interpretation is surely not aimed—even partially—at hewing to an aesthetically pleasing arrangement of words that might have been put into the text. It is rather the clarity of the error that justifies the adjustment. Thus when a consensus intention can be clearly discerned, displacing even clear conventional meaning in the service of that intention seems appropriate even if quite a lot of textual violence is required.[95]

In any event, Justice Scalia is not alone among originalists in appreciating that some ascription of human purposes is necessary to give meaning to the barren marks of constitutional language.[96] His stance on the reach of First Amendment speech and press protections is even suggestive of an inclination to give meaning to constitutional silence in that way. But like Justice Scalia, several academic originalists seem to want to argue that the ascription of purposes can be done objectively, routinely leading to right answers about language meaning or perhaps even about the meaning of silence.[97] A number of commentators make the point even more emphatically by insisting that the inquiry into meaning is a pure factual matter. Gary Lawson and Guy Seidman, for example, argue that the "[d]ocuments [like the Constitution] that address themselves to the public have objective meanings that are capable of being grasped or missed, even by the authors."[98] Taken very far, however, any such claim is simply courting mischief.

No doubt there are many instances where the meaning to be assigned to words, in particular contexts, would be uncontroversial. But it hardly follows that words produced by a multiplicity of people for inclusion in a constitution will typically have objectively ascertainable meanings. We have seen that different people may attach different meanings to the same words. If anything, constitutional silences create a greater danger of disparate understandings. And disparate understandings are what led to the summing problem in the first place. The move to original meaning may shroud that problem, much as the move to original understanding did, but it does not eliminate the necessity for some sort of amalgamation in elaborating that meaning. The shift to original meaning as the object of the originalist's concern thus presents in a different guise the problem we touched upon earlier: choices will often have to be made in order to interpret constitutional language produced in fact by collections of real people.[99]

Choices in the Ascription of Original Meaning

The choices that must be confronted are of various sorts. The debates about originalism and a living Constitution have often focused on the level of generality or specificity at which to conceive of the meaning originally intended or conveyed, and we will return to that choice below. But there are many other choices that will be required. If broad social purposes are to be attributed to words, how does the person who is to decipher meaning sort out the relevant purposes? How much is he or she allowed to learn about the conditions of the day? Some of those conditions may have motivated the real people involved, but is the decipherer of meaning assumed to understand which of the actual social, political, and economic concerns may have moved one or more of the actual authors to vote for the words? A related but arguably different question is whether the meaning fathomer is allowed to know about constituent argumentation or pressure of one sort or another that was in fact brought to bear on the decision makers as the words were crafted or voted upon. If the fathomer of meaning is assumed to know those influences and considerations, how is one to choose among influences if different ones operated on different persons who played a decision-making role? And what is our decipherer to assume about practices or assumptions in the use of language? Is legal training to be assumed or familiarity with other specialized vocabularies? Regardless of the answer to that question, is language—and punctuation—taken to be used with great care?[100] Or can a degree of casualness or sloppiness occasionally—or even often—be taken to have intruded? If words are assumed to be used meticulously, does that nonetheless allow the use of rough synonyms or variant forms for elegance or rhetorical flourish? And when a given word or phrase is in issue, how much consistency across usages is to be assumed? In the case of the Constitution, for example, does any assumed consistency extend to a given clause only, or does it extend to the section in which it is found or to the article that contains the section? Or is the usage taken to be consistent across the entire Constitution? And even apart from the use of a given word or phrase, how much awareness of related or contrasting ideas elsewhere in the same document should be assumed? Is a phrase to be interpreted in isolation or in the context of words around it, and if the latter, how close must those other words be?[101] And what about other documents extant at the time?

Problems of these sorts have long dogged legislative interpretation, and I think it fair to say that in that context there is little in the way of a settled set of answers to them.[102] In the context of constitutional interpretation there has been only occasional overt recognition of such questions, except that those drawn to emphasis on text and its original meaning often proceed as if the decipherer of that meaning is to assume consummate consistency and coherence in language usage.[103]

The original-meaning originalists Lawson and Seidman offer the following response to these problems: "[T]he [original unamended] Constitution means what a reasonable person in 1787 would have understood it to mean after considering all relevant evidence and arguments. Under this approach, original meaning represents *hypothetical* mental states of a legally constructed reasonable person.[104]

The authors thus deploy a hypothetical construct, but, unlike Mr. Intender, theirs is presented as a decipherer of meaning rather than an intender.[105] Other originalists of the original-meaning stripe use somewhat different formulations about how to think of this meaning decipherer. Vasan Kesavan and Michael Paulsen insist on "an average, informed speaker and reader of language at the time of its enactment into law."[106] John Manning puts the point this way: "[M]odern textualists...ask how a reasonable person, conversant with the relevant social and linguistic conventions, would read the text in context."[107] Randy Barnett would refer questions to "the meaning a reasonable speaker of English would have attached to the words, phrases, sentences, etc. at the time the particular provision was adopted."[108] Each of these formulations raises a version of the same related questions we can ask in Lawson and Seidman's terms: (1) What makes evidence and arguments relevant and the legally constructed person reasonable? (2) Is there any difference to be expected between a "legally constructed reasonable person" in the guise of a decipherer of meaning and a reasonable version of Mr. Intender or, for that matter, a similarly reasonable hypothetical understander?

It is certainly possible to think differently about the knowledge base and about the use of language for the different hypothetical role players. We might imagine, for example, that Mr. Intender knew of some interest group pressure, while neither an understander nor a decipherer of meaning did. Or vice versa. It appears that the inclusion of the necessary-and-proper clause in the listing of congressional powers in Article I was rather uncontroversial at the constitutional convention but became contentious in the state-based ratification process, no doubt because some of those involved in the process had a more focused concern about the threat posed to state prerogatives.[109] Or, in the name of realism, we might indulge in an assumption of more looseness in the use of language for Mr. Intender than we would for a fathomer of meaning, who, after all, was not the one who "used" the language. Or we might posit that Mr. Intender was given to some rhetorical flourishes here or there, whereas the other role players were not. It might be that we would imagine an intender who was versed in the law and used language in a technical legal sense, whereas an understander or a meaning fathomer was a nonlawyer who understood the same language in a different way. I do not mean to suggest that any of these assumptions is required, only that such choices must be confronted—implicitly, if not explicitly—regardless of the choice of role players. And those choices, rather than the designation of a particular role for the player, will often bear directly on a conclusion about the meaning to be assigned to the language.[110]

An example employed by Lawson and Seidman can bring the point into sharper focus. In an article on the executive power "to make treaties [by and with the advice and consent of the Senate]," they provide an extended discussion of the vesting clause of Article II and the differences in phraseology between that clause and the vesting clause of Article I.[111] In Article I, legislative powers "herein granted" are vested in Congress, whereas in Article II the executive power is vested in a president, without any reference to some delineation of those powers "herein." Building in part on this contrast, the authors argue, as others have before them, that except as specifically qualified elsewhere and despite some explicit delineation in Article II of the powers of the president, the vesting clause of Article II reposes in the president all of what might reasonably be understood as the "executive power." I take it that they might concede that, considered by itself, the language of Article II does not necessarily mean that the president is assigned all executive power, but for Lawson and Seidman the contrasting language makes that meaning clear.

The authors discuss a variety of arguments against this interpretation, including the possibility others have advanced that the differences in phraseology between Article I and Article II "may have been the product of a drafting accident rather than conscious design."[112] While acknowledging that this "may be true," Lawson and Seidman view that truth or falsehood as irrelevant, because their "reasonable person originalism ... is concerned with how the Constitution's language would be perceived by a reasonable person rather than with the motivations behind the language."[113] But left entirely unclear is why they have their reasonable person assuming that language was used in the contrasting vesting clauses with great care, attention to detail, and consistency across usages. If in fact the actual authors—who were after all paying attention to concerns in and around the interpretational question that Lawson and Seidman are discussing—might not have honed in on possible implications of the contrasting language, why should we conclude that a reasonable decipherer of meaning would have? The answer, I think, is that we would reach such a conclusion only by ascribing nonobvious traits to our decipherer of meaning, in this case consistency and careful attention to language usage. And if we ascribed less of such attentiveness to a perfectly reasonable fathomer of meaning and more to the author, we might reach Lawson and Seidman's interpretive conclusion in the name of original intention but just the opposite conclusion in the name of original meaning.

Lawson and Seidman are more explicit than some of the other original-meaning enthusiasts in claiming that the ascription of meaning is a factual matter that can be done objectively. No doubt they recognize that language can be characterized by ambiguity and vagueness, but they seem to believe that their reasonable-person construct can ferret out clear meaning when it is there. And they also seem to believe that clear meaning is frequently there to be found. What they—and others less explicit—do not seem to appreciate is that the construct of a reasonable person brings normative dimensions with it. The reasonable person is, of course, familiar from the law of torts, and torts scholars have long recognized that a judgment of reasonableness is not a purely factual matter.[114] Thus the reasonable person of torts is not the average person in the world (whatever that might mean), or even the average of some defined class of people, but an idealized person who will apply *appropriate* norms. And that is also true of Lawson and Seidman's construct. The clear normative judgment that they bring to the discussion is that language should be understood as used with care and consistency. There is nothing obvious or objective about that assumption and hence nothing obvious or objective about any conclusion about meaning to which it might lead. Short of an authorial consensus possibility that allows us to rely on actual role players rather than hypothetical ones, it is the choices interpreters make for whatever role player they choose to deploy that will typically determine the meaning to be assigned.[115]

Specificity and Generality in Intention or Meaning

As originalists have struggled to find their grounding, the problem that has probably attracted most of the scholarly attention has been the appropriate level of generality or specificity at which to conceive of the intentions—or understandings or meanings—to be ascribed to constitutional language. This problem of choosing the level of generality may arise when one is faced with relatively precise enacted language. The interpreter might in the name of some general purpose give language a broader sweep than the words alone seem to suggest. To be sure, such moves are often criticized by originalists as failing to respect the authoritative language. Thus originalists poke fun at the possibility that the thirty-five-year age requirement to be president of the United States might really be conceived as a requirement of maturity, which in the present day could be satisfied with a different age.[116] And Justice Douglas's opinion for the Supreme Court in *Griswold v. Connecticut* is often derided by originalists.[117] The Court in *Griswold* held unconstitutional Connecticut's laws restricting the use of contraceptives and the giving of advice about that use. In support of that conclusion Douglas cited several provisions of the Bill of Rights protecting interests of privacy. These specific provisions, he argued, "have penumbras, formed by emanations from those guarantees, that help give them life and substance." With this grounding Douglas concluded that there was a more general constitutional interest in privacy that was "created by several specific constitutional guarantees."[118] Despite the disdain, self-styled originalists occasionally indulge in reasoning that bears some similarity to Douglas's. I mentioned above that Justice Scalia says that the First Amendment protections of speech and press are available for other vehicles of "communicative expression" as well because the two that are mentioned "stand as a sort of synecdoche for the whole."[119]

It is, however, general or vague constitutional language that has posed most insistently the level-of-generality problem. By now the classic example is the question of whether state-required racial segregation of public schools violated the original intention behind (or, for that matter, the original understanding or meaning of) the equal protection clause. Though the historical question is the subject of some debate, most of those who have delved into the history have concluded that the predominant assumption among those responsible for promulgating the clause was that segregation of schools would continue to be permissible.[120] If this reading of history is accepted, it might seem that the original intention behind the clause specifically understood would pose no obstacle to a modern-day state law requiring segregation. But if the intention is pegged at a high level of generality, it easily leaves room for finding that racially segregated public schools are—and even *were* back then—forbidden by that intention.

It is often said that the intention behind the equal protection clause was to forbid discrimination with regard to *fundamental* rights or interests.[121] This is then taken to justify a finding that laws requiring segregation are forbidden because public schooling is now seen as fundamental even if it was not at the time the clause was adopted. We might even conclude now that schooling was fundamental at that time, even if it was not appreciated as such.[122] Jack Balkin's examination of the implications of the equal protection clause for regulation of abortion finds "principles" attached to the clause of "equal citizenship" and a prohibition of "class legislation." Balkin calls his approach "the method of *text and principle*."[123] Applied to the question of school segregation, these general formulations also seem to leave ample room for finding the practice forbidden by the clause.

Additional tensions between specificity and generality of intentions (or understandings or meanings) lurk in the underbrush of essentially all general constitutional language. We touched earlier on the phrase "executive power" in Article II. Does it refer to a specific list of powers that executives exercised at the time, or is it a more general characterization? Is the notion of cruel and unusual punishments to be conceived as a series of punishments that were specifically disapproved at the time the Eighth Amendment was passed or as a general characterization that can then be fleshed out by an interpreter? Is due process of law a set of specific procedural requirements or a more general requirement that must be given content as it is applied?[124] Is the "public use" for which property cannot be taken without "just" compensation to be conceived as a set of uses defined at that time or as a more sweeping category?[125] Is the establishment clause to be understood in reference to specific practices approved and disapproved at the time it was made law or as a general prohibition?[126] Does the general language of the equal protection clause allow court review of state legislative apportionment even if the historical evidence shows that the amendment was specifically intended to reach a set of concerns that did not include apportionment?[127]

Levels of generality and specificity do not necessarily come at two ends of a simple spectrum. If generalities associated with the equal protection clause leave some room for programs of racial affirmative action, what about particular subcategories, like job placement, education, or medical care?[128] And levels of specificity and generality can be teased out of constitutional silence. The disdain for political parties could be a general one. But it might also take more specific form, as in the assumption that parties would be particularly mischievous in the selection of a president. Moving among levels of specificity and generality of conceptions about what enacted language was supposed to accomplish is also a problem familiar from statutory interpretation. In that context, though usage is not as settled as one might wish, legislative *purpose* is often used to express legislative aims at a high degree of generality, while legislative intention is used to characterize more concrete aims.[129]

The level of specificity and generality does not present a choice in quite the same sense as the choices we discussed above. A given individual who voted for the equal protection clause could simultaneously harbor both an understanding that a legislative requirement of racially segregated schools would be permissible (or impermissible) and an understanding expressed in more general terms of what the clause required. If real people could simultaneously harbor intentions at different levels of generality and specificity, then so presumably could our hypothetical constructs.[130] Still, the originalist interpreter is faced with the question of whether original conceptions of what generally phrased provisions require at the level of the specific should be heeded in the process of interpretation. And they have been sharply divided on the question.[131] Recall that we caught a glimpse earlier of Justice Rehnquist seemingly torn about whether or not the intention ascribed to the generalities of the Fourteenth Amendment was to be limited to "abuses in which the states had engaged prior to that time."[132]

This division among originalists is not focused exclusively on intention, for a parallel distinction is made by those who see the search as one for meaning. In the *Blaisdell* case we saw the Supreme Court disparaging any "fine distinction," between the "intended meaning of the words of the

Constitution and their intended application."[133] But just such a distinction has proved attractive in the recent original meaning literature. Thus Larry Solum, my partner in this exchange of essays, relies on a distinction between "semantic meaning" and applications, arguing that only the former is relevant in the search for original meaning.[134] And Balkin, also flying under the banner of original-meaning originalism, argues that original expected applications are not a part of that original meaning. He criticizes Justice Scalia—also an original-meaning enthusiast—for finding meaning in mere expected applications.[135] In what follows I will occasionally add *Mr. Meaning* to a discussion group (or substitute him for Mr. Intender) to help draw out the implications of this level of generality choice in fathoming meaning.

The choice of whether to accede to intention or meaning at the level of the specific has implications for the process of constitutional interpretation and indeed for the clash between originalism and living constitutionalism, though the implications are not nearly as momentous as is often assumed. We have already discussed the limited reach of intentions, and we will return to a similarly limited reach of original applications. But first I should voice my doubts that self-respecting originalists can coherently subordinate "mere" expected applications to generalities in their approach to constitutional interpretation. This appears to be the stance of the most recent wave of originalist theorists, but for several reasons the basis for that preference is questionable.

First, it is not at all clear why the values caught up in applications are not as authoritative as the generalities—not of the language but of the purposes used to give meaning to the barren marks of the language. It might well be that Mr. Intender or Mr. Meaning would have felt particularly strongly about some of the value judgments he harbored as he sought to craft or to understand constitutional language. If we could discover that hierarchy of values, we might then accede to it out of respect for our authoritative character. Confronted by Constitution Man with the school segregation question, for example, Mr. Intender might say that though he meant to allow state-required segregation of schools, if there was a clash between school segregation and the requirement of equal citizenship, the latter must prevail. Mr. Meaning might give comparable responses about the meaning he ascribed to the constitutional language. It is also entirely plausible, however, to imagine a directly contrary position for either character, an insistence that segregation of schools was simply too important to allow it to be subordinated to the views of others about what equal citizenship implied (or meant). I see no particular reason to imagine that the general would usually rank higher on the hierarchy of such originally held values. Indeed, it is often observed that even generally phrased laws are typically responses to specific problems.[136] Of course, the historical record will seldom make it easy to uncover any such hierarchy of values, but the possibility suggests that when the general and specific seem to clash, the specific might often command priority if the aim of interpretation is to respect an originally held hierarchy.

More fundamentally, one might wonder whether the general and the specific can regularly be disentangled in the way suggested by talking of a choice between the two. The originalists John McGinnis and Michael Rappaport, commenting on Balkin's exploration of the abortion problem, say that "[a]n expected application might be so much at the core of a provision that the application is constitutive of its meaning."[137] Or, as Brest put it, one might doubt that "[a] principle...exist[s] wholly independently of...exemplary applications."[138] Indeed, a variety of levels of generality may have mingled in the minds of those who promulgated or sought to understand constitutional language. In discussing the abortion question, Balkin cites views he finds in the historical record about the role of women in addition to those he uncovers about equal citizenship and class legislation. The views about women are not particularly helpful to the argument he wants to make about abortion, but they are part of a complex mix, at once more general than any views about abortion itself and more specific than those about, say, equal citizenship.[139]

For another look at the complexity, let us return to our imagined interrogation by Constitution Man, this time of Mr. Meaning cast as a defender of school segregation. Mr. Meaning would presumably be able to present reasons for his stance. And those reasons might well be expressed in terms of generalities. He might say that schooling was not important enough to be taken as fundamental or even that it was too important to allow good schooling for whites to be compromised by mingling with former slaves. Such generalities do not, of course, appeal to modern sensibilities; but they are generalities, and any judgment that they are unprincipled would be that of the interpreter rather than the original actors. In a classic article on constitutional interpretation, Terrance Sandalow saw right through the problem: "Choice from among the various alternative [principles] is inescapable, and through that choice contemporary values are given expression."[140]

Sometimes commentators who disdain applications in favor of generalities or principles seem to be relying on the meaning of the word *meaning*.[141] Equal protection of the laws might mean equal citizenship, they may be arguing, but it could not possibly mean that racially segregated schools are permitted (or for that matter forbidden). Sometimes the argument seems to be that the meaning of vague or general language must itself be general. Balkin tells us that for original meaning, "principles underlying the constitutional text should be as general as the text itself."[142] It is hardly clear, however, that the word *meaning* has such a limited meaning in ordinary—or judicial—parlance. Thus it is a perfectly conventional use of the word to ask what the equal protection clause *means* for specific matters like the school segregation question.[143] Even more fundamentally, however, why should the meaning of *meaning* matter?

Let us assume that generalities could effectively be identified in the historical record, abstracted from specific problems that may have inspired them, and then be associated with the constitutional language to the exclusion of those specifics. Quite apart from any definition of the word *meaning*, there would remain a serious question about whether such association of language with the generalities was appropriate for at least much of the activity that we call constitutional interpretation. The courts deploy constitutional interpretation in the resolution of particularized disputes. Given that task, it might seem that judicial application of general constitutional language would find more real guidance from specific applications uncovered in the historical record than from the generalities. And ignoring that guidance would be to disdain things that mattered to those with the authority to make things constitutional.

Consider the extreme example of a case that comes to court within days or months of the passage of a constitutional amendment posing a problem that is normatively indistinguishable from one that had rather clearly inspired the amendment. Could a court then appropriately decide the case contrary to the expectation? That would represent the substitution of a judicial decision for one made (or at least thought by the makers to have been made) in the crucible of constitution making. To be sure, there may be doubt in the historical record about an expected application, or the case that arises may not seem normatively congruent with an application that was expected. Over time we can expect a fair amount of such incongruity, and we will return to the questions that it poses. But if there were no problem of incongruity, refusing to afford authoritativeness to the expected application would represent a serious challenge to the amendment process itself.[144] That would be a strange thing to do in the name of respect for the Constitution.

A serviceable example of the power of expected applications is provided by the Supreme Court's 1983 decision in *Marsh v. Chambers*.[145] Nebraska's practice of opening legislative sessions with a prayer offered by a chaplain who was paid for that service was challenged as a violation of the First Amendment's establishment clause, which is taken to be applicable to the states on account of "incorporation" into the Fourteenth Amendment.[146] In upholding the practice, the Court paid scant attention to establishment clause principles as gleaned from the historical record or as elaborated in prior decisions. Instead it dwelt on legislative—including congressional—practice at the time the First Amendment was promulgated, concluding that "the men who wrote the First Amendment Religion Clause did not view paid legislative chaplains and opening prayers as a violation of that Amendment."[147] The Court, in other words, rested its decision squarely on original expected applications. Of course, a lot had happened between the time the First Amendment was passed and 1983. That might have opened up possibilities for distinguishing the issue raised in *Marsh* from those expected applications—i.e., for finding the kind of incongruity mentioned above. The Court did not venture into that territory, however, and the decision can comfortably be viewed as acceding to original expected applications.

The Problem of "Erroneous" Precedent

It is commonly conceded—indeed, emphasized—by many originalists that courts have more than occasionally deviated from an originalist path.[148] It was just such a conviction that Meese articulated. But constitutional decision making by courts in particular is traditionally viewed as an ongoing enterprise, building on its own past. Originalists then must come to grips with how to deal with aspects of that decision-making past that come to be seen as originally erroneous. The most wrenching version of this problem for originalists has been the doctrine of stare decisis, the notion that a degree of fidelity is owed to prior judicial decisions, even those that are later taken to have been mistaken when rendered.

There is not much controversy among originalists about the appropriateness of examining the extant body of judicial decisions for what they might teach about sound originalist decisions.[149] If those decisions were rendered fairly close to the time that the constitutional language was made law, they may even seem to have been informed by sensitivity to originalist sources. And even if a prior decision resolved a genuinely debatable question one way or another, for an originalist there might be a great deal to be said for adhering to it in the future rather than inviting constant revisiting of the debatable issue. But much could also be said for following prior judicial decisions that come to be seen as clearly wrong by originalist lights.[150]

Following precedent can avoid the litigation costs of revisiting issues. Even more important are broader societal costs of unsettling what appears to be settled law. Judicial decisions stimulate reliance by all manner of private and public actors. Overruling decisions can cause loss on investments that seemed sound or otherwise rattle accustomed ways of doing things. And a willingness to revisit a decision might induce less faith in the stability of judicial decisions more generally—even those treating genuinely debatable issues—providing less guidance about the state of the law than might seem optimal. This last point should have special bite for originalists, since a part of the case often made for originalism rests on the stability of written law. Indeed, the unresolved troubles of originalism that we have discussed earlier might accentuate the peril in a willingness to discard precedent. For if originalists cannot agree on the proper approach to decision making, all manner of prior decisions may seem constantly up for (originalist) grabs, as first one school of originalist thought is ascendant and then another.

There is, to be sure, a bit of circularity in the argument about the stability that would follow from judicial adherence to precedent. Judicial decisions induce reliance, it might be argued, only because we do in fact adhere to them. If courts were always willing to fully revisit prior decisions and follow pure originalist decision making wherever it might lead, that willingness would become apparent over time, and private and public actors would not rely on prior decisions beyond any originalist appeal. To this argument about circularity there are both practical and theoretical responses.

As a practical matter, there seems to be no real prospect that courts will change their supposedly errant ways anytime soon, even if originalists could reach more agreement than they have on elements of some right way. On a theoretical level, even if originalists could reach basic agreement on elements of the approach, originalism could not hope to bring the degree of stability in the law that following precedent does. This would likely be so even if intention or meaning were pegged at the level of the specific, for time will produce a multitude of specific problems that will bear only attenuated resemblance to things that were the subject of attention (or of subconscious assumption) at the time of constitutional enactment. Over time, the number of judicial precedents will overwhelm those to be found in the historical record. Precedent will then provide a much richer set of applications of constitutional language to offer guidance for the ongoing flow of controversies that come to court. And if original intention or original meaning is conceived to be quite general, proliferating judicial decisions can be mined for guidance that the generality of language could not possibly provide.[151]

It is therefore not surprising that self-styled originalists are all over the map on the question of whether deference should be paid to prior judicial decisions.[152] Some would leave any precedent routinely vulnerable to challenge on originalist grounds.[153] And there are many variations in originalist positions on precedent between utter disdain and more conventional strong attachment to precedent.[154] Moreover, the rationales for these various positions differ dramatically. Some originalist defenders of stare decisis acknowledge that their stance is unprincipled, flatly inconsistent with their originalism. They adopt the position as a bow to practical realities.[155] Others, in contrast, see no inconsistency, usually because they claim that a doctrine of precedent forms an originalist part of the conception of judicial power.[156] Still others, as we have seen, claim that their originalism is a purely descriptive or factual inquiry into the meaning of words, which, they seem at times to claim, is without normative implications. For these originalists, getting the facts straight in interpretation is one thing, but what to do with that interpretation is presumably another.[157] A doctrine of precedent might then have normative appeal, I suppose, as long as it was recognized as not really interpretation of the constitutional text.

Despite these differences, originalists are largely agreed that incorrect precedents should be narrowly confined so that the damage from infection of the decision-making process by nonoriginalist decision making is contained.[158] But this position brings its own problems because the reach of a precedent is itself a matter of judgment. At one extreme a prior judicial decision could be confined to the specific facts of the dispute that occasioned it. At the other, an opinion would reach as far as its rationale. The first would essentially strip a prior decision of precedential effect, whereas the second would provide little limitation on the sway of precedent. Following precedent only a little bit, moreover, introduces the possibility of treating differently cases that are in many respects quite similar. In any event, there does not appear to have been serious originalist probing of just how originalism in particular might define an appropriate middle ground on the force of precedent.

The Problem of Constitutional Amendment

The ongoing process of constitutional decision making poses yet another problem for originalists, this time one that has received little explicit attention in originalist literature. Constitutional amendments build on a past and pose the question of how an amendment and the past on which it is built are to be integrated into some coherent—or at least workable—whole.

The Amendments can, of course, pose language problems much like those we surveyed earlier. For example, the Eleventh Amendment explicitly addresses lawsuits against a state by "citizens of another state," denying the reach of the "judicial power of the United States" to such proceedings. But it says nothing explicit about suits against a state by citizens of that very state. The courts have examined the historical setting in which the amendment was passed, however, and concluded that those responsible took for granted that suits against a citizen's own state were equally offensive.[159] If this reading of history is accepted, the Eleventh Amendment might be interpreted to forbid such suits despite its silence.

But the silence of amendments can be even more deafening, and, like judicial precedent, amendments can be built on a reading of the past that originalists see as erroneous. The problem is most acute where the language of an amendment is similar or identical to preexisting constitutional language, as with the Fourteenth Amendment's privileges and immunities and due process clauses.[160] Assuming there was originalist error in interpretation of the language before the amendment, is an interpreter of the original language working after the amendment still looking for the original meaning of that original language or for the different meaning on which the amendment's use of the same language was predicated?[161] (Some originalists actually endorse yet another possibility: the hypothesized role player for all amendments should be situated at the time of the original, unamended Constitution.)[162] A similar question can be imagined for amendments that do not closely track earlier constitutional language and even for failure to amend. It is easy to imagine that amendment efforts might be abandoned because existing constitutional interpretations—even if erroneous by originalist lights—make amendment seem unnecessary.[163] If initial constitutional silence might carry meaning, then failure to amend might do so as well.

The problem of the constitutional status of political parties that we touched on earlier can illustrate the dilemma. Despite the early disdain for political parties, two antagonistic political groupings did develop during Washington's presidency, and, as we saw, they injected themselves into the process of selecting presidential electors. Under the original constitutional provisions governing presidential selection, electors were to cast two votes for president—for two different candidates with no designation of a favorite. If one (or more) candidates commanded electoral votes equal to at least a majority of the number of electors, the candidate with the highest number became president. The runner-up was to be vice president, whether or not he commanded a majority. Before the intrusion of parties into the process, a tie vote among electors, with each of the tied candidates commanding the required majority, seemed possible but decidedly unlikely, as electors in uncoordinated state meetings met and debated who were the two people in the country who would be suited to fill the office of president. The Constitution provided for selection of the president in the House of Representatives if no candidate commanded an electoral college majority (with a majority of state delegations in the House required to prevail there), and basically the same backup procedure was provided for the seemingly unlikely possibility of a tie between two (or even three) candidates with electoral college majorities.[164]

The involvement of political parties in the process considerably complicated the picture. If all electors were party loyalists and each cast his two votes for the party's presidential and vice presidential candidates, the result would be a tie, albeit through a mechanism that had apparently been given no consideration in constructing the constitutional scheme. And that is just what happened with the Republican electors of 1800. Thomas Jefferson and Aaron Burr were the party's candidates for president and vice president, respectively. The party's electors commanded a majority of the electoral college, and they all cast their two votes for Jefferson and Burr. Burr did not gracefully step aside, and the House backup procedure was engaged. It required thirty-six votes for the House to resolve the impasse in Jefferson's favor.[165]

This wrenching drama led to the Twelfth Amendment, which separated the electoral college votes for president and vice president. The amendment was clearly necessitated because political parties had become a looming reality in American political life, but it makes no mention of parties. How, then, is an originalist to think about the relevance of the amendment for questions that keep arising in constitutional law about the role of political parties? The electoral college is now the least of those problems. Political parties are in the center rather than at the margins of political life in the country, officially assigned all manner of electoral responsibilities. The Twelfth Amendment might be taken to legitimate party activity, but its silence on the subject makes that an awkward move for an interpreter who insists on assigning meaning to words in the name of some reasonable fathomer of meaning. Constitutional meaning before the Twelfth Amendment presumably was one of disdain for parties, and there is no language in the amendment that might seem to change that meaning. Of course, if a reasonable fathomer of meaning is allowed to know about the real-world background of the amendment and apply the amendment with that background in mind, it might open up space for political parties to assume a place of honor in American politics and governance. But even so, would that place be limited to the presidential elector context that prompted the amendment—and that its words address—or would it extend more generally? And if it extended more generally, we would still be faced with trying to integrate original attitudes toward political parties and Twelfth Amendment attitudes. For example, contemporary questions about political parties arise under the First Amendment, which, of course, preceded the Twelfth and also preceded the movement of political parties to center stage in American politics. Are originalists to interpret the First Amendment in or out of some shadow cast by the Twelfth?

Claiming the mantle of original-meaning originalism, Steven Calabresi urges a startling resolution of dilemmas like this (at least on a theoretical level). He would interpret the necessary-and-proper clause of the original Constitution to withhold authority from the federal government to discriminate on the basis of race, a restriction that would presumably include race-based affirmative action programs. Calabresi's explanation is that for originalists like him, "texts should be read holistically," and thus congressional power "is logically read in light of the...Fourteenth Amendment."[166] It is not at all clear that history justifies Calabresi's reading of the Fourteenth Amendment to forbid affirmative action.[167] But if we grant that move, it would seem that for Calabresi the original public meaning of parts of the Constitution can be changed by amendment, without any actor's having been aware that he was instituting such a change—and without the inclusion of any language suggestive of it. Nor does Calabresi probe at all deeply into the implications of his suggested integration. It is thus unclear whether a holistic reading of the amended Constitution might operate in the opposite direction (in the time dimension) from Calabresi's, causing amendments to be brought into alignment with preexisting provisions even though those responsible for the amendments may have had change in mind.

Problems of integrating meanings harbored at different points in time arise in the legislative context. If there is a direct clash, the later enactment governs, but beyond that little is settled, except that attaching significance to failure to enact legislation is often disdained on account of the ambiguity of such failure.[168] The great difficulty of constitutional amendment might then justify even greater reluctance about attaching significance to failure to amend. But those who adopt this stance must appreciate that it does further unsettle any attempt to depict the interpretational enterprise as some straightforward fathoming of meaning—or intention, for that matter.

Implications for Living Constitutionalism

Constraint Based on Original General Principles

We have seen that many originalists disdain any claim for the authoritativeness of specific original intentions or meanings (or expected applications) that attended general constitutional language. This then opens space for the use of contemporary values in the adjudication of cases where that general language is to be applied. For as Justice Holmes instructed in his dissent in *Lochner v. New York*, "general propositions do not decide concrete cases."[169]

Increasingly, originalists are acknowledging, or even relishing, the space created by general language. In his original-meaning defense of *Roe v. Wade* Jack Balkin acknowledges that there was no original intention to forbid or restrain state regulation of abortion. Balkin justifies *Roe* instead by invoking general "principles" associated with the general language of the equal protection clause. His conclusion with regard to *Roe* is, of course, particularly striking, since disapproval of that decision undoubtedly provided much of the political impetus for Meese's introduction of the originalism debate onto the public stage.

To be sure, reliance on general principles need not mean that contemporary interpretation of general language is unconstrained, that judges must simply decide cases as they think they should come out as a matter of contemporary social policy. A good dose of realism about the judicial task would advance the cause of understanding constitutional interpretation. But constraining influences are potentially available, even when generally phrased constitutional language is understood in terms of generally phrased principles. Conventional or semantic meanings of constitutional generalities are not unlimited. The "cruel and unusual" limitation applies to "punishments." The Fourth Amendment "reasonableness" requirement is for "searches and seizures." Even the grand generalities of the Fourteenth Amendment are expressed in terms of what a "state" can do.

It may also be that history could be mined for constraint in interpreting general constitutional language. It is possible that a diligent search of the historical record might unearth some general principles that were associated with the adopted language and that those historically grounded principles might carry different implications than did other principles that the constitutional language might accommodate but that did not surface in the historical record.[170] In such a case, the contemporary originalist judge might find some self-discipline by following only historically grounded general principles.[171]

Consider, for example, the appropriate interpretation of the guarantee clause, the provision of Article IV that "the United States shall guarantee to every State in this Union a Republican form of government."[172] Of course, the federal courts have long held that direct application of this clause raises nonjusticiable political questions.[173] Putting that aside, however, the historical record provides a discernible measure of support for at least two rather different meanings of a republican form of government. There is some evidence that it was understood to mean government responsible to the citizenry at large. But most historians would gravitate instead to a definition that insisted on some intermediation between the public and the making of policy. In this latter view a legislature would be an essential vehicle for public decision making under a republican form of government because it would provide insulation from popular pressure.[174] A conscientious originalist seeking guidance from original general principles might then prefer this latter interpretation. And the choice might well affect his approach to troublesome questions about the use of the popular initiative process on the part of the states.[175]

To be sure, clarity in the historical record about the principles to be associated with constitutional generalities may still provide relatively little guidance for particular problems that arise. Clarity may also be hard to come by. When hundreds, or even thousands, of individuals were actually involved in formulating and enacting general phraseology—and did so against the backdrop of a variety of perceived evils—we should hardly be surprised to find support in the historical record for a variety of generalities associated with the language. In addition to the guarantee clause example, we saw some of this complexity about Fourteenth Amendment principles in our earlier discussion of Balkin's exploration of the abortion problem.[176] After receiving criticisms of his text and principle analysis of the constitutional status of abortion, Balkin retreated from any suggestion of clarity about principles to be found in the historical record. Indeed, he went so far as to insist that authoritative principles need not actually have been embraced by any of the real actors responsible for enacting the constitutional language.[177] Instead, for Balkin, what is required is simply that the principles be ones that "the text can bear."[178] Obviously such a relaxation of any requirement of historical validation of applicable principles opens additional space for reliance upon contemporary values.

Constraint from More Particular Original Aims

With constitutional generalities providing modest constraints on judges even as fleshed out by general principles, a number of originalists have insisted that the purposes behind general constitutional language should be pegged at the level of the particular. In addition to Justice Antonin Scalia, Justice Clarence Thomas seems to have adopted this stance (albeit not always consistently), and it clearly was the position of Raoul Berger, who pursued originalist interpretations of the Fourteenth Amendment decades before Meese entered the picture.[179] It is also the working assumption of Johnathan O'Neill's exploration of the history of originalism.[180] I argued earlier that treating those specific judgments as authoritative is an entirely justifiable move for an originalist because it bespeaks respect for values that were originally associated with the language. But this move to the specific does not bring the stability to constitutional interpretation that these originalists usually assume. In fact, reliance on originally assumed applications has little capacity to hold the line against a living constitution.

To lay bare the frequent futility of relying on original intentions or applications in this way, let us return to our interrogation of Mr. Intender, cast as a defender of school segregation. And this time we will imagine that Constitution Man travels through time—from the 1950s, when the *Brown* case was before the Supreme Court, back to the nineteenth century, when Mr. Intender was producing the equal protection clause. In this way the discussion between the two of them can be informed by the history of racial segregation of schools in the United States. We will assume, as this class of originalists suggests, that mere original applications of general constitutional language have fully as much status to guide us in constitutional interpretation as do original general principles associated with that language. Just what guidance can we hope to glean from the values caught up in those specifics?

Suppose that Constitution Man set about interrogating Mr. Intender about how he would reconcile the general and the specific. Constitution Man might ask whether legislatively required racial segregation of schools was consistent with equal protection of the laws, and Mr. Intender would presumably respond that he did not understand the clause to pose an impediment. "Well," Constitution Man might then continue, "it is helpful to know that, because state-required racial segregation of public schools became quite contentious over the years in the United States, and an historic court challenge to such laws was mounted toward the middle of the twentieth century." That might elicit some surprise, or at least interest, on the part of Mr. Intender, who might then probe for more information. Constitution Man might then recount the history of race relations since passage of the Fourteenth Amendment, including a complete explanation of the role that schooling had come to play in the mid-twentieth-century United States and a realistic assessment of the inequality of black schools in segregated systems in that era. The discussion I have in mind would, in short, educate Mr. Intender so that he could think about twentieth-century school segregation as if he had lived through all that happened between promulgation of the Fourteenth Amendment and the 1950s. Seeing the full picture, Mr. Intender might be given pause about his earlier response. He might say that the issue as he now understood it was not the one he had had in mind when he first responded. With the education he has received, he might conclude instead that the equal protection clause would forbid legislatively required segregation of schools as he now understands it as a phenomenon of the middle of the twentieth century.

My point is not that Mr. Intender would surely answer the question this way. He might insist that racially segregated schools in the twentieth century were permissible under the equal protection clause. The point, rather, is that we have no way of knowing whether he would view the contemporary issue as being the same as the one he had a clear opinion about in the nineteenth century. The one has a history and a social and economic setting that is very different from the other. Those differences might well lead to a conclusion that they posed quite different issues. The mid-twentieth-century issue was not one about which Mr. Intender had any view at all as he originally fathomed the meaning of the equal protection clause for school segregation.[181]

Nor is this unusual for constitutional questions. There may be occasional contemporary questions of application of constitutional generalities, the normative dimensions of which are basically congruent with those that informed original intentions or original applications.[182] The legislative prayer issue posed by *Marsh v. Chambers* that we discussed earlier strikes me as a plausible candidate for such congruence. If we conclude that there are such issues, however, that conclusion will almost surely be debatable for most of them. But more to the present point, the conclusion will be rare.

For example, less than two decades after enactment of the Fourteenth Amendment, the Supreme Court found in *Yick Wo v. Hopkins* that the reason for discriminatory enforcement of San Francisco building ordinances was simple "hostility to the race and nationality" of the resident alien plaintiffs—"subjects," in the Court's words, "of the emperor of

China."[183] The Court found the discrimination offensive to the "broad and benign provisions" of the amendment.[184] That conclusion would not seem to follow, however, if the principle of choice was one of equal citizenship. Nor could the court garner much guidance from the applications of the amendment that had been the near-exclusive focus of concern in the debates leading up its passage. For obvious reasons, that concern was with the newly freed slaves. Disfavor of (legal) resident aliens poses very different questions than does disfavor of the freedmen.[185] (Recall Justice Rehnquist's focus on "abuses" that the framers of the amendment had in view.) There is, in other words, no knowing what answer Constitution Man would have gotten had he probed Mr. Intender as the Fourteenth Amendment was being made law about what to do in solving problems like that posed by *Yick Wo*. The Supreme Court's decision in *Yick Wo* has not been a controversial decision—I know of no originalist criticism of it—but the value judgments that informed it could simply not be found with any degree of certitude either in original general principles or in original, specifically focused, intentions or applications. By default, much of the value structure that informed *Yick Wo* simply had to be supplied by the judges charged with deciding.

And so it is with myriad issues embedded in some latter day's social, political, and economic world. Issues that are posed today will often bear scant resemblance to what the constitutional framers—or any meaning decipherer of that time—envisioned, and thus the normative questions joined in today's litigation must typically draw on a host of considerations—a configuration of values—that have no real roots in any plausible recounting of Mr. Intender's understanding back then.[186] In his classic concurrence in *Youngstown Sheet & Tube Co. v. Sawyer* Justice Robert Jackson put it this way: "Just what our forefathers did envision, or would have envisioned had they foreseen modern conditions, must be divined from materials almost as enigmatic as the dreams Joseph was called upon to interpret for Pharaoh."[187] In something of a rejoinder to Meese, Justice Brennan made much the same point: "[O]ur distance of two centuries [from our constitutional beginnings] cannot but work as a prism refracting all we perceive."[188] I see no escape from the point. And if this is so, resolution of today's questions, if relegated to the judiciary, must be guided in large measure by contemporary values as discerned and explicated by that judiciary.[189]

The Seduction of Verbal Formulations

The reconfiguration of issues with the passage of time is often obscured by the verbal formulations that are used to characterize issues. Consider, for instance, the contemporary problem of *faithless* presidential electors— those who cast their electoral votes for a candidate other than the one to whom they were pledged before the election. Can a state forbid this practice? As suggested by our earlier discussion of presidential electors, if Constitution Man were to have posed this question at the time the electoral college provisions were being crafted, there is little doubt that he would have been told that electors were free agents and could cast their votes as they saw fit.[190] Nobody could instruct them. But it was not long after the Constitution was adopted that the world of presidential selection took on a very different cast. As noted earlier, this was due to the emergence of political parties and their formation of elector slates in support of presidential and vice presidential nominees of the parties. And as those political parties moved from the margins of American politics to its center over the ensuing two hundred and some years, presidential selection has changed in additional ways that would be entirely unrecognizable to the constitutional framers. Today, for example, the ballots that most voters mark up on election day give no hint whatsoever of a role to be played by presidential electors some forty days later. It would thus be pure fiction to assume that those who crafted or originally understood the electoral college provisions of the Constitution had a ready answer to the question of whether modern state laws forbidding elector faithlessness are permissible.

This is so no matter how the issue is articulated. If the constitutional question is presented as, Are presidential electors constitutionally entitled to exercise discretion in their choice? then we know the original answer, whether cast in terms of intention, understanding, or meaning. Electors not only were entitled to exercise discretion but were surely expected to do so. The same articulation could be used for today's question, but that provides only the appearance that the questions are the same. The mere fact that what was once laudable discretion is now seen very broadly as lamentable faithlessness betrays the changes. Today's presidential selection process is simply worlds apart from that originally envisaged. And so it is not only with school segregation and the status of resident aliens under the equal protection clause but with political parties as holders of free speech rights and even with the constitutional status of abortion. Yesterday's questions in those forms only faintly foreshadow the reality of today's questions.[191]

Justice Antonin Scalia recognizes the point in the First Amendment context, acknowledging the genuine difficulty of the question, "How...does the First Amendment guarantee of 'the freedom of speech' apply to new technologies that did not exist when the guarantee was created—to sound trucks, or to government-licensed over-the-air television?" But he insists that such genuine questions will not arise "very often."[192] Scalia does not explain the basis for that judgment, and I find it hard to fathom. Maybe he thinks that the only changes that can count are technological. Or perhaps he appreciates the emergence of new questions in the context of speech and press protections because, as we have seen, he is sensitive to the important purposes behind those protections. But the appearance of television and sound trucks does not begin to capture societal changes in the United States since the Constitution was adopted. The relevance of television and sound trucks to First Amendment questions strikes me as at the easy end of the spectrum of constitutional problems posed by change over time. The importance and applicability of purposes that help us today to find and apply meaning for contemporary problems in the barren marks of constitutional language are simply not something that history can often settle. In other words, even if history provides some clear answer about the important purposes that were associated with constitutional language long ago, judgment will still be required in identifying changes and assessing their significance. That process of assessment will itself be suffused with value judgments. And the values will necessarily be contemporary ones—for Justice Scalia as well as for others who have a responsibility to decide.

The Place of Precedent

The changes that the march of time so often brings to constitutional issues provide a clue to the role of precedent in constitutional adjudication, a role that, as we have seen, distresses and divides originalists. A contemporary question that has been the subject of a prior judicial decision, one that has generated substantial reliance, is simply not the same question that may originally have engaged an intender—or a decipherer of meaning. There is thus typically no knowing what his answer would be to a question of whether that precedent should be followed. Nor can we even know more generally the intender's or meaning decipherer's general attitude toward constitutional precedent in today's setting. Regardless of what he may have thought more than two hundred years ago about the role of precedent, given the incredible drama of judicial review in the name of the Constitution since that time, he might well view that role differently today than he did back then.[193]

To be sure, both specific problems that helped stimulate constitutional generalities and specific problems that have been addressed in judicial precedents do have some power to guide and constrain in the ongoing process of constitutional adjudication. It may appear that there are no normative differences between an identifiable historical example and a question under adjudication. As mentioned, that conclusion may well be contestable, but a judgment that the issues are the same is certainly possible. Indeed, through just such a mechanism, it is likely that many problems never get to court in the first place. And even if there are normative differences between present issues and earlier ones, a measure of guidance can still be found. Both similarities and differences can be noted and evaluated. Resident aliens are different from newly freed slaves, but they are also similar in important respects. Indeed, descendants of slaves are both different from and similar to ex-slaves in ways that might be thought to bear on how Fourteenth Amendment protections are applied. Precedent is in fact used in just this way in constitutional (and other) adjudication, providing examples on the basis of which litigants can argue about—and courts can decide—how to think about new problems that those courts are called upon to address. The process requires choice through the exercise of judgment; there is simply no escape from judges bringing that judgment to the decision-making mix.

The Judicial Decision-Making Process

There is a larger point that emerges from thinking about the judicial decision-making process in this way. Originalists pay much too little attention to that process, concentrating instead on an abstract enterprise of constitutional interpretation. Federal courts in particular sit in judgment of cases and controversies, and they interpret the Constitution as a means to that end. Thus at least from an historical perspective Keith Whittington seems to have it backwards when he asserts that "the purpose of judicial review is to interpret the Constitution" and that "the [Supreme] Court justifies itself ... with the claim that it engages in interpretation [of the Constitution]."[194] The classic justification for the Court as constitutional expositor is that it adjudicates cases.[195] That, at least, was the justification for judicial review that was offered in *Marbury v. Madison*.[196] Constitutional interpretation is a means to that end and cannot be readily disentangled from the process that occasions it.

To be sure, over the years the Supreme Court has increasingly come to see itself as a lawgiver rather than simply as an adjudicator using the elaboration of law (including constitutional interpretation) as a tool. But in many ways the process of adjudication still conditions the Court's behavior. To a great extent the Supreme Court grapples with issues that litigants define and shape. And it does so in a time frame that is seldom if ever of its own exclusive choosing. The facts of cases to be adjudicated are developed at great length and then understood to be fair game in the argumentation and decision of cases.[197] Litigants often have incentives to develop records that emphasize the particulars of cases, and that emphasis then draws the attention of judges. That is not an accidental byproduct of judicial activity but constitutive of it. Each side in litigation will typically emphasize similarities to and differences from some problems that history may be thought to have settled. In this setting it would be quite surprising if judges put those particulars out of their minds as they puzzled about constitutional meaning. Indeed, it is doubtful that they could do so if they tried. Thus although the question of Washington's eligibility for the presidency never got to court, it seems entirely unrealistic to imagine that a court faced with that question could somehow have put out of its mind the consequences of its answer. In addition, as courts address new questions, they are often prompted to think about dimensions of problems that had not earlier come into focus. The process of deciding *Yick Wo*, for example, might open minds to ways of dealing with problems posed by illegal aliens in a way that would have been harder to come by when emancipated slaves had been the only real object of attention.[198]

Instructive examples of the role of contemporary values abound. Robert Bork's struggle with the school segregation question is one. In his first published discussion of the problem in 1971, Bork assumed that history was unclear about whether the Fourteenth Amendment "authors" had a clear answer one way or the other about the relevance of the amendment for racially segregated public schools. But if it were clear that there was an "intention" to allow segregated schools, Bork insisted that courts would be obliged to follow that intention. "If the legislative history revealed a consensus about segregation in schooling," he wrote, "I do not see how the Court could escape the choices revealed and substitute its own, even though the words are general and conditions have changed."[199] When he treated the subject at greater length in 1990, however, Bork's analysis had changed. By then, he took the teaching of history to be clear that those responsible for the equal protection clause thought that it would interpose no obstacle to segregated schools. This then posed a clash for Bork between the general and the specific, as to both of which he thought there was a well-established original intention (or understanding). But now the clash was to be resolved in favor not of the specific but of the general. And this was because "[t]he text itself demonstrates that the [*sic*] equality under law was the primary goal.... [E]quality, not separation, was written into the text."[200]

As suggested earlier, the general phraseology does not resolve primacy of goals, and Bork does not tell us what else might establish primacy in this clash. Moreover, the equality that was written into the text of the equal protection clause was for "protection of the laws." Judgments about equal protection of law necessarily draw on normative evaluation of justifications for distinctions that laws inevitably make.[201] And one can probably be confident that Bork did not believe that once protection of the laws was provided equally, equality of results was also required by the equal protection clause. The fact that segregated schools were in fact unequal then posed an equal protection question but did not provide the answer without inquiry into the justifications offered. But one thing is clear. By 1991 the *Brown* case had become a part of the constitutional culture. Bork wrote of "the obvious moral rightness of its result" and indeed of *Brown* as "the greatest moral triumph constitutional law had ever produced."[202] He was certainly not alone in this judgment, and it is clear that he could not have hoped to be taken seriously if he had disavowed the result in *Brown*. Bork was honest enough to note that his rationale for that result had changed, but what had remained constant was room for the result in *Brown*.[203] I cannot, of course, read Bork's mind and pronounce on what was really going on in producing this constancy, but guidance from values of Bork's own day seems like a pretty good bet.

The guarantee clause provides the backdrop for a second telling instance of the pull of values drawn from the here and now. On account of the nonjusticiable political question doctrine mentioned earlier, the federal courts have refused to rule on guarantee clause challenges to state use of the mechanisms of direct democracy, including the popular initiatives that have come to play a prominent role in a number of states.[204] At the same time, however, they have not thought they could avoid review of particular pieces of initiated state legislation (or particular initiated state constitutional amendments) under other provisions of the United States Constitution.[205] But there is no comfortable way to disentangle many of those latter constitutional questions from the question of the republican bona fides of the popular initiative.

Just how, for instance, are the courts to treat the question of the motivation—or intention—for a popular initiative when it is challenged under the equal protection clause? The summing problem that we discussed earlier for legislation and constitutional provisions is compounded manyfold for popular initiatives, since the legislators may be hundreds of thousands of individual voters.[206] And the secrecy of the ballot makes inquiry into the motivations of those voters even more problematic than it is for the members of legislatures and the makers (and ratifiers) of constitutions. What is particularly telling is that justices Scalia and Thomas— the two self-proclaimed originalist judges on the Supreme Court—cut through these difficulties, using something of a presumption of constitutionality for initiatives because of their democratic credentials.[207] In other words, they not only avoid the question of the meaning of *republican form of government* but they adopt a normative stance that is oblivious to the most likely historical meaning of the language. Again, I cannot read minds, but there is no mystery about where those originalist judges find their favor for democracy. Were they to have delved into the history books, they would have found originalist materials that provided at least as much evidence that *democratic*—at least when used in the sense of governmental policymaking by the public at large—was a term of disparagement in our constitutional beginnings as that it was a label of praise.[208] In all likelihood the embrace of democracy by Scalia and Thomas is a product of values they absorbed as they came of age in the twentieth century.

Earlier we discussed a variety of choices other than the level of generality that must be made in assigning meaning to constitutional language in the name of a hypothetical construct, whether cast as an intender, understander, or fathomer of meaning.[209] The Supreme Court's 2008 opinion in *District of Columbia v. Heller* provides a telling illustration of the exercise of those choices to shape decisions.[210] The case presented a challenge to District of Columbia laws that essentially prohibited the possession of handguns in the home. By a five-to-four vote the Court held that the district's prohibition was forbidden by the Second Amendment, which provides (in full) as follows: "A well regulated Militia, being necessary to the security of a free State, the right of the people to keep and bear Arms, shall not be infringed." The *Heller* opinions on both sides are lengthy, and I will not rehearse all the twists and turns in their reasoning. But it is noteworthy that each relies on three different types of arguments, reaching diametrically opposed conclusions in each of those three realms. Emphasizing different parts of the historical record, they draw different historical conclusions. They diverge on the significance to be attached to the extant judicial precedent. And they urge different readings of the spare language of the amendment, the dissent emphasizing and the majority opinion minimizing the significance of the introductory language. I think it fair to say that both majority and dissenters advance arguments in each of those three realms with at least surface plausibility. And what is particularly striking is that in each realm both majority and dissenters reach conclusions that are consistent in the sense of reinforcing the conclusion that each reaches on the ultimate issue. In the case of the majority opinion by the originalist justice Scalia, we also have evidence that the conclusion reached was one the author had embraced more than a decade earlier.[211]

In minimizing the significance of the introductory language, Justice Scalia characterizes that language as articulating the purpose of the amendment. But he insists that the right referred to in the second part of the amendment is not to be read as constrained to service of that purpose. This is at the least in some tension with the stance we have seen him adopt toward the First Amendment, where he would extend the literal reach of its speech and press protections to effectuate the purpose they were designed to serve.[212] It is hard to imagine a fair reading of the clash in *Heller* that did not conclude that each side mined the choices available to reach conclusions each found congenial to its own—contemporary—scheme of values.[213]

I want to be clear that the contemporary *values* on which judges draw might be quite complex. I am not using the word as basically synonymous with public policy outcomes that might be at stake. Judges may, for instance, harbor important values about how the job of judging should be done. They may bring attitudes toward precedent to the task of judging or views about appropriate deference to other branches of government in general or particular sorts of cases. They may think it appropriate in opinion writing to paint with a broad brush to provide guidance for related problems or with a fine brush because of a conviction that courts should tread lightly in constitutional law. They may even bring to the task of judging views about guidance that can be gleaned from history. Indeed, it is possible that views of these sorts can be held quite sincerely but also be simplistic in the ways we have encountered for the uses of history, to the extent that some judges will fail to appreciate how much substantive value judgments are actually affecting their decisions. Whether consciously appreciated or not, views about matters of social policy will certainly be a part of the mix, but that decidedly does not mean that they are all that will be in play in the realm of contemporary values.

The Possibility of More Originalist Guidance

Could the conscientious originalist hope for more originalist guidance in the process? If originalists would more forthrightly acknowledge the choices involved, they might, I suppose, strive for discipline in the exercise of those choices. They might settle on an approach to precedent, for example. Steven Calabresi has urged a rule that a necessary and sufficient condition for a precedent to be binding is that all three branches of the federal government must have accepted it as "well settled."[214] Perhaps originalists could rally around that rule. They might agree that language will always be assumed to have been used consistently and with consummate care. And they could try to specify in some detail just what a reasonable decipherer of meaning might have known. They might, for instance, try to purge their reasonable construct of normative dimensions by insisting that he was the average citizen of the time in terms of age, values, education, occupation, or what have you. They might insist on a literal reading of all constitutional language or, conversely, that all language must be understood in light of the purposes that history shows it was designed to serve.

I have very serious doubts that any such efforts would yield some significant degree of determinacy in the originalist effort.[215] On the attempt to
construct an average citizen, for example, even if one could settle on what
is to be averaged, the historical work to find out how that citizen would
likely have understood constitutional language would be daunting. And
any such disciplinary regime would still leave room for a neooriginalist
countermovement that did not accept one or more of the constraints. In
any event, there is no real prospect of agreement on any significant set of
disciplining rules. In truth, the ongoing troubles of originalism result from
basic sources of imprecision in the enterprise of constitutional interpretation. The result is that there are quite plausible arguments to be made—
even in originalist terms—on different sides of so many of originalism's
disagreements. Given that state of affairs, there seems little reason to expect originalists as a whole to settle their differences anytime soon or, for
that matter, ever.

This being said, there is one kind of constitutional question with a bit
more potential to bring its own discipline to the decisional process—a kind
of question for which the constitutional language seems to clearly dictate
an answer. If the Constitution says that each state is to have two senators,
it would seem easy and comfortable to follow that instruction without getting diverted by inquiries into purpose. It might still be, of course, that very
weighty arguments could be mounted against the most natural reading of
the language. Woeful consequences could be cited. The ratio of populations
in the most and least populous states, for example, is wildly different today
than it was in 1787, and thus the malapportionment of the Senate with two
senators for each state might seem considerably more problematic now.[216]
Indeed, values might have changed. What is called federalism is a different
phenomenon now than it was back then. For one thing, since the Seventeenth
Amendment, senators do not represent states in the way they originally did.
And we think very differently now about distribution of the electoral fran-
chise. Whether caused by changing values or a cause of them, the Supreme
Court's "one person, one vote" apportionment decisions of the 1960s seem to
have won widespread acceptance.[217] Those decisions held up representation
based on population as the obvious ideal in American democracy, and as the
Court essentially recognized, the United States Senate seriously offends that
ideal.[218] Contemporary values that bear on Senate apportionment might
thus seem to be different from those that prevailed as the Constitution was

being crafted. But despite the potential tug of such arguments, the Senate formula is clear and seems easy to apply, so an originalist approach to interpretation of the two-senator requirement can be made to work. And serious problems are easy to imagine if courts were to break loose from the articulated formula, inviting one state or another to argue for more representation on the basis of one or another way of calculating.[219]

Still, even for such precise language, events may occasionally create quite a strong temptation to skirt the language in favor of some liveliness in the Constitution. Consider, for example, the nineteenth-century fate of constitutional language closely related to the stipulation that each state is to have two senators. Article IV provides that "no new State shall be formed...within the jurisdiction of any other State...without the consent of the Legislatures of the States concerned."[220] When Virginia was in the process of seceding from the Union in the wake of Abraham Lincoln's election to the presidency, a rival Virginia government was formed in a part of the state that was opposed to secession. An allied effort was made to form a brand-new state in the same geographic area, one that would remain in the Union. The would-be new state applied as West Virginia for representation in the United States Senate, and its allied rival Virginia government purported to give Virginia's permission. No permission was given by the sitting Virginia government, but both President Lincoln and the Senate concluded that the illegality of Virginia's secession justified recognizing the permission that was given as that of Virginia. On this basis, a new state was born.[221]

This history is hardly surprising given Lincoln's views on secession, views that may well have been broadly shared in the nation at large. And the legality of West Virginia never made its way to court. What is surprising is that Vasan Kesavan and Michael Paulsen, two twenty-first-century original-meaning originalists, revisited the problem and concluded that the constitutional requirement of Virginia's consent had been satisfied. They recognized that the "real" government of Virginia had not given its permission, but, following Lincoln, they employed a "legal fiction" to allow a breakaway portion to speak for the state. This was, in their words, "one of the great constitutional legal fictions of all time."[222] If this seems strained, recall our earlier discussion of the frequent necessity for normative judgments in fathoming constitutional meaning.[223] Kesavan and Paulsen could have Mr. Meaning employing legal fictions if that seemed the right way to go about constitutional interpretation for resolution of the issue that was posed.

Nonetheless, Kesavan and Paulsen's conclusion seems jarring because it so clearly exposes that normative component of their original-meaning originalism. It seems quite unlikely that any sincere decipherers of constitutional meaning at the time would have made use of such a legal fiction. At least unless one assumed that they were pretty much just like Lincoln in what they knew and assumed and were trying to accomplish, they would likely have thought that consent of a state meant real consent of the real state. In other writing, Kesavan and Paulsen want to claim that constitutional words have "'objective' and...*fixed* meaning[s]," a stance that is especially hard to accommodate to the position they take on the rather precise language bearing on the West Virginia problem.[224] And note that if the admission of West Virginia to the Union and the Senate is taken to have been constitutionally impermissible, Virginia has now for a long time had four senators instead of the constitutionally mandated two.

I am actually a little puzzled about why Kesavan and Paulsen succumbed. To be sure, in a variety of ways, it was much easier to accede to West Virginia's request to join the Union than it would be today to afford California more representation in the United States Senate than other states receive. With civil war looming, the press of events was very compelling. The West Virginia problem was also sufficiently different from concerns that loomed large when the two-senators formula was put into the Constitution that a decision maker could easily conclude that admitting West Virginia did not give offense to some focused matter of original concern. And, originalist concerns aside, there was a reasonably easy way to accede to the West Virginia request that would not create additional unwelcome complications elsewhere in the system. In contrast, giving California additional representation in the Senate today would raise a host of intractable problems regarding other states. But Kesavan and Paulsen were writing an academic article and could presumably have cast these mere policy arguments aside in favor of a conclusion that would have provided better cover for originalist bravado.

I am not sure that an absurd-results exception to the reach of constitutional language would capture the justification for a West Virginia exception to the state consent and two-senator requirements. Emergency or extreme extenuating circumstances seem more apt characterizations. Moreover, there are other instances in which the literal reach of constitutional language has been put to the side without much cover from an absurdity or even an emergency. We have seen Justice Scalia's willingness to do just that with the language of the First Amendment.[225] Another example got some attention when President-elect Obama announced that he would nominate New York senator Hillary Clinton to be his secretary of state. The emoluments clause of Article I provides that "No Senator or Representative shall, during the Time for which he was elected, be appointed to any civil Office under the Authority of the United States...the Emoluments whereof shall have been encreased during such time."[226] The remuneration of the secretary of state had been increased during the senator's term, but the emoluments clause problem was to be "cured"—as it had been with past appointments raising similar problems—by legislation that lowered Senator Clinton's secretariat salary to what had prevailed before the increase. That might well deal with the likely "purpose" of the constitutional provision—perhaps to discourage members of Congress from pressing for salary increases for jobs they covet—but the literal reach of the words seems to preclude the appointment anyway. And it is hard to argue that the ineligibility of Senator Clinton would have presented a national emergency or that an inability to appoint her would have been an absurd result.[227]

Still, a great deal of clear constitutional language is heeded by all relevant actors, probably because, as with the two-senator requirement, skirting the language might invite eruption of a hornets' nest of particularly mischievous uncertainties. Thus, despite the ballooning disparities in state ratios of population to senators, no state other than Virginia has laid serious claim to more than two senators. And even the least populous state has seen no challenge to its constitutionally guaranteed minimum of one member of the House of Representatives.[228] The president serves for four years, members of the Senate for six, and members of the House for two.[229] Only the House initiates impeachments, and only the Senate tries them.[230] When the president is subjected to an impeachment trial, the chief justice presides.[231] Constitutional amendments are effective when three-fourths of the states approve them.[232] And the emoluments clause and the two-senator and state-consent requirements do at least reveal a sensitivity to the constitutional language by the actors involved. Lincoln's argument for the admission of West Virginia may have been built on a legal fiction, but he felt obliged to construct it. And Secretary Clinton will not receive the enhanced salary. It thus seems that relatively precise constitutional language does have an effect on the actors involved even if it is not always the tightly drawn effect that originalists seem to crave in the abstract. In that sense, it is precise language that comes closest to realizing the originalist ambitions for an antidote to a living Constitution. And that is not surprising. For, as originalists have long insisted, it is constitutional language that is voted upon and enacted.

Living with a Living Constitution

The American institution of judicial review essentially guarantees a judicially enforced living Constitution. If we did away with judicial review, constitutional liveliness would be injected by other actors. In any event, and despite the pleas of some commentators, there seems little chance that we will abandon judicial review in the foreseeable future, or even drastically pare back its reach.[233] Should we then be concerned that our democracy is subject to the whim of nine lawyers?

On this matter I think there is cause for concern, but for rather different reasons than those that seem to trouble most originalists. The originalist criticism of judicial review, and of the judicial choice that characterizes it, often seems to proceed on the assumption that there is some canonical version of democracy that this judicial choice offends. In fact, the notion of democracy is not particularly well defined. As Winston Churchill's much-quoted sally suggests, democracy is a messy process that is desirable not because it implements some well-understood ideal of government but because it has fewer of the abuses that characterize nondemocratic forms of government.[234] And the American version of this ill-defined democracy is messier than many. Putting judicial review aside for the moment, consider these aspects of the American polity: bicameralism; apportionment of the House of Representatives by states and the use of districts to elect those state delegations; the equal state representation in the United States Senate regardless of the state's population; the peculiar way we select the nation's president and vice president: the proliferation of administrative agencies, some of which operate with significant independence of the (peculiarly) elected executive; the division of functions among federal, state, and local governments; the shifting nature of that division over time; and the large—but shifting—areas left to individual prerogatives. All of this

gives form to a complex whole, in which influence on public policy decisions is distributed quite unevenly across the population. It is plausible to
suppose that appreciable elements of happenstance affect public policy outcomes. In this context, a good measure of influence for unelected judges is
not nearly so awkward an element as is sometimes suggested. With different phraseology, the historian Gordon Wood captures the essential point:
"[J]udges have exercised...[a] sort of presumably undemocratic authority from the very beginning of our history....[But w]e have never had a
purely democratic system of government, in any traditional meaning of
that term."[235]

Those judicial choices, moreover, are not nearly as unconstrained as the
word *whim* might suggest. We have seen that specifically worded constitutional provisions bring a good measure of constraint and that general
phraseology may bring some as well. Deference to precedent has even
greater potential to guide and constrain judicial choice. And that deference is part of the larger professional culture into which judges are social-
ized. Deference to the political branches is actually an important part of
that culture.[236]

Supreme Court justices, moreover, do not initiate issues but rather
decide matters that are brought to them and shaped in good measure by
litigants. The Court typically engages issues after a substantial time lag
in which the issue has been allowed to percolate in the lower courts and
in the society at large. There are also potentially more muscular external
constraints on the judiciary, which the Congress and the executive can assert with their power over judicial appointments, budgets, and Supreme
Court jurisdiction.[237] There is even reason to believe that the president and
the Congress could pack the Supreme Court and lower federal courts with
additional judges congenial to them, as Franklin Roosevelt famously tried
to do with the Supreme Court. Roosevelt's plan failed, of course, and that
is indicative of another complication in the picture. The Court's growing
power over the years has been tolerated and, some would argue, encouraged, by the political branches of government. As one commentator puts
it, there is an "emerging consensus in law and political science that judicial
review is politically constructed."[238] That toleration and encouragement
might itself bolster the democratic credentials of judicial review.

For me, at least, this is not a source of much solace. The embrace of robust judicial review by the legislative branch may provide too convenient an

excuse for American legislatures to fail to engage issues in ways that might in turn engage the populace. There are differences among various centers of government authority, and one of the differences is the opportunity for widespread popular engagement. The legislative branches are most susceptible to popular pressure and—what may be equally important—popular interaction. If legislators can beg off from such pressure and participation with the excuse that the matter lies in the realm of constitutional decision making and hence of the courts, that may drain a measure of vibrancy, and even of popular approval, from the system as a whole. It is not clear that the large reach of judicial review in the contemporary United States is having that effect—or that we would easily spot it if it were occurring—but to my mind the possibility has to be counted a concern.

Jack Balkin depicts his method of text and principle as furthering a "vibrant multigenerational undertaking, in which succeeding generations pledge faith in the constitutional project and exercise fidelity to the Constitution by making the Constitution their own." The result, according to Balkin, is a "conversation between past commitments and present generations" that "is at the heart of constitutional interpretation."[239] Given the contemporary place and reach of judicial review, the primary conversationalists in this undertaking seem to be the justices of the United States Supreme Court. They may well be reasonable surrogates for their generations or even for the generations living at the time they are doing their judging. But none of that is self-evident, and there is certainly a danger that the great body of members of those generations will hardly know the undertaking is in process.

If this is a danger, however, the cure would presumably be to inhibit judicial review to some degree. That would cut back on the extent to which the judiciary injected life into the Constitution, but it would do nothing to make constitutional doctrine any less susceptible to modern influences. It would presumably substitute a measure of legislative interpretation for judicial, but the result would still be a Constitution very much alive to contemporary values. In any event, for a Constitution like ours with sweeping generalities, "the values to which constitutional law gives expression" are destined to be "more nearly those of the present than those of the past."[240] It is only in that framework that something called originalism can survive—as a part, one hopes, of a vibrant and evolving constitutional life and certainly not as an antidote to it.

The Failure of Originalism as Restraint

Some originalists who focus on the world of adjudication express reverence for the Constitution while simultaneously disparaging constitutional
law. These commentators insist that in constitutional cases a large vol-
ume of mistakes have been made by the courts over the years and that
many have found their way into the fabric of the nation's life. Steve Calabresi puts it this way: "One could make a powerful case that the history
of judicial review has been largely one of errors and tragedies."[241] At the
same time, however, Calabresi tells us that the "United States is the freest
nation on earth because we have a better Constitution" than other coun-
tries.[242] And the originalists John McGinnis and Michael Rappaport seem
to agree: "[P]eople are loath to amend...[the Constitution since operating
under it] the United States has become the most prosperous large nation
on earth."[243] But if commentary in this vein is correct in asserting a causal
connection between the vitality of the United States and the Constitution,
surely the only Constitution entitled to the credit is the one that commentary insists has been infected by a multitude of errors and tragedies.

The only path through this muddle, I fear, is to disentangle two different goals entertained by many—perhaps most—originalists. Virtually all
originalists see their approach as the right way to elaborate the content of
constitutional law. This seems to be the grounding for the claim of error.
But most truly value their approach as a way to rein in judicial discretion. No matter how powerful the sentiment in favor of restraint, however,
originalism is simply not up to the task. For though the words of the Constitution may be unchanging, many of them have virtually no capacity to
dictate results in the unending set of problems that American courts decide
in the name of the Constitution.

This is so for four different, albeit interrelated, reasons.

1. The instructions of many of those words are very general or ambiguous.
2. Those general or ambiguous formulations had to be agreed upon by a large
   number of people, who could entertain different views—or no views at all—
   about implications of the language for problems of their time.
3. Because a great deal has happened since those words were formulated, the
   problems presented today often bear scant resemblance to those for which
   the words may have been a response.

4. The dynamic of court decision making in the United States emphasizes specific consequences of what must be decided, consequences that reside in the
here and now. A sense of responsibility in the resolution of the problems of
today is then hard—as a practical matter, probably impossible—for courts to
avoid. Even if judges could find a lot of guidance from yesterday, that sense
of responsibility would propel them toward thinking in terms they can comfortably relate to today.

If originalists would see more clearly that the goal of restraint through
originalism is essentially unattainable for a large swath of the problems
that arise, they might have less certitude about originalism as the only right
way to do constitutional law. They might instead become comfortable with
the interdependency of the United State Constitution and constitutional
law. What are now seen as errors and tragedies of constitutional law could
then be discussed straightforwardly in normative terms, without pretense
that they are erroneous and tragic because they are at odds with objective
facts that can somehow be demonstrated by comparing the Constitution
and the law announced in its name. Reverence for the Constitution could
still be entertained, but it might then be leavened by recognition that that
Constitution will remain a lively one, no matter how much originalists
might wish that it were otherwise. Decision making will surely vary with
the identity of the judges doing the deciding because choices will have to
be made that draw heavily on contemporary values. Some or even all of
those judges might still identify themselves as originalists, but those who
do should not be allowed to insist that embrace of the label means that
their decisions are—even largely—free from the influence of those contemporary values.

LIVING WITH ORIGINALISM

A Response by Lawrence B. Solum

Can Original Meaning Constrain?

A major theme of Robert Bennett's critique of originalism focuses on the question whether the original meaning of the Constitution can constrain constitutional decision making. His answer to this question is a mostly emphatic *no*. Although Bennett recognizes that the constitutional text imposes some constraints on constitutional interpretation, he insists that this constraint is modest at best. And to the extent that constitutional practice is constrained, much of the work is done by nonoriginalist devices like precedent and the structure of judicial practice.

Bennett advances a variety of arguments in support of his claim that original meaning cannot strongly constrain constitutional practice. For example, he claims that the constitutional text consists of "barren marks" that are given meaning only by "social practices." And Bennett explains, "social practices are themselves often imprecise or ill defined. They may also be variable at any given time—by and among individuals—and they may change over time" (p. 84). Bennett is right about this. Language is a social practice, and the meanings associated with particular words and phrases do change over time. Indeed, the fact that linguistic meanings change over time is one of the most important motivations for originalism. If it were not for the fact of linguistic drift, what we now call *originalism* might be called *textualism*. Originalists claim that the relevant social practices for determining the semantic meaning of a text are the linguistic practices that create conventional semantic meanings and the regularities we call rules of grammar and syntax.

What about the fact that social practices are imprecise, ill defined, or variable at any given time? It is not clear what Bennett means here. He might be arguing that the linguistic practices that ground natural languages are (in general) so indeterminate that words cannot have fixed meanings, but that argument (a version of the radical-indeterminacy thesis associated with the critical legal studies movement) cannot be squared with the fact that language is used to communicate in precise and invariable ways. The owner's manual for a digital video recorder can give precise and invariable instructions for recording a television program. An instructor can communicate precise and invariable instructions for the format and length of a term paper. The fact that social practices can be variable and imprecise does not mean that they must be so.

Bennett's comments about social practices may not be intended as an independent argument against the constraining force of originalism. He may instead believe that the potential imprecision and variability of social practices provides the explanation for the fact that some words and phrases are "open-textured." He gives "due process of law," "equal protection of the laws," "unreasonable searches and seizures," and "cruel and unusual punishment" as examples and correctly observes that many contemporary constitutional controversies center on these constitutional words and phrases (p. 85).

We need to be very careful here. Originalists can and should embrace the fact that the Constitution includes some provisions that are ambiguous, others that are vague, and a few that are both. Ambiguities can almost always be resolved by resorting to context. Vagueness is another matter. Recall that a word or phrase is vague if it admits of borderline cases. Thus, some searches may be clearly reasonable and others clearly unreasonable, leaving a group of borderline cases that could fit in either category. If the linguistic meaning is vague, then we have a case of constitutional under-determination. A line will need to be drawn, but the line will not be found in the linguistic meaning of the word *unreasonable*—because the meaning of that word is vague. So constitutional construction is required. Originalists can and should embrace this conclusion.

The vague provisions of the Constitution are frequently litigated, and the results of that litigation are frequently controversial. And that is exactly what we should expect. Easy cases may not be litigated, either because the claim clearly lacks merit or because it can be settled before a lawsuit is filed. Of course, in some cases where the law is clear, the facts may be disputed, but in these cases there is no reason to ask an appellate court to review the trial court's rulings of law. And it will be very rare indeed for the Supreme Court to grant certiorari on a question of law that involves the core of determinate meaning; the Court will want to hear the border-line cases involving an unsettled or controversial question.

The fact that constitutional litigation frequently involves issues in the construction zone should not obscure the fact that the constitutional text provides clear guidance on countless questions that are never litigated or are easily decided in the early stages of a dispute. This is obvious in the case of constitutional provisions that are neither vague nor ambiguous, including those that have the greatest practical importance. The constitutional text clearly defines the basic structure of the national government, which includes three branches—an executive, a bicameral legislature, and a judiciary—and the procedures by which these branches are constituted. Even the vague and abstract provisions of the Constitution have constraining force. There are paradigm cases of due process, freedom of speech, and judicial power.

But Professor Bennett might have a more radical idea about the meaning of words like *unreasonable* and phrases like *due process of law*. When he suggests that language is open-textured, Bennett might be making the claim that there is no core of settled meaning (p. 85). The phrase *open texture* is a technical term that comes from the philosophy of language. The idea originated in an essay by Frederic Waismann, who contrasted open texture with vagueness:

> Vagueness should be distinguished from open texture. A word which is actually used in a fluctuating way (such as "heap" or "pink") is said to be vague;

a term like "gold," though its actual use may not be vague, is nonexhaustive or of an open texture in that we can never fill up all the possible gaps through which a doubt may seep in. Open texture, then, is something like possibility of vagueness. Vagueness can be remedied by giving more accurate rules, open texture cannot. An alternative way of stating this would be to say that definitions of open terms are always corrigible or emendable.[1]

Waismann's claim is roughly that an open-textured term like *gold* (when used in the sense in which it refers to a metal) does not have a meaning that can be taken as settled in advance. The question whether particular words and phrases in the Constitution are open-textured is certainly interesting, but we do not need to answer that question in the present context. Open texture does not imply indeterminacy of meaning. If Waismann was right and the word *gold* is open-textured, it could turn out that some things we think are gold really aren't (or that there are things that are gold that we didn't previously know about), but this doesn't imply that just anything could be gold. Likewise, even if constitutional phrases like *due process* were open-textured, the consequence would not be that the original meaning of due process imposes no constraints. Quite the contrary. For the idea of open texture to make sense, there must be enough stability in the meaning of words like *gold* for the variations and amendments to make sense as continuations of the same concept. For originalism to make sense, there must be a core of settled meaning, but the notion of open texture at the margins is perfectly consistent with the notion of stability at the core.

So far, we have assumed that Waismann's theory that language is open-textured is correct, but that claim is certainly controversial. Take Waismann's example, the word *gold*. Is it really the case that we lack determinate criteria for determining what substances are gold and which aren't? A powerful case might be made that the reference of gold is now fixed by our theories of physics and chemistry. If something has the atomic structure of gold (with the atomic number 79), then it is properly called gold, period. If the critics of originalism believe that language is open-textured, they need to tell us what they mean by open texture and to provide the arguments from linguistic theory and the philosophy of language that vindicate their theory.

Bennett introduces another objection when he asserts that seeming clarity can shroud an ambiguity. In the abstract, Bennett is surely correct. Some ambiguities become apparent only on close inspection. But the example that Bennett introduces actually demonstrates the constraining force of originalist interpretation. Bennett notes that the provision that restricts eligibility for the presidency to persons who are thirty-five years of age seems to draw a bright line but then notes, "There are cultures that calculate age differently than we do, as the number of (lunar) calendar years in which one has been alive for any length of time rather than the number of calendar recurrences of the date of one's birth" (pp. 85–86). And it is imaginable that our linguistic practices might change; we might calculate age from the date of conception or of fetal viability. All of that is true, but originalists are right to insist that the meaning of "the Age of thirty-five Years" in the Constitution is determined by linguistic practices in America in that era. The fact that the Constitution would have meant something different had it been authored in another time and place demonstrates the originalist point that linguistic meaning is a function of the linguistic practices that prevailed at the time and place where the text originated.

Many of Bennett's arguments against the constraining force of originalism simply do not apply to original-public-meaning originalism. For example, he discusses the summing problem, which does pose a serious objection to original-intentions originalism (if intentions are viewed as mental states of individuals), but his objection is off the mark as applied to the contemporary versions of originalism that rely on conventional semantic meanings derived from the regularities of linguistic practice.

When Bennett turns to original public meanings, it is not clear to me what his objections actually are. He writes, "Meanings do not exist in the ether. Meaning is always meaning to a person or persons, whether existing out there or constructed in our imaginations" (pp. 97–98). Of course, there is a sense in which this is true. There would be no meanings without language users. But this does not entail the further conclusion that the meaning of words and phrases is always their meaning to a particular person or group of persons. The whole point of conventional semantic meanings is that words and phrases can have public meanings that are not reducible to the psychological states of particular persons on particular occasions. This is simply a fact about language.

If the linguistic meaning of an utterance were reducible to the psychological states of particular persons on particular occasions, the consequences would be very strange indeed. Consider the phenomenon of misunderstanding. Common sense tells us that sometimes we get linguistic meanings wrong. Ben believes that the word *tortuous* is formed from the word *torture*, but the actual meaning is twisting, bending, or curving. If the meanings of texts reduced to mental states of readers, then Ben couldn't have made a mistake about meaning. But this result is absurd. Of course we can be mistaken about the conventional semantic meaning of a word—such mistakes happen all the time. A similar problem would arise in the case of ignorance of meaning. If meanings depended on psychological states, then ignorance of meaning would be impossible. Alice reads the word *prolixity* for the very first time. If the meaning of the word were reducible to Alice's psychological state on this occasion, then *prolixity* would have no meaning at all. But that isn't what Alice would be likely to say. Instead, she would most likely search the Internet for a definition or other examples of usage from which the meaning could be inferred. Our commonsense beliefs about language do not support the claim that the linguistic meaning of a text is identical to some mental state of individual readers of the text.

The point of our investigation of linguistic mistakes and linguistic ignorance is to show that meanings are not reducible to the psychological states of particular individuals on particular occasions. The conventional semantic meanings of the words and phrases that make up the Constitution are determined by linguistic practice—systematic regularities of usage, syntax, and grammar. There is nothing mysterious about this—no meanings in the ether. If meanings were reducible to individual mental states, then the summing problems that Bennett attributes to original-intentions originalism would carry over to original public meanings. But once we recognize the existence of conventional semantic meanings based on systematic regularities in linguistic practice, the summing problem disappears.

The Levels-of-Generality Pseudoproblem

Another objection to original-intentions originalism is sometimes framed in terms of levels of generality and particularity. Bennett gives this objection a forceful and seemingly persuasive formulation (pp. 108–14). In fact, there is no such problem for original-public-meaning originalism. To see why this is the case, it is helpful to understand something about the origins of the levels-of-generality problem in contemporary legal theory.

Legal scholars have noted that the principle for which a case stands can be stated at various levels of generality, from a holding that is particular to the case at hand to one that is more abstract and would apply to a wider range of future cases. Similarly, in fundamental rights jurisprudence, the question whether a given right has been recognized by existing legal practice may vary with the level of generality with which the right is described. Legal practice has recognized a right to privacy (very general) but not a right to engage in sexual activity outside the confines of marriage (more particular). Likewise, Brest argued in 1975 that the framers' intent could be stated at various levels of generality.[2] And it is true that an action can be intentional under a variety of different descriptions; one way that such descriptions can vary is in terms of levels of generality. Thus, when I drank a cup of coffee while writing this response, it is true that I intended that action under all of the following descriptions: (1) drinking a beverage, (2) drinking coffee, (3) drinking Peet's coffee, (4) drinking Peet's Major Dickason's Blend coffee, and (5) drinking a filter-brewed cup of Peet's Major Dickason's Blend coffee. My action was intentional under all five of these descriptions, which vary in levels of generality from the very general beverage to the fairly particular filter-brewed cup of Peet's Major Dickason's Blend.

This fact about the relationship between levels of generality and intentions does not carry over to linguistic meaning generally. The meaning of the word *coffee* is not the same as the meaning of the phrase *Peet's coffee*, which in turn is not equivalent to the meaning of the phrase *Peet's Major Dickason's Blend coffee*, and so forth. Originalism is concerned with the linguistic meaning of the Constitution. Each operative unit of meaning (a word, phrase, or whole clause) can be general or particular. The Constitution uses the term *State*, which is general and the name *Delaware* (which is a state) but is (as compared with *State*) particular. The Constitution uses the phrase "legislative power," which is general, and also the phrase "to establish Post Offices and post Roads," which is more particular. Of course, general provisions can have particular applications. For example, the power to establish a post office includes the power to establish a post office in Champaign, Illinois. But from that fact it does not follow that the linguistic meaning of the phrase *to establish post offices and post roads* might be to establish a post office in Champaign, Illinois. The linguistic meaning of the phrase is the more general meaning. To think otherwise would involve a conceptual mistake—confusing linguistic meaning with application meaning.

In sum, there is no levels-of-generality problem for original-meaning originalism or for any form of originalism that focuses on the linguistic meaning of the constitutional text. *Purposivism*—the theory that the meaning of the Constitution is the same as the purposes for which it is adopted—does suffer from a levels-of-generality problem, but purposivism should not be confused with any sophisticated contemporary form of originalism.

The Role of Values in Constitutional Construction

In his main essay, Robert Bennett's discussion of originalism does not have much to say about the distinction between interpretation and construction, but in his reply Bennett observes that constitutional construction may open the door to judicial reliance on values or morality in constitutional decision making. Bennett would count that as a virtue of an originalism that embraces the interpretation-construction distinction, but there are likely many originalists who will worry about the possibility that decision making in the construction zone will simply reintroduce the problem of ideological judging driven by the personal morality and politics of individual judges. Bennett might argue that this shows that originalism cannot meaningfully constrain constitutional practice; some originalists might argue that this is a reason to avoid constitutional construction altogether.

This raises an important question for originalists who embrace the interpretation-construction distinction: Is constitutional construction consistent with the rule of law? This is an important question, but answering it requires that we exit the discussion of originalism as a theory of interpretation and enter a conversation about theories of constitutional construction. What can originalists say about constraint in the construction zone?

Almost all originalists will agree that constitutional construction should be constrained by constitutional interpretation. When the meaning of the text is clear, then constructions should respect that meaning. Even when a provision is vague, originalists should insist that constitutional construction should respect the core of settled meaning. I have suggested that most originalists will see these constraints as defeasible. But defeasibility is not equivalent to a lack of constraint. For example, an originalist might allow for amending constructions of the Constitution in the case of emergency.

If a terrorist attack on the Capitol during the State of the Union address were to prevent Congress from functioning, the successor to the president might assume a temporary legislative power. Originalists should insist that this kind of defeasibility condition is limited to cases of true necessity. Of course, defeasibility does open the door to normative considerations to enter into constitutional decision making in a very narrow class of cases. But this is no embarrassment for originalism.

But what should originalists say about decision making within the construction zone? How should an originalist proceed when faced with the abstract, general, and vague provisions of the Constitution? It might be argued that construction of these provisions requires judges to rely on their own values or beliefs about political morality and justice. If this were the case, then it might follow that much of the originalist critique of living constitutionalism would lose its force. Originalists seem to be arguing that courts should avoid judicial legislation, but if originalists allow judges to make law in the construction zone, it might be argued that the difference between originalists and living constitutionalists is only a matter of degree. Given the practical importance of the abstract, general, and vague provisions (legislative power, freedom of speech, and so forth), living constitutionalists might well claim that originalist endorsement of the interpretation-construction distinction effectively concedes the most important constitutional questions to nonoriginalists.

At this point, originalism cannot speak with a single voice. It does not entail any particular theory of constitutional construction. There is a range of options available to originalists that avoids judicial lawmaking in the construction zone. But before we discuss these options, we should discuss an approach to construction that will not apply to many originalists. Some theorists may believe that decision making in the construction zone must be discretionary. Of course, this discretion does not need to be vested in the hands of individual trial judges. Rather, it could be assigned to the Supreme Court, which would then be empowered to make law to fill the gaps opened by the general, abstract, and vague provisions of the Constitution. How should the justices exercise their discretionary power? One answer to that question would be, Do justice! Of course, different justices have different values and beliefs about political morality. Presidents and senators would inevitably take this into account in the nomination and confirmation process.

Is there an alternative to judicial discretion in the construction zone? Can legal decisions that are underdetermined by the constitutional text nonetheless be constrained by law? This brings us back to our earlier discussion of the originalist approaches to construction. One originalist option (*the model of construction as politics*) would involve a rule of deference to democratic political processes. When a case is in the construction zone, the judicial branch should defer to decisions made by the political branches— Congress, the president, or elected state officials. A second option (*the model of construction as principle*) might involve the attempt to derive guiding purposes or principles from the Constitution itself; the idea would be for judges to search for the values that are immanent in the specific provisions and overall structure of the Constitution. A third option (*the model of construction by original methods*) might involve the search for constraint in the original methods of constitutional construction.

Living constitutionalists are likely to challenge originalist claims that any of these three methods can substantially constrain judicial discretion. For the purposes of this book, the important point is that there are plausible originalist stories about the constraining force of law in the construction zone. The legal realist story, that the construction zone must be governed by discretion, may be credible, but it is not inevitable.

Dead Hands

Can we live with originalism? Or is a return to the original meaning of the Constitution costly, impractical, and unrealistic? And in particular, can contemporary Americans live with an originalism that would result in many of the most important legal and political questions of the twenty-first century being governed by the dead hands of the framers and ratifiers of an eighteenth-century constitution?

The dead-hand objection should be taken seriously by originalists. Originalists believe that contemporary Americans, the living, are morally and legally obligated to respect decisions made decades and centuries ago by those now dead—by the framers and ratifiers of the Constitution, by the Reconstruction Congress that proposed the Thirteenth, Fourteenth, and Fifteenth amendments, and by Progressive-Era legislators who framed and ratified the Seventeenth Amendment (providing for popular election of the Senate). Why should we respect their decisions, given the barriers that Article V creates for any effort to amend the Constitution?

Of course, the dead-hand objection needs to be put in context. Article V makes amendment difficult but not impossible. The Constitution has, in fact, been amended on twenty-seven occasions, with the most recent amendment approved in 1992 (although this particular amendment—which deals with the effective date of changes in the salaries of members of Congress—had been proposed almost two centuries earlier in 1789 along with the Bill of Rights). When contemporary American opinion supports an amendment, the lesson of history is that Congress and state legislatures will rarely resist the tide. Of course, this is not equivalent to *majoritarian constitutionalism*. The Constitution requires the approval of two-thirds of each house of Congress and three-quarters of the state legislatures for an amendment to become effective. An amendment desired by a majority of Americans could be defeated by a minority—theoretically (but rarely practically) a minority that represented only a fraction of the citizenry. And this fact might form part of the case for a political system that is much different from American constitutional democracy: the British system of parliamentary supremacy does a much better job of translating the political preferences of contemporary majorities into law (at least in theory).

But the debate between originalism and living constitutionalism is not a debate about the comparative merits of a written constitution and parliamentary majoritarian democracy. Living constitutionalists do not believe that Congress should have the right to overrule either the Constitution itself or the decisions of the Supreme Court. To the extent that living constitutionalists believe that the Supreme Court should have the authority to adopt amending constructions of the Constitution, their philosophy substitutes the living hands of five (or more) justices for the dead hands of the framers and ratifiers of the Constitution. It may well be that the justices read the public opinion polls (or that they respond to democratic majorities in more subtle and sophisticated ways), but living constitutionalism is not plausibly understood as democratic majoritarianism in disguise.

There is another difficulty with a critique of originalism that rests on the normative premise that contemporary democratic majorities should not be ruled by the dead hands of the framers and ratifiers. It is far from clear that contemporary Americans object to the dead hand of the Constitution. Indeed, the Constitution itself may be far more popular than the majoritarian institutions (the presidency, Congress, state governments) that it rules with a dead hand. Of course, it might be argued that the American people would object to the Constitution if only they knew what it really said (the text's original meaning). But the same might be said about the American public's generally favorable attitude toward the Supreme Court—the opinion polls may measure the gravitas and dignity the Court holds in the popular imagination and not the actual content of constitutional doctrine or the reality of the Court's sometimes messy and unattractive decision-making processes.

There is another important version of the dead-hand objection: the problem with the dead hand is not that it is undemocratic but that it is insufficiently sensitive to the changes in American values and circumstances that separate the twenty-first-century superpower from the eighteenth-century agrarian republic. This version of the dead-hand objection is best known in a roughly utilitarian form.[3] Boiled down to its essentials, this argument rests on the premise that the content of the Constitution is out of date—and that living constitutionalism (as a method for constitutional interpretation and construction) can do a better job of providing constitutional doctrines that can work in contemporary circumstances.

The utilitarian version of the dead-hand objection has its greatest appeal if leveled at a particular version of the old originalism. If originalism were a theory stating that contemporary constitutional questions should be answered by imagining how a majority of the framers or ratifiers would have voted on the issue, then a strong case could be made that originalism has passed its shelf life. The values and beliefs of the framers and ratifiers may have enduring validity on some important questions of constitutional principle, but the constitutional problems of twenty-first-century America involve both values and circumstances that were unknown to the founding generation.

Does contemporary originalism privilege the preferences and beliefs of the founding generation in this way? The new originalism is committed to the linguistic meaning of the constitutional text and not the mental states of the framers and ratifiers. It acknowledges the fact that the text contains a number of provisions that are written in abstract, general, and vague language—with the consequence that their application to particular cases will require construction. This means that new originalists can endorse the adaptation of constitutional doctrine to changing circumstances and values—even while they insist that the construction zone in which this evolution occurs is bounded by the fixed linguistic meaning of the constitutional text (unless truly extraordinary circumstances obtain).

So the utilitarian version of the dead-hand objection has much less force as an objection to the new originalism. In the end, the soundness of the objection will depend on our evaluation of the Constitution itself. Does it provide a practical framework for governance in the twenty-first century? Or do we need a better Constitution, whether adopted through the Article V amendment process or by the Supreme Court? The question whether the letter of the Constitution has passed its shelf life is enormously complicated. A good answer should acknowledge that the Constitution contains a mix of relatively rigid structural provisions with flexible generalities. The structure of Congress is rigidly fixed by the original public meaning of the text: Senate and House of Representatives, two senators per state, the House apportioned by population, the requirement that bills must pass both houses, and so forth. But these rigidities are embedded in the highly abstract scheme of separation of powers—which allocates legislative power to the Congress, executive power to the president, and judicial power to the Supreme Court and such inferior courts as Congress shall establish. The operative phrases (*legislative, executive,* and *judicial power*) are general, abstract, and vague—permitting adaptation to changing circumstances. The leading Supreme Court case on the subject, the *Steel Seizure Case*,[4] takes as its basic operative premise the flexibility created by the fixed linguistic meaning of the text: the Court endorsed the idea that the Congress could work with the President to assign greater power to the Executive as needed. Arguably, a similar flexibility is built into the most important individual rights provisions of the Constitution—due process, equal protection, and freedom of speech.

The observation that the constitutional text contains "majestic generalities"[5] is hardly enough to defeat the dead-hand objection. It is possible that the more particular provisions of the Constitution are now badly out of date. For example, it is at least arguable that the antimajoritarian structure of the United States Senate is now intolerably out of sync with contemporary values.[6] (Indeed, one of the most rigid and inflexible parts of the Constitution is Article V, with its cumbersome and antidemocratic process for amending the text.) But when it comes to comparing originalism with living constitutionalism, it becomes apparent that most living constitutionalists are unwilling to push their theory to its logical conclusion. Many of them profess the belief that the Court is never bound by the text. The First Amendment says, "Congress shall make no law," but living constitutionalists applaud the Court for extending the protections of free speech and free exercise of religion to executive and judicial action. But if the linguistic meaning of the text does not bind the Supreme Court, then why shouldn't the Court direct a lower court to issue an injunction requiring reapportionment of the Senate? Of course, the linguistic meaning of the text (of both Article I and Article V) would be an obstacle, but that is the question, Should the Supreme Court possess a power of amending construction?

At this point, living constitutionalists might divide into two camps. One group, the moderates, might accept much of what the new originalism has to offer. They might accept the fixation thesis and the constraint thesis—so long as originalists concede that the construction zone is large enough to permit the Constitution to achieve a tolerable degree of adaptation to changing values and circumstances. Of course, the moderates may suggest that the construction zone is where the action is and complain that originalists have been making a mountain out of a molehill.

Another group of living constitutionalists, the radicals, reject any form of originalism, even a new originalism that acknowledges a substantial construction zone. Radical living constitutionalism might be motivated by the belief that the construction zone is too narrow to accommodate important parts of constitutional doctrine. For example, some living constitutionalists may believe that the New Deal Settlement (roughly, the endorsement of greatly-expanded federal power and the legitimation of the administrative state) cannot be reconciled with the original meaning of the text. Like some originalists, they may believe that the original meaning of the commerce clause cannot be squared with the massive expansion of federal legislation that occurred during and after the New Deal. Likewise, some living constitutionalists may believe that the original meanings of *legislative power* and *executive power* cannot accommodate the modern administrative state, which is predicated on the delegation of rulemaking and adjudicative authority to administrative agencies (e.g., the Federal Communications Commission, the Environmental Protection Administration, and so forth).

If acceptance of originalism entailed the consequence that the New Deal Settlement must be undone (with all deliberate speed), then the utilitarian version of the dead-hand objection would be strong indeed. Much of the United States Code is premised on an expansive construction of Congress's legislative power under the commerce clause and the necessary-and-proper clause. Almost all of the Code of Federal Regulations would be struck down under an interpretation of legislative power that entailed a strict version of the nondelegation doctrine. There may be room for argument, but it is at least reasonable to suppose that suddenly undoing the New Deal Settlement would be a seismic event that could do substantial damage to the fabric of national life.

Transitions and Precedent

This utilitarian version of the dead-hand objection is premised on the assumption that acceptance of originalism would entail a rapid transition to a new constitutional order and a vastly diminished role for the doctrine of stare decisis in constitutional cases. When we evaluate this assumption, we should remember that living constitutionalists who reject the dead hand of originalism are unlikely to embrace the equally lifeless grip of decisions by long-deceased justices of the United States Supreme Court. Both originalism and living constitutionalism are committed to constitutional change; the question is whether the driving engine should be the text of the Constitution itself or the views of the justices about changing circumstances and values. In this regard, both originalism and living constitutionalism may have a common foe in a jurisprudence of conservatism that draws its inspiration from the philosophy of Edmund Burke.[7]

But even if both originalists and living constitutionalists are committed to constitutional change in principle, that commitment need not entail willful blindness to the harms that could be created by a rapid reconstruction of the constitutional order. No responsible originalist has advocated a constitutional big bang in which the Supreme Court would bring all of constitutional doctrine into line with the original meaning of the Constitution in a single term of nine months. Even if every single justice of the United States Supreme Court were a committed originalist, the Court might proceed at a cautious pace, moving to originalism one case at a time over a period of years or decades.

Moreover, originalism is actually consistent with a relatively strong version of the doctrine of stare decisis. Almost all originalists believe that the linguistic meaning of the constitutional text was fixed at the time each provision was framed and ratified. And almost all of them believe that courts are bound to respect that meaning as far as it goes. But those beliefs are consistent with a vigorous doctrine of precedent in both constitutional interpretation and constitutional construction.

Consider the role of precedent in constitutional construction. When the Court operates in the construction zone, it can respect precedent without running afoul of original meaning. When the original meaning of the constitutional text is vague, then construction is required. This means that the Court could adopt a rigorous doctrine of precedent for issues involving constitutional construction without compromising its duty of fidelity to the original meaning of the text. And what about issues of constitutional interpretation? Doesn't originalism require judges to reverse prior decisions if those decisions are contrary to the original meaning of the constitutional text? It is tempting to leap to the conclusion that the answers to these questions must be yes. Most originalists believe that the constitutional text is the supreme law of the land and that it stands higher in the hierarchy of authority than do the pronouncements of the Supreme Court. But the temptation to adopt this simple position should be avoided. Consider a simple point first. The doctrine of stare decisis does not specify the criteria by which novel questions are to be decided: even judges who believe in a strict doctrine of stare decisis could adopt an originalist framework for the resolution of open (or novel) questions of constitutional law. Originalism and precedent are not always inconsistent.

The relationship between stare decisis and originalism becomes more complicated when the constitutional issue is not an open question, especially for the relatively narrow set of cases in which there is a prior decision that is on all fours with the new case (that is, the cases in which the precedent cannot be distinguished on the basis of legally salient characteristics). Even in these cases, an originalist can accept the doctrine of stare decisis so long as the prior decision was made on the basis of a good-faith effort to ascertain the original meaning of the Constitution. The doctrine of stare decisis allocates authority chronologically—it allows judges in the past to resolve issues for the present. Of course, a present judge might believe that the decision of the past judge was in error, but any rule that allocates authority will insulate some erroneous decisions from revision. Just as a lower court judge could accept originalism but recognize that final authority to determine original meaning rests with the Supreme Court, so too could a Supreme Court justice accept originalism but recognize that the doctrine of stare decisis allocates authority to determine original meaning to a prior incarnation of the Supreme Court itself.

Nothing in the core commitments of originalism entails wholesale rejection of the doctrine of stare decisis itself. But originalism does undermine the basis for adherence to decisions that cannot be viewed as good-faith attempts to determine the original meaning of the Constitution. Nonetheless, some originalists may believe that even nonoriginalist precedents should not be overruled at any cost. Originalists are no more committed to irrational absolutism than any other group. One might believe that the duty of fidelity to the original meaning of the Constitution is serious and weighty but also believe that departures from original meaning can be justified if the costs of adherence to the original meaning would be enormous.

One might wonder whether originalism will make any practical difference at all if originalist judges are willing to follow precedents that reach nonoriginalist results on the basis of nonoriginalist reasoning. There can be no doubt that this kind of compromise would slow the transition to a thoroughly originalist jurisprudence. But slow and steady advance is one thing, whereas headlong retreat and perpetual stalemate are different things altogether. Originalist judges are likely to move forward most quickly in those rare areas of constitutional jurisprudence where the precedents are few and far between—as was the case in *District of Columbia v. Heller*. Where the nonoriginalist precedents are piled on thick, originalist judges are likely to make small inroads at the edges of existing doctrine. As such inroads accumulate, isolated exceptions may come to be seen as large exceptions, then as contrary doctrines, and finally the exception may become the rule. In some areas of the law, the transition to originalism might take decades, but glacial change is not uncommon in the law.

There is nothing inherent in originalism that commits originalists to a constitutional big bang, the elimination of the doctrine of stare decisis, or an irrational absolutism. Of course, there may be particular originalists who believe in rapid constitutional change. And by the same token, there may be particular living constitutionalists who believe that their social vision (perhaps of an egalitarian society with constitutional rights to equal distribution of wealth and income) ought to be realized immediately. The important point is to avoid confusion between the views of particular originalists or living constitutionalists and the core commitments of originalism or living constitutionalism as theories.

Original Intent Revisited

Originalism is young as academic theories go. Its precursors can be found in discussions of intention and plain meaning that predate the Constitution itself. The earliest versions of contemporary originalism date back to the 1970s. But originalism as a distinctive academic theory began to emerge only after Paul Brest coined the term in the 1980s, and the new originalism (with its emphasis on original public meaning and the interpretation-construction distinction) was not articulated until the 1990s. And it is only very recently (in the second half of the first decade of the twenty-first century) that sophisticated criticisms of the new originalism have been developed.[8]

So it is not surprising that many critics of originalism continue to focus on original-intentions originalism as that theory was specified by Brest, its first major critic.[9] One of the objections to a jurisprudence of original intentions is based on the assumption that the intentions relevant to the meaning of an utterance are mental states. We think of mental states as properties of individuals. If a group has a mental state, that simply means that each member of the group has the mental state. And this leads to a familiar series of objections to original-intentions originalism. Foremost among these is the problem of multiple intentions. If the relevant intentions are individual mental states and if the Constitution has multiple authors with a multiplicity of nonidentical and perhaps even inconsistent mental states, then how do we combine or aggregate them into the original intended meaning of the Constitution? In his essay Robert Bennett provides a compelling version of this argument (pp. 87–91). It is precisely this sort of objection that led many originalists to turn to public meaning: the conventional semantic meaning of words and phrases is determined by patterns of usage and not by the mental states of any particular individual.

Nonetheless, those who embrace originalist theories still include original-intentions originalists, and the question whether they can defend themselves against the multiplicity-of-mental-states objection is interesting for this reason. How might an original-intentions originalist answer Bennett's powerful objection? The first step is to ask what sorts of mental states are relevant to original-intentions originalism. This first question leads to a second one: What intentions determine linguistic meaning? There can be only one answer to that question—semantic intentions. Once this point is understood, the multiplicity-of-mental-states objection turns out to be much weaker than it might at first appear. This is because multiple authors themselves know that coordination of their individual semantic intentions will be difficult unless they rely on conventional semantic meanings. For this reason, it would be quite odd for an individual engaged in group authorship to have deviant semantic intentions: it would be possible but not likely.

The importance of this convergence between original-intentions originalism and original-public-meaning originalism is frequently underestimated. A jurisprudence of original intentions leads to the conclusion that the framers and ratifiers of the Constitution likely intended meanings that converge with public meanings.

Critics sometimes charge originalism with theoretical fragmentation, but in fact, originalists converge on conventional semantic meanings in all but the most unusual cases. Moreover, the criticisms of original-intentions originalism rarely focus on semantic intentions. The critics focus instead on purposes or expectations. And the mental states that are associated with the purposes or expectations that are associated with a jointly authored text are less likely to align than are semantic expectations. The reason for this is obvious. The process of drafting a jointly authored text calls explicit attention to word choice and sentence structure; the drafters must agree on the words. In the course of negotiating the words, there may be discussion of purposes or expectations, but agreement on the text does not require agreement on these additional matters. Different authors can agree to the text for different reasons with different expectations about the effects the text will have.

The multiplicity-of-authors problem would be a serious one if original-intentions originalism held that the meaning of a text is a function of purposes or goals, but these are not in fact the mental states that are relevant to the linguistic meaning of a text. Even if original-intentions originalism were committed to the notion that meaning is a function of individual mental states and that agreement in mental states is required in order to produce meaning, it would be hard to argue that the necessary agreement is impossible or unlikely once we understand that the relevant kind of intention is semantic in nature.

Defenders of original-intentions originalism have another line of defense against the multiplicity-of-authors objection. They can argue that the relevant intentions are not individual mental states but are in fact a property that emerges from the coordinated action of the group. Many legal theorists assume (without much reflection) that group intentions are impossible. If pressed, they would likely argue that by definition intentions are mental states that are internal properties of individuals. Mental states are in your head. This leads to the conclusion that a group mental state could only mean that identical mental states were independently in the heads of all the members of the group. Call this the *shared-mental-states model* of group intentions.

But this assumption can be challenged because it seems inconsistent with a variety of familiar phenomena that seem to involve group intentions that cannot be explained on the shared-mental-states model. Consider a simple example. A group of friends agree to a plan to have a picnic on Sunday. Some members of the group organize the food while others organize the transportation. Various individuals and subgroups know various aspects of the plan. It may be that no single aspect of the plan is known by all the members of the group. Most of them know the time and place, but Sally, who is making dessert, never checked her e-mail and just assumes that Jill will pick her up. Bill, who is under intense deadline pressure, remembers that the picnic is at 1:00 p.m. in Barnes Park, but he skipped the part of the e-mail that says "next Saturday"; he knows that Sally and Jill will tear him away from work on the right day, whatever it is. The group has a plan to have a picnic next Saturday at Barnes Park at 1:00 p.m., with roast chicken, ham sandwiches, coleslaw, beer, and apple pie, but there are no mental states corresponding to each of these elements of the plan that are shared by all the group members. The plan is intended by all, but the set of intended elements of the plan might not exist in any one person's head. In other words, there can be group intentions that do not reduce to mental states that are shared by all the members of the group.

Just as a group can intend a plan without sharing mental states about all the elements of the plan, so the authors of a text can intend the meaning of the text without shared mental states. Planning can involve a division of labor, and so can authoring. In neither case is the multiplicity of participants (and diversity of mental states) an obstacle to the development of content that is intended by all.

Most contemporary originalists believe that the meaning of the Constitution is its original public meaning—fixed by linguistic facts at the time each provision of the Constitution was framed and ratified. But even if original-intentions originalism were the only form of the theory, the multiplicity-of-authors objection is not fatal. Agreement in individual semantic intentions can be produced through coordination on conventional semantic meanings. And even if that were not the case, group intentions can emerge through complex social interactions without identical mental states in each member of the group.

I am not an original-intentions originalist, and these remarks are not intended as an endorsement of the intentionalist approach to constitutional interpretation. But I do believe that the best forms of intentionalism can avoid many of the objections that Bennett offers in this book and that Brest offered in his 1981 essay. The final chapter in the history of originalist theory has yet to be written.

Originalism and Politics

A final set of concerns about originalism involves the relationship between originalism and politics. One such objection expresses a hermeneutics of suspicion—the fear that originalist judges and scholars are flying a false flag, disguising their political ideology as fidelity to the constitutional text. One version of this worry is that originalists practice law-office history. The suspicion is that they pick the results they want on ideological grounds and then find historical evidence to support a predetermined conclusion. Whatever the merits of this objection as applied to particular judges, it is not an objection to originalism as a theory of constitutional interpretation. Judges of every stripe—originalists and nonoriginalists alike—may be insincere, but to draw conclusions about the truth of a theory from the insincerity of its adherents is simply a version of the ad hominem fallacy.

A particularly strong form of the objection that originalism is insincere argues that a truly originalist jurisprudence is simply impossible. This strong version might be premised on the belief that good-faith originalism is psychologically impossible—human judges simply lack the capacity to set aside their political preferences and reach impartial conclusions about the linguistic meaning of legal texts. The question whether fidelity to law is psychologically possible is an interesting one, but it is far from clear that there is sufficient evidence for the proposition that it is psychologically impossible. This is an empirical hypothesis—and its validation would require empirical evidence.

Another strong version of the objection is based on the politics of judicial selection. Even if there are some individuals who can practice good-faith originalism, they will never become Supreme Court justices because presidents and senators will inevitably nominate and confirm candidates who are politically reliable. These critics might prefer living constitutionalism to originalism on the ground that living constitutionalism that openly acknowledges the role of politics in constitutional adjudication is more honest—and hence that it is more transparent to democratic politics.

There is, however, a question-begging quality to the objection that originalism is impossible given the institutions of judicial selection. After all, the debate about originalism and living constitutionalism is not just about academic theories or the judicial philosophies of individuals. The debate is (and should be) part of democratic politics. Fidelity to the Constitution is something that citizens and their representatives can endorse or oppose. Political actors (presidents and senators) can be evaluated by citizens, in part, on the basis of their performance in the judicial selection process. The politicization of this process—with attendant media coverage, political advertisements, and all the rest—may be regrettable, but it surely demonstrates that judicial selection is open to debate and discussion by citizens and officials. The recent history of the process provides evidence that presidents and senators are sensitive to public opinion on these matters.

Should Americans endorse originalism or reject it? Should presidents favor originalists for appointments to the Supreme Court? Should individual judges adopt an originalist approach to constitutional interpretation? Robert Bennett and I have provided the arguments on both sides of these important questions. We hope that our efforts have contributed to public debate and discussion.

Are We All Living Constitutionalists Now?

A Response by Robert W. Bennett

The Interpretive Role of Nonoriginalism in Solum's Scheme

This exchange between Professor Solum and me has certainly uncovered disagreements, large and small, and I will turn to some of them shortly. But it is at least as important to appreciate a large area of agreement. In my principal essay, I argued that once judicial review was in place, a continuing injection of contemporary values was essentially inevitable in our judiciary-centered constitutional decision-making process. In particular, I claimed that no plausible version of what is called originalism has the resources to stem a substantial flow of evolving values into our constitutional law, even if they are different from original animating ones. Typically those values will be drawn from the time decision is to be made. In that sense we have no real choice about whether our Constitution will be a living one, and that even apart from controversial normative arguments about the desirability of keeping the Constitution in touch with changing times.

Solum proudly styles himself an originalist. Those who embrace that label used to speak with near unanimity in looking to original intention as the key to giving meaning to constitutional language. But Solum and a number of others who today claim the mantle of originalism now see the construct of original meaning as decidedly preferable. And at least Solum's version of this original-meaning originalism finds a good deal of room for the expression of values drawn from decision-making time. Solum actually adverts to three different occasions when what he thinks of as nonoriginalist decision making might be appropriate, though only two of them would clearly open the way for the introduction of values drawn from the time the courts (or presumably any other constitutional decision makers) join issue on constitutional questions.

First, Solum mentions in passing that "an originalist might accept that a long-standing historical practice that has generated substantial reliance might be lawful, even though it turns out to be contrary to original meaning." (p. 35). In my principal essay I had drawn on the possibility of reliance as a justification for judicial deference to court precedent in particular (p. 115), and Solum's point can be seen as generalizing the appropriate influence of long-standing practice outside the realm of the judicial doctrine of stare decisis.[1] Of course neither Solum nor I was the first to urge that reliance might justify continued adherence to practices or decisions that come to be seen as having initially been erroneous on originalist or other grounds. But recognition of the point in this exchange is nonetheless important because (as both Solum and I discussed in our principal essays, pp. 71–73, 116–17), some self-styled originalists remain resistant to any deference to what they see as erroneous precedent. It seems quite likely that the resistant contingent would hold out more generally against the Solum generalization of the reliance-based argument for moving beyond originalist decision making.

This being said, the other two openings that Solum discusses more clearly arouse the specter of living constitutionalism because they identify possibilities for the injection into the decision-making mix not of tested values but of fresh ones. For Solum, originalist interpretation heeds the "semantic meaning" of the constitutional text. But some of the text takes the form of general or vague language, where Solum concedes that semantic meaning alone cannot provide closure for the range of questions that may arise. As he puts it "the stable meaning of the text must be supplemented by other

modes of constitutional decision making." (p. 54). I, as well as others before me, had also placed heavy emphasis on vague constitutional language
as necessitating the injection of values that originalist sources could not
supply (p. 82). Adopting the vocabulary of some recent originalist writing, Solum tells us that in these circumstances constitutional "construction" becomes appropriate, perhaps even inevitable.[2] This takes place in
what Solum (wonderfully) calls the "construction zone." This is the first—
and seemingly most important—way in which Solum's conceptualization
opens the way for a degree of liveliness in our Constitution.

Here too the acknowledgment is important. Solum counts himself
among a class of "new originalists," and, as he explains, many older versions of originalism saw little or no room for the entry of contemporary
values, in some construction zone or elsewhere. He associates this latter
position with what he calls "constitutional determinacy," the position that
"the resolution of every issue of constitutional law is determined (in principle) by the meaning of the constitutional text." According to Solum, this
older originalist thinking found that determinate meaning in something
like authorial intention. As he puts it, those earlier originalists thought
that the right answers to constitutional questions could always be forged
by asking what the constitutional framers either did think or would have
thought about an issue that had arisen. Solum insists instead on "constitutional underdeterminacy," the view that "many of the most important
questions of constitutional law are underdetermined by the linguistic
meaning" of the text. (pp. 21–22).

Solum refers to the embrace of this idea as representing a "seismic shift"
in originalist thinking (p. 20). Whether or not there actually are (or were)
originalists who staked out the extreme old originalist position that Solum
explains,[3] it is important to appreciate that no seismic shift has swept away
all originalists who embrace a large measure of constitutional determinacy.
There are even echoes of that old originalist faith in determinacy in what
Solum has to say, and I will return to that point. For present purposes,
however, I should note that although Solum is not entirely explicit that the
supplemental modes of decision making required in the construction zone
employ contemporary values, at a minimum his construction zone opens
an inviting door.

The second opening for contemporary values is what Solum variously
calls "an emergency," "horrendous evil," "exceptional circumstances," and

"special or extraordinary reasons" (pp. 35, 48, 61, 69).[4] He tells us, that though "[o]riginalism must claim that the original meaning acts as a substantial constraint on constitutional doctrine,... it need not claim that the constraint is absolute and indefeasible" (p. 35). Thus when the condition of extraordinariness is met, Solum's position is that originalist answers, even though available, may be unacceptable or at least that a conscientious originalist could opt not to accept them. This is different from construction, where the semantic meaning of vague language provides no answer to many questions that arise. Typically, when the exception for extraordinariness is appropriate in Solum's scheme, there *will be* originalist answers, but courts may appropriately set them aside, presumably injecting a contemporary scheme of values that helped elicit the judgment of extraordinariness in the first place (p. 35).

Though Solum adverts to this possibility at several places, and at one point refers to a "national emergency exception" (p. 35), he does not elaborate on what might justify the judgment of extraordinariness, with the possible exception of a discussion he provides of the Supreme Court's path-breaking school desegregation decision, *Brown v. Board of Education.*[5] As I pointed out in my principal essay, several commentators have argued that *Brown* cannot be justified on originalist grounds (p. 109). Solum dissents from that view, albeit without elaboration (p. 46). But, he tells us, even if *Brown* could find no justification in originalism, it would still have been a justifiable decision, not because of any construction zone but presumably because of the overwhelming moral case for ending state-mandated racial segregation in public schools (p. 48).

Solum's acknowledgment of these last two openings in particular creates an obvious tension in his defense of originalism. His overarching argument for originalism is a normative one, in which the desirability of stability and predictability in the law looms large. At least those two openings compromise any such stability. They invite arguments in a wide swath of cases that one or even both of the openings are presented by that case. And the courts would presumably then be obliged to give those arguments serious attention, signaling that the existing stability can be put in play in yet other cases. It should also be noted that Solum derides what he calls the "justice-trumps-text" view that he associates with many living constitutionalists (p. 50). And he faults what he calls "pragmatic living constitutionalism" because it cannot "guarantee[] a stable core of fixed constitutional meaning," endorsing as it does "the power of judges to override the original meaning of the text for pragmatic reasons" (p. 41). Solum's "extraordinariness" opening could seemingly be subjected to criticism that bears some kinship to these criticisms.

I imagine that Solum would respond that any kinship is pretty distant and that since the latter opening is limited to extraordinary occasions, there is a large difference of degree between this concession and the claims of living constitutionalists. And the vagueness opening would simply be following originalism where it leads. But some originalists might fret that openings like those Solum provides could jeopardize the whole idea of originalism. Indeed, in a classic article, the originalist Randy Barnett accused Justice Antonin Scalia of "infidelity" to originalism because of the multiplicity of openings he would provide for nonoriginalist decision making.[6] Justice Scalia's openings are not identical to Solum's, but it would hardly be surprising if Solum's openings generated similar unease among some originalists.

By no means do I count Solum's openings as fatal to his defense of originalism. I, too, place some value on the guidance for decision makers provided by interpretational resources, even though the liveliness I find inevitable compromises that guidance to a significant degree. It should be open to Solum (as I would insist it is to me) to advance an approach to interpretation that achieves a degree of predictability—and that counts that measure as a virtue—even if the approach falls far short of complete determinacy. In any event, Solum's openings—and indeed the new originalist literature as a whole—suggest a measure of accommodation between originalism and liveliness in our Constitution.

Extent of Liveliness in Solum's Constitutional Law and Bennett's

This being said, Solum and I likely have important differences about the reach of that living constitutionalism. I put the point about our differences somewhat tentatively because Solum assiduously avoids discussion of specific constitutional problems. With the minor exceptions of some approving comments on the *Brown* case and on the originalism of the Supreme Court's recent Second Amendment *Heller* decision,[7] he provides no concrete examples of good or bad decision making by originalist lights. Even in discussing *Heller*, he does not extend any particular praise of cogency to the Court's analysis. Instead, he confines his approval to the terminology used in the majority's opinion. Without more specific examples and an explanation of their appropriate steps and their missteps, it is hard to be confident about the nature of the living constitutionalism that would be produced by decision making in Solum's construction zone. And apart from the different phrases he uses for the extraordinariness opening, his summary discussion of *Brown* is all we have to go on to judge the size of that opening. But even so, and despite his occasionally expansive language ("many of the most important questions...are underdetermined," p. 22), it seems pretty clear that the field for living constitutionalism that I see as inevitable is a good deal larger than what Solum has in mind.[8]

This is suggested by our respective treatments of ambiguity. Solum makes note of the possibility of ambiguity but then basically dismisses it in the constitutional context. At one point he tells us that "[i]n most cases...problems of constitutional ambiguity can be resolved by reference to context," mentioning "three dimensions of context," which, taken together, are *"the publicly available context of constitutional utterance"* (p. 25). These three dimensions are the "surrounding words and phrases" of the language being interpreted, "the structure of the Constitution as a whole," and "those aspects of the framing and ratification of a given constitutional provision that would have been available to the general public." At another point, ignoring the possibility of ambiguity, Solum tells us that "construction is required [for borderline cases] when the meaning of a constitutional text is vague" (p. 25).[9] Taken as a whole, these passages suggest that consulting context thoroughly enough will wrestle down virtually all ambiguity, leaving little—and perhaps no—construction zone openings for the injection of contemporary values when choosing among plausible meanings of ambiguous language.[10]

I am not sure why Solum thinks there is so little genuine constitutional ambiguity. He acknowledges that the Constitution "is a complex document filled with political tensions" and that might well suggest a mechanism by which a host of ambiguities found their way into the text.[11] I will return to that point below. My best guess about what leads Solum to discount ambiguity in the Constitution is related to what is probably the most fundamental difference between us. He believes that constitutional meaning is in principle a simple matter of fact, unsullied by normative considerations. He makes no bones about that position. Language meaning, he insists, is a question of "the way the world is" (p. 12). For Solum, aside from the extraordinariness and long-standing practice possibilities, constitutional language is forever to be given the "conventional semantic meaning" that it had at the time it was adopted. This is the "meaning to ordinary speakers as determined by patterns of usage" (p. 12). At one point he refers to "the linguistic meaning that the words and phrases of the text had for...['ordinary American citizen[s] fluent in English'] (including farmers, seamstresses, shopkeepers, and even lawyers) in the 1780s." (p. 3). To determine that meaning with supreme confidence one might ideally be informed by "large-scale empirical investigation," but in principle for Solum there is nothing normative involved. He tells us that his "fixation thesis"—that "[t]he linguistic meaning of the constitutional text was fixed at the time each provision was framed and ratified"—is "not normative." Rather it is a claim "about linguistic facts" (pp. 4, 12). This is not to say that he dismisses the very possibility of ambiguity. He clearly thinks that meaning itself can be ambiguous. But he seems to believe that virtually all claims of constitutional ambiguity are simply the result of not struggling hard enough with the language "in context" to get to that single, clear, objectively knowable meaning.

It is interesting that this view of language meaning as objective fact appears for Solum *not* to be inherent in the nature of communication through language but rather to be contingent on other aspects of that communication. For he seems to acknowledge that the meaning appropriately ascribed to language that is used by a "single speaker in face-to-face communication" is (Solum says "may be") not something "objective" but rather what that speaker intends, as long as the "listener[] can reliably grasp the speaker's intention and the speaker can count on that fact" (pp. 8, 13–14). What seems to make that approach inappropriate for Solum in the constitutional context is the "multiple authors" and "multiple audiences," both spread over space and time, so that "there is no such thing as *the* intentions of the author" (p. 14). And in addition, "the readers of a constitution...are unlikely to have reliable information about the [possibly multiple] intentions that do exist," and thus "the *success conditions* for speaker's meaning...are not met" (p. 14).

If I am right in tying Solum's dismissal of ambiguity as a real problem to his view of original meaning as a factual matter, that is not to say that I truly fathom some connection he may sense. Rather, he appears to resurrect in the context of ambiguity something like the belief in determinacy that he objects to in older originalist thinking. In Solum's telling, that older originalist determinacy tied it to intention, whereas Solum ties his to meaning in context, but at least the lure of determinacy seems to be common to both. In my principal essay I urged in contrast that ascribing meaning to the Constitution's words will often be a process suffused with normativity, or value judgments. I also argued that intention should be—for the originalist—a more appropriate lens than meaning for the interpretive enterprise (p. 102). But even if one insists on meaning and views that meaning as strictly a matter of fact, I still do not see why one would think that there is little if any genuinely ambiguous language in the constitutional text.

In my principal essay, I discussed several places where the Constitution might be thought ambiguous.

1. Article V provides two avenues for proposal of constitutional amendments, in one of which action by "two thirds of both Houses" of Congress does the trick. That might seem unambiguous in *not requiring* "presentment" to the president for his approval or veto, except that Article I says that "[e]very ... vote to which the concurrence of the Senate and House of Representatives may be necessary (except on a question of Adjournment) shall be presented to the President" for his approval or veto. Taken alone, the Article I language might also be thought to be unambiguous in *requiring* presentment for amendment proposals, that is, just the opposite resolution of the presentment question that examination of Article V alone seems to require. Taken together, those two apparently unambiguous—but contradictory—pieces of language in the unamended Constitution seem to create an ambiguity (pp. 86–87).
2. Article I states that "[t]he number of Representatives shall not exceed one for every thirty thousand," but it does not say whether that limitation applies separately to each state or only to the House of Representatives as a whole. Early on in our constitutional history there arose a dispute about which of those two interpretations was to govern (p. 86).
3. Article II says that "[t]he executive power shall be vested in a President of the United States of America" and then later mentions some specific powers of the president. This might be thought to create an ambiguity about whether the vested executive power is confined to what is later spelled out or extends

more broadly to everything that might be encompassed within the notion of executive power (pp. 106–7).

4. If ambiguity created by silence is fair game, the failure of the Constitution to explicitly provide a mechanism for selection of a chief justice of the United States Supreme Court provides another example. That there was to be such a position is made clear by Article I's reference to "the Chief Justice," but state chief justices were chosen in a variety of ways at the time. As president, George Washington assumed the power to nominate someone for the position, subject to Senate confirmation, and that mechanism has been employed by presidents (and the Senate) ever since (p. 99).

Examples like these of at least potential constitutional ambiguities could easily be multiplied.[12] To evaluate Solum's apparent belief that these and other ambiguities can be resolved if one struggles hard enough with the language in context, let us first be clear about why at least surface ambiguities might appear in the Constitution.

First, ambiguity can be used quite intentionally, for at least two separate reasons. Some commentators argue that draftsmen might use ambiguous language in order to delegate choices to "future generations."[13] The same might be said of vague constitutional language. Perhaps more important, even more than vagueness, constitutional ambiguity might be used intentionally because it can be a powerful tool to mollify external constituencies. Solum seems not to appreciate either of these possibilities. As noted above, he does acknowledge that the "Constitution is a complex document filled with political tensions" (p. 53). But in discussing the possibility that we would today draft a new Constitution, he tells us that in pursuing such an enterprise, we would be "acutely aware of the perils of private meanings" and that we "would attempt to use words and phrases with clear public meanings." "We would," he tells us, "try to avoid ambiguity and minimize unnecessary vagueness" (p. 75). None of this is self-evident, at least unless the word *unnecessary* carries a lot of baggage and extends to ambiguity. Indeed, I would say that the exact opposite will sometimes be likely, even putting aside the delegation possibility. Of course, drafters might use vagueness and ambiguity to defuse opposition from segments of those whose approval of the document is legally required—the ratifiers, a part of what might be taken as the document's authors. In that case, there might well be divergent views about meaning among authors. But it is also possible that drafters and ratifiers alike, or at least substantial portions of them, will knowingly employ vagueness and ambiguity to defuse concern in the population at large outside the world of authors.

Perhaps even more important than intentional ambiguity is unintentional. Individuals can use language loosely or carelessly or in some specialized way that could later be read as only one of several plausible meanings. The multiplicity of authors further increases the chances that language will not be crafted with consummate care. Indeed, in the case of the Constitution, with various groupings of individuals playing different roles in creating the language of the document and then in making it law through a process of voting, the shared responsibility could easily encourage inattention by individual participants, as each assumes that others will keep (or already have kept) a watchful eye. We do not like to acknowledge fallibility in our constitutional framers, but one need look no further than the first example cited above for evidence of their human frailties in the use of language. All this is seemingly irrelevant for Solum because his concern in interpretation is not with the authors but with that objective original meaning. The trouble is that the shift from intention to meaning is quite unlikely to provide any escape from ambiguity—of the intentional or unintentional variety—that may have found its way into the text when the authors were doing their work.[14]

Recall that meaning for Solum is a function of patterns of usage among ordinary speakers. If anything, the shift from intention to meaning should increase, not diminish, the chances of varying understandings. For the constitutional authors surely had more in common with each other than did farmers, seamstresses, shopkeepers, and lawyers, whom Solum invokes as the grounding for meaning. Of course, that large crowd may have converged on usages, but it also may not have. It should hardly be surprising on occasion to find divergent patterns along the lines of occupation, region, or age. For that matter there could easily be variations among, for example, seamstresses of the same age and region. I will return to the specialization of much constitutional language, but even for more ordinary usage, I cannot fathom how Solum thinks his construct of original meaning provides an escape from the summing problem that he seems to acknowledge for the audience as well as the authors of the Constitution. At times he seems to think that he is no more ascribing meaning to audience than to authors, but it is not apparent to me where one might then turn—until one introduces into the picture normativity and hence choice.

Just to revert to one of the choices that I mentioned in my principal essay, originalists often indulge in an assumption that constitutional language is internally consistent and carefully crafted. One need look no further than the four examples above for evidence that this is simply false. When originalists assume consistency and care nonetheless, they are making a normative judgment, not probing any raw fact of the matter. Because of that choice—and lots of others—resolving ambiguity or, for that matter, concluding that language is ambiguous in the first place will often be a function of the interpreter's normative choices. Originalists like Solum shroud this problem by insisting, for example, that the meaning decipherer is a reasonable or ordinary or competent user of English, who would then obviously be routinely consistent and careful in the use of language (pp. 3, 25). Call it what you will, that is not taking the world as it is. Rather, it is normativity.

Normative Choices in Interpretation

When finding or resolving ambiguity—or vagueness for that matter—draws on normative considerations, there is, of course, room for disagreement in interpretation. This is not simply, as with factual inquiry, because the evidence is sparse or contradictory. Rather, it is because people can harbor normative differences that more evidence alone could never hope to resolve. In the first of my four examples of ambiguity, for instance, there is no semantic fact of the matter about whether presentment is required for congressional proposal of a constitutional amendment. If the question were to be posed on a clean slate, any sensible interpreter would be heavily influenced by a normative judgment about whether presentment would be salutary in that process. It might, for instance, seem pointless to require presentment under Article I when, numerically speaking, the vote necessary to override any veto had already been obtained under the Article V procedure. But that normative argument could be undermined if there were reason to think that a second legislative look after a veto could be salutary, could, for instance, occasionally lead to genuine legislative reconsideration and a different result. Any such normative judgment about a salutary second look might, of course, be influenced by experience in the real world of legislative voting—not two hundred years ago, but since, all the way up to today. If political parties utterly dominate the process, then there might seem to be little to be gained from a second look, whereas a more freewheeling process (free, that is, of political party partisanship) might suggest the real possibility of a change of mind by some legislators after a presidential expression of disapproval.

The mention of political parties suggests another reason why contemporary values will inevitably come to bear on interpretation of ambiguous and also vague language. As I argued in my principal essay, twenty-first-century American politics is embedded in a radically different world from the one the constitutional authors confronted. Political parties in particular play an entirely different role now than they did then. A contemporary issue that is framed in some significant way by the role of parties is thus likely to bear scant resemblance to any issue that the framers might even have considered. For vague language, Solum would no doubt think that questions of mere application back then are irrelevant today, since the original semantic meaning of vague language must forever be vague. For reasons discussed in my principal essay, I disagree about the relevance of original "applications" of vague language (pp. 111–14). But for ambiguous language, it seems to me that Solum can find no refuge in semantic meaning. Where political parties are part of the picture that the application of ambiguous language today may conjure up, the choices for resolving the ambiguity may all be quite awkward. If any fit the language at all, however, every one of them may well be quite different from *any* that were available to the framers back then—and likely different as well from what was available to ordinary citizens.

The *Heller* case provides an example of choices (often shaped by normative considerations) that will often be required in interpretation. Solum rightly depicts Justice Scalia's majority opinion in *Heller* as sounding in original-meaning originalism (p. 28). But Scalia's approach focuses attention alone on the meaning of the words *the right to keep and bear arms*, with no particular concern for the rest of the Second Amendment language (p. 29). Solum may well disapprove of that stance, for he insists that linguistic context can help wrestle down meaning, and he tells us that "[t]houghtful critics of Justice Scalia's opinion believe that the Second Amendment was intended to apply *only* to weapons used in connection with service in a state militia" (pp. 31–32). In any event, when the introductory language of the amendment is brought into the interpretational picture, the possibility emerges that some quite ordinary readers of the amendment as a whole would think the right announced was to be constrained by the announced introductory purpose. This latter interpretation, however, is hardly an objectively verifiable fact of the interpretive matter. To the contrary, the Second Amendment provides yet another example of serious ambiguity, the resolution of which would inevitably turn on normative considerations. These include the policy question of whether in this day and age a generalized right to bear arms is a good idea. Solum might claim that the ambiguity could be resolved by struggling hard enough with the words of the Second Amendment in context, but until he has done the struggling and produced that objectively verifiable ambiguity-resolving meaning that others would clearly rush to embrace, the claim rings pretty hollow. There is simply no reason to think that either language in context or patterns of language usage are up to the task that Solum insists on assigning to them.

Ordinary or Technical Meaning

Justice Scalia's *Heller* opinion also illustrates how perverse the public meaning emphasis on "publicly available context" can be. In a passage Solum quotes with apparent approval, Scalia—himself quoting a prior decision—tells us that the Constitution's "'words and phrases'" are to be taken "'in their normal and ordinary as distinguished from technical meaning.'" This, Justice Scalia explains, leaves room for "idiomatic meaning" but not for "secret or technical meanings that would not have been known to ordinary citizens in the founding generation" (p. 28). Those ordinary citizens might, however, simply shake their heads in bewilderment if asked to assign meaning to technical phrases like "Letters of Marque and Reprisal."[15] And even if ordinary citizens at the time might have assigned some single coherent meaning to the constitutional phrase "Corruption of Blood," it is entirely possible that that phrase would have had a technical meaning to the draftsmen that would not have occurred to all—or perhaps any—of the farmers, seamstresses, shopkeepers, and lawyers whom Solum invokes as representative of those ordinary citizens.[16]

Solum is clearly aware of this tension, but he is not very convincing in grappling with it. In a separate discussion in his essay, he invokes the possibility of a *division of linguistic labor* (p. 34). He explains that an ordinary citizen encountering "the phrase *letters of marque and reprisal* might say, 'That sounds like a term of art'" and then "consult a lawyer or judge" to find out "what it means" (pp. 34–35). First, one might wonder just what Solum means by "might." Does the decipherer of meaning have a choice of whether or not to hunt for the technical meaning? And then, how obvious does it have to be that some technical meaning is at work before the meaning decipherer might (or must) search out that technical meaning and accede to it? To the modern ear, at least, the phrase *letters of marque and reprisal* is comfortably outside the realm of ordinary daily discourse. It alerts a meaning decipherer to the likelihood of a technical meaning. But other words in the Constitution could have been used by the draftsmen in a technical sense, and a meaning decipherer might fail to appreciate that possibility. Article I, for example, refers to "Piracies," to "Felonies committed on the high Seas," and to "Captures on Land and Water."[17] Those could well have had technical meanings, but that might not have been apparent to the population at large, for whom there might have been nontechnical meanings.[18] Is it open to Solum's interpreter to give those words some nontechnical meaning because they happen to match some discoverable pattern out there in the world? And then most fundamentally, why consult a lawyer or judge rather than the authors of the language that might have been used in a technical way? For the consultation that Solum advises has already broken loose from the objective moorings that he had claimed, revealing, I think, that he is himself a "faint-hearted" original-meaning originalist.[19] Deep down he senses that the law is a purposive enterprise, in which objective meaning is basically attractive because, if available, it is good evidence of what the authors were trying to accomplish.

The Limits of Constraint Based on Language

To be clear, I am not arguing that inquiry into patterns of usage of constitutional language in the world beyond the authors must routinely come up empty. When some widespread consistent pattern is discoverable, Solum's objective meaning exists. The two-senators-per-state allotment and the thirty-five-year age requirement for president, for example, are plausible candidates for the authorial consensus that I argued in my principal essay should be the touchstone for clarity of meaning, and likely as well (not surprisingly) for the clarity of semantic meaning upon which Solum relies. But I also argued that that should not be the end of the constitutional inquiry if it seems to command results the normative dimensions of which were clearly outside the field of vision of the authors of the seemingly clear language (pp. 123–25). That is how the absurd-results exception works (p. 101). Even then, however, I would indulge in a very heavy presumption in favor of clear language meaning—like that of the two-senator provision—on account of the (normatively relevant) complications that are often invited by putting that clear meaning aside.

Nor is clear meaning the end of the constitutional inquiry for Solum. We have seen that he leaves an opening for putting semantic meaning aside—inviting a living Constitution—in the case of extraordinary circumstances or the like. Aside from his discussion of *Brown*, which I mentioned above, Solum does not elaborate, but perhaps he would include the secession crisis that provided the background for the admission of West Virginia to the Union and the allocation to that supposedly new state of two members in the United States Senate. If so, then I should note that Solum would ground such a conclusion a lot more solidly than did Vasan Kesavan and Michael Paulsen, the original-meaning enthusiasts whose approach I discussed in my principal essay (pp. 135–36). For Solum seems to acknowledge that his exceptional circumstances opening is justified by normative considerations, whereas Kesavan and Paulsen give no such ground, at least that I can detect.

I hope this discussion has brought into focus the most fundamental difference between Solum and me. For Solum constitutional language falls into one of two or three categories, the ambiguous—of which there is little or none—the vague, and the clear. He provides an extraordinary circumstances safety valve for escape from thoroughly undesirable consequences of clear language and would occasionally accede to established practice, even if it was "erroneously" derived. Putting those possibilities aside, placement in one or another of the three categories is a matter of semantic meaning, a pure matter of fact. Meaning may come into focus as clear only when the interpreter does his homework, but diligence will regularly be rewarded with decisively clear answers. In contrast, I find it more realistic and instructive to think of constitutional interpretation as a complex enterprise that eludes reduction to something resembling an objective inquiry. It is fully as much art as science. There may occasionally—or even often—be decisively better and worse answers to interpretational questions. They may be grounded in an authorial consensus about which well-established patterns of language usage in the society at large can provide weighty evidence. Apart from the consensus possibility, interpretation will be the result of judgment that draws on normative considerations. And even in the face of an original consensus about meaning, these considerations may provide an overwhelming case for putting that consensus to the side.

Many of the answers to interpretational questions that we think of as clear are really ones where the clarity is produced by the weakness of any normative considerations that seem to cut in a different direction. Often the normative argument for putting the semantic meaning aside may simply not seem worth it, as in the hypothetical case of California's claim today that it should have more than two senators. We could make a normative case for such a claim—and we might even accede to the argument if it were truly compelling, as we did in the case of West Virginia. But the confusion and disruption of the processes of government that would be invited by acceding to an argument based simply on California's huge population provide powerful reasons to accede instead to the consensus—or, if you will, the clear semantic—meaning. Those powerful reasons are normative. So it seems fair to say that even when semantic language meaning seems clear, normativity repeatedly casts its shadow in the process of constitutional interpretation.

NOTES

Preface

1. 290 U.S. 398, 448–49 (1934) (Sutherland, J., dissenting).
2. 290 U.S. at 442–43 (citing McCulloch v. Maryland, 17 U.S. [4 Wheat.] 316, 407 [1819]).

We Are All Originalists Now

1. The term *originalism* appears to have been coined by Paul Brest. See Brest, "The Fundamental Rights Controversy: Essential Contradictions of Normative Constitutional Scholarship," *Yale* Law Journal 90 (1981): 1090; Brest, "The Misconceived Quest for the Original Understanding," *Boston University Law Review* 60 (1980): 234.

2. West Coast Hotel v. Parrish, 300 U.S. 379, 404 (1937) (Sutherland, J., dissenting) (quoting T. Cooley, *A Treatise on the Constitutional Limitations Which Rest upon the Legislative Power of the States of the American Union* 55 (1868; repr., Cambridge, MA: Da Capo Press 1972).

3. The phrase *original public meaning* was introduced by Gary Lawson. See Lawson, "The Rise and Rise of the Administrative State," *Harvard Law Review* 107 (1994): 1249–50.

4. See Keith E. Whittington, *Constitutional Construction: Divided Powers and Constitutional Meaning* (Cambridge, MA: Harvard University Press, 1999); Whittington, *Constitutional Interpretation: Textual Meaning, Original Intent, and Judicial Review* (Lawrence: University Press of Kansas, 1999); Randy E. Barnett, *Restoring the Lost Constitution: The Presumption of Liberty* (Princeton: Princeton University Press, 2004).

5. Brown v. Board of Education, 347 U.S. 483 (1954).
6. Griswold v. Connecticut, 381 U.S. 479 (1965).

7. Miranda v. Arizona, 384 U.S. 436 (1966).

8. Roe v. Wade, 410 U.S. 113 (1973).

9. Lochner v. New York, 198 U.S. 45 (1905).

10. *Id*. at 74, 75 (Holmes, J., dissenting).

11. Alexander Bickel, *The Least Dangerous Branch: The Supreme Court at the Bar of Politics*, 2nd ed. (New Haven: Yale University Press, 1986), 16–18; see also Barry Friedman, "The History of the Countermajoritarian Difficulty, Part One: The Road to Judicial Supremacy," *New York University Law Review* 73 (1998): 333–433; Friedman, "The History of the Countermajoritarian Difficulty, Part II: Reconstruction's Political Court," *Georgetown Law Journal* 91 (2002):. 1–65; Friedman, "The History of the Countermajoritarian Difficulty, Part Three: The Lesson of *Lochner*," *New York University Law Review* 76 (2001): 1383–1455; Friedman, "The History of the Countermajoritarian Difficulty, Part Four: Law's Politics," *University of Pennsylvania Law Review* 148 (2000): 971–1064; Friedman, "The Birth of an Academic Obsession: The History of the Countermajoritarian Difficulty, Part Five," Yale Law Journal 112 (2002): 153–259.

12. Mark Graber, "The Nonmajoritarian Difficulty: Legislative Deference to the Judiciary," *Studies in American Political Development* 7 (1993): 35–73.

13. John Hart Ely, *Democracy and Distrust: A Theory of Judicial Review* (Cambridge, MA: Harvard University Press, 1980).

14. Robert H. Bork, *"Neutral Principles and Some First Amendment* Problems," *Indiana Law Journal* 47 (1971): 1–35.

15. William H. Rehnquist, "The Notion of a Living Constitution," *Texas Law Review* 54 (1976): 706 (1976).

16. Edwin Meese III, "Speech before the American Bar Association (July 9, 1985)," in *The Great Debate: Interpreting Our Written Constitution*, ed. Paul G. Cassel (Washington, DC: The Federalist Society, 1986).

17. Raoul Berger, *Government by Judiciary* (Cambridge, MA: Harvard University Press, 1977).

18. Brest, "The Misconceived Quest."

19. H. Jefferson Powell, "The Original Understanding of Original Intent," *Harvard Law Review* 98 (1985): 885–948.

20. Charles A. Miller, *The Supreme Court and the Uses of History* (Cambridge, MA: Belknap Press, 1969), 157–58.

21. David Hume, *A Treatise of Human Nature*, ed. David F. Norton and Mary J. Norton (Oxford: Clarendon Press, 2000), 334.

22. Paul Grice, *Studies in the Way of Words* (Cambridge, MA: Harvard University Press, 1989), 3–143.

23. U.S. Const. art. VI, cl. 2.

24. Andrew Coan, "The Irrelevance of Writtenness in Constitutional Interpretation," *University of Pennsylvania Law Review* 158 (2010): 1077–81.

25. Akhil Reed Amar, "Intratextualism," *Harvard Law Review* 112 (1999): 747–827.

26. District of Columbia v. Heller, 554 U.S. 570, 128 S. Ct. 2783 (2008).

27. United States v. Miller, 307 U.S. 174 (1939).

28. United States v. Cruikshank, 92 U.S. 542, 553 (1876); Presser v. Illinois, 116 U.S. 252, 264–65 (1886); Miller v. Texas, 153 U.S. 535, 538 (1894).

29. *Heller*, 128 S. Ct. at 2788.

30. These passages occur at pages 2823, 2825, 2827, and 2836 of Justice Stevens's dissenting opinion.

31. *Heller*, 128 S. Ct. at 2847 (Breyer, J., dissenting).

32. *Id*. at 2816–17 (majority opinion).

33. *Id.* at 2821 (emphasis added).

34. H. L. A. Hart, *The Concept of Law*, 2nd ed. (Oxford: Clarendon Press, 1984), 56–57.

35. See John Rawls, *Political Liberalism*, exp. ed. New York: Columbia University Press, 2005); Rawls, "The Idea of Public Reason Revisited," in *The Law of Peoples* (Cambridge, MA: Harvard University Press, 2001), 129–75 (1999).

36. See, e.g., Douglas H. Ginsburg, "Originalism and Economic Analysis: Two Case Studies of Consistency and Coherence in Supreme Court Decision Making," *Harvard Journal of Law and Public Policy* 33 (2010): 225–26.

37. Albert Venn Dicey, *Introduction to the Study of the Law of the Constitution*, 8th ed. (1885; repr., London: Macmillan, 1902).

38. Barnett, *Restoring the Lost Constitution*, 101–3.

39. Kurt T. Lash, "Originalism, Popular Sovereignty, and Reverse Stare Decisis," *Virginia Law Review* 93 (2007): 1437–81.

40. U. S. Const. art. V.

41. Bruce Ackerman, "The Living Constitution," *Harvard Law Review* 120 (2007): 1762.

42. Jack M. Balkin and Reva B. Siegel, "Principles, Practices, and Social Movements," *University of Pennsylvania Law Review* 154 (2006): 927–50.

43. Brown v. Board of Education, 347 U.S. 483 (1954).

44. Cass R. Sunstein, *Radicals in Robes: Why Extreme Right-Wing Courts Are Wrong for America* (New York: Basic Books, 2006), 64.

45. Michael W. McConnell, "Originalism and the Desegregation Decisions," *Virginia Law Review* 81 (1995): 947–1140.

46. Clinton Rossiter, ed., *The Federalist Papers* (New York: New American Library, 1961), no. 10 at 77 (James Madison).

47. Walter M. Merrill, *Against Wind and Tide: A Biography of Wm. Lloyd Garrison* 205 (Cambridge, MA: Harvard University Press, 1963), 205 (quoting resolution adopted by the Antislavery Society, January 27, 1843).

48. Randy E. Barnett, "Was Slavery Unconstitutional before the Thirteenth Amendment? Lysander Spooner's Theory of Interpretation," *Pacific Law Journal* 28 (1997): 977–1014.

49. Plessy v. Ferguson, 163 U.S. 537 (1896).

50. Brown v. Board of Education, 347 U.S. 483 (1954).

51. Herbert Spencer, *Social Statics* (London: John Chapman, 1851).

52. John Rawls, *A Theory of Justice* (Cambridge: Belknap Press, 1971).

53. Robert Nozick, *Anarchy, State, and Utopia* (New York: Basic Books, 1974).

54. Brian Z. Tamanaha, *Beyond the Realist-Formalist Divide: The Role of Politics in Judging* (Princeton, NJ: Princeton Univeristy Press, 2009).

55. Saul Cornell, "Originalism on Trial: The Use and Abuse of History in *District of Columbia v. Heller,"* *Ohio State Law Journal* 69 (2008): 625–40.

56. Quentin Skinner, "Meaning and Understanding in the History of Ideas," *History and Theory* 8 (1969): 3–53.

57. Philip Bobbitt, *Constitutional Fate: Theory of the Constitution*, rev. ed. (Oxford: Oxford University Press 2006).

58. Brest, The Misconceived Quest," 238.

59. 290 U.S. 398 (1934).

60. *Id.* at 442–43 (quoting McCulloch v. Maryland, 17 U.S. (4 Wheat.) 316, 407 (1819)).

61. Charles A. Reich, "Mr. Justice Black and the Living Constitution," *Harvard Law Review* 76 (1963): 735–36.

62. William J. Brennan, Jr., "The Constitution of the United States: Contemporary Ratification," *South Texas Law Review* 27 (1986): 437.

63. Ronald Dworkin, *Law's Empire* (Cambridge, MA: Belknap Press, 1986), 400.

64. Whittington, *Constitutional Interpretation*; Whittington, *Constitutional Construction*.

65. Jack M. Balkin, "Framework Originalism and the Living Constitution," *Northwestern University Law Review* 103 (2009): 549–614.

66. John O. McGinnis and Michael B. Rappaport, "Original Methods Originalism: A New Theory of Interpretation and the Case against Construction," *Northwestern University Law Review* 103 (2009): 751–802.

67. Compare Lash, "Originalism, Popular Sovereignty, and Reverse Stare Decisis," with Lawrence B. Solum, "The Supreme Court in Bondage: Constitutional Stare Decisis, Legal Formalism, and the Future of Unenumerated Rights," *University of Pennsylvania Journal of Constitutional Law* 9 (2006): 155–208.

68. Antonin Scalia, "Originalism: The Lesser Evil Justice," *University of Cincinnati Law Review* 57 (1989): 849–65.

69. James E. Fleming, "Fidelity to Our Imperfect Constitution," *Fordham Law Review* 65 (1997): 1335–55.

Originalism and the Living American Constitution

1. Johnathan O'Neill, *Originalism in American Law and Politics: A Constitutional History* (Baltimore: Johns Hopkins University Press, 2005), 12.

2. See, e.g., Keith E. Whittington, "The New Originalism," 2 *Georgetown Journal of Law and Public Policy* 2 (2004): 599–613.

3. See Ethan J. Leib, "The Perpetual Anxiety of Living Constitutionalism," *Constitutional Commentary* 24 (2007): 355 n.7 (collecting authority).

4. See Paul Brest, "The Misconceived Quest for the Original Understanding," *Boston University Law Review* 60 (1980): 236.

5. See Lino A. Graglia, " 'Interpreting' the Constitution: Posner on Bork," *Stanford Law Review* 44 (1992): 1031; Antonin Scalia, "Originalism: *The Lesser Evil,*" University of Cincinnati Law Review 47 (1989): 854.

6. See Randy E. Barnett, *Restoring the Lost Constitution* (Princeton: Princeton University Press 2004), 92; Scalia, "Originalism," 855 (" 'nonoriginalism' represents agreement on nothing except what is the wrong approach").

7. Associated Press, "Scalia Slams 'Living Constitution' Theory," March 14, 2006; see William H. Rehnquist, "The Notion of a Living Constitution," *Texas Law Review* 54 (1976): 695 ("nonelected members of the federal judiciary … [are] responsible to no constituency whatever").

8. Academic debates about originalist ideas had certainly predated Meese's entry onto the stage. See Raoul Berger, *Government by Judiciary* (Cambridge, MA: Harvard University Press 1977); Whittington, "New Originalism," 599–600, points to an exchange about originalism (albeit without using the word, which had not yet made its appearance) and living constitutionalism between North Carolina's senator Sam Ervin and (soon to be) Justice Thurgood Marshall at the latter's 1967 confirmation hearing.

9. Edwin Meese, "Speech before the D.C. Chapter of the Federalist Society Lawyers Division (November 15, 1985)," in *Originalism: A Quarter-Century of Debate*, ed. Steven G. Calabresi (Washington, DC: Regnery, 2007), 71, 80.

10. 410 U.S. 113 (1973).

11. 25 U.S. (12 Wheat.) 213, 332 (1827) (separate opinion).

12. See Davison M. Douglas, "Foreword: The Legacy of St. George Tucker," *William and Mary Law Review*. 47 (2006): 1112–13.

13. William Blackstone, *Commentaries on the Laws of England*, facsimile of 1st ed. of 1765–1769 (Chicago: University of Chicago Press, 1979), 91.

14. O'Neill, *Originalism*, 13.

15. Ibid., 12–28. Something of an embarrassment to originalists has been Chief Justice Taney's originalist language in his opinion in the infamous *Dred Scott* decision. Dred Scott v. Sandford, 60 U.S. 393, 426 (1857). For an example see O'Neill, *Originalism*, 23.

16. See Philip Bobbitt, *Constitutional Fate: Theory of the Constitution* (New York: Oxford University Press 1982).

17. 290 U.S. 398 (1934).

18. U.S. Const. art. I, § 10, cl. 1.

19. 290 U.S. at 442–43.

20. Brest, "The Misconceived Quest."

21. "At various points in American history, originalism was not a terribly self-conscious theory of constitutional interpretation." Whittington, "The New Originalism," 599.

22. Rehnquist, "The Notion of a Living Constitution," 698.

23. Ibid., 694.

24. Ibid., 695.

25. Ibid., 700.

26. See, e.g., Edwin Meese, "Speech before the American Bar Association (July 9, 1985)", in Calabresi, *Originalism*, 47. As Henry Monaghan put it in the early eighties "For the purposes of *legal* reasoning, the binding quality of the constitutional text is itself incapable of and not in need of further demonstration. It is our master rule of recognition." Monaghan, "Our Perfect Constitution," *New York University Law Review* 56 (1981): 383–84 (emphasis in original).

27. Keith E. Whittington, *Constitutional Interpretation* (Lawrence: University Press of Kansas, 1999), 94; see Caleb Nelson, "Originalism and Interpretive Conventions," *University of Chicago Law Review* 70 (2003): 561–62; Gary Lawson and Guy Seidman, "Originalism as a Legal Enterprise," *Constitutional Commentary* 23 (2006): 54–55. Sometimes recognition of the point is not so clear, as many originalists routinely invoke the "text" of the document as if to suggest that it is self-defining. See, e.g., Antonin Scalia, "Response," in *A Matter of Interpretation: Federal Courts and the Law* (Princeton: Princeton University Press, 1997), 129, 132. At one point, Justice Scalia recognizes the problem but then dismisses it by suggesting that "broader social purposes that a statute is designed, or could be designed, to serve" will simply be obvious. Scalia, "Common-Law Courts in a Civil-Law System: The Role of United States Federal Courts in Interpreting the Constitution and Laws," in *A Matter of Interpretation*, 3, 23.

28. See Barnett, *Restoring the Lost Constitution*, 108.

29. See U.S. Const. art. I, § 3, cl. 1, *amended by* U.S. Const. amend XVII, cl.1.

30. U.S. Const. art. II, § 1, cl. 5.

31. See Keith Pratt and Richard Rutt, *Korea: A Historical and Cultural Dictionary* (Richmond, UK, Curzon Press 1999), 2.

32. U.S. Const. art. I, § 2, cl. 3.

33. See United States Department of Commerce v. Montana, 503 U.S. 442, 447–49 (1992).

34. U.S. Const. art. I, § 7, cl. 3.

35. For a very different interpretation, see Seth Barrett Tillman, "A Textualist Defense of Article I, Section 7, Clause 3: Why *Hollingsworth v. Virginia* Was Rightly Decided, and Why *INS v. Chadha* Was Wrongly Reasoned," *Texas Law Review* 83 (2005): 1265–1372.

36. See Hollingsworth v. Virginia, 3 U.S. 378, 381 (1798); Bruce Ackerman, "The Living Constitution," *Harvard Law Review* 120 (2007): 1759 ("the Founders...excluded the presidency from any role in constitutional revision").

37. Meese, "Speech before the American Bar Association," 52.

38. See, e.g., Griffin v. Oceanic Contractors, Inc., 458 U.S. 564, 571 (1982) ("in rare cases the literal application of a statute will produce a result demonstrably at odds with the intentions of its drafters, and those intentions must be controlling") (Rehnquist, J.). Justice Scalia is one of the few

critics of this emphasis on intention, but even he acknowledges its overwhelming prevalence. See Scalia, "Common-Law Courts," 16.

39. To be sure, there were exceptions. See, e.g., Max Radin, "Statutory Interpretation," *Harvard Law Review* 43 (1930): 863–85.

40. See Scalia, "Originalism," 857.

41. Jack N. Rakove, *Original Meanings* (New York: Knopf, 1996), 6. The document, moreover, reads as if it were a product of "the People of the United States," and some have urged that we must somehow construct a state of mind for that group as our guiding intention. See Lawson and Seidman, "Originalism as a Legal Enterprise," 49.

42. See Brest, "The Misconceived Quest," 212.

43. See Steven G. Calabresi, "A Critical Introduction to the Originalism Debate," in Calabresi, *Originalism*, 12 (quoting Meese to that effect and characterizing the position as "right"); Meese, "Speech before the D.C. Chapter of the Federalist Lawyers Division," 76. Keith Whittington seems to take the position that such a consensus is required. Whittington, *Constitutional Interpretation*, 194–95; but cf. Gary Lawson and Guy Seidman, "The Jeffersonian Treaty Clause," *Illinois Law Review*, 2006, 44 n. 159 ("under reasonable-person originalism, even a strong historical consensus ... would not be conclusive").

44. See Scalia, "Common-Law Courts," 32; Michael S. Moore, "The Semantics of Judging," *Southern California Law Review* 54 (1981): 265–68.

45. See, e.g., National Labor Relations Bd. v. Catholic Bishop of Chicago, 440 U.S. 490 (1979); Griffin v. Oceanic Contractors, Inc., 458 U.S. 564, 573–74 (1982); Bankamerica Corp. v. United States, 462 U.S. 122 (1983).

46. Still, the suggestion of agency does come up in the literature about legislative interpretation. See, e.g., Lawrence M. Solan, "Private Language, Public Laws: The Central Role of Legislative Intent in Statutory Interpretation," *Georgetown Law Journal* 93 (2005): 428.

47. E.g., FDIC v. Philadelphia Gear Corp., 476 U.S. 426, 433 (1986); see Gerald T. Dunne, "*Philadelphia Gear*—Hard Case, Bad Law," *Banking Law Journal* 103 (1986): 507.

48. Scalia, "Common-Law Courts," 35.

49. I take it that Ronald Dworkin has basically this idea in mind when he refers to the "personification" of a lawmaking institution that we employ in ascribing an "intention" to it. See Dworkin, "Comment," in Scalia, *A Matter of Interpretation*, 115, 117. Keith Whittington disparages this idea, referring to it as "the anthropomorphic error." But later he says "whether the author is implied or actual, he comes with the text." Whittington, *Constitutional Construction*, 164, 177.

50. See pages 86–87.

51. See Brest, "The Misconceived Quest," 216 and 216n41.

52. See Jack M. Balkin, "Original Meaning and Constitutional Redemption," *Constitutional Commentary* 24 (2007): 455–57; Barnett, *Restoring the Lost Constitution*, 118–19.

53. U.S. Const. art. II, § 1, cl. 5.

54. "Contest: Was George Washington Constitutional?" *Constitutional Commentary* 12 (1995): 137–38.

55. See Jordan Streiker, Sanford Levinson, and J. M. Balkin, "Taking Test and Structure *Really* Seriously: Constitutional Interpretation and the Crisis of Presidential Eligibility," *Texas Law Review* 74 (1995): 237–257; Calvin H. Johnson, "RE: Was George Washington Constitutional?," letter to the editor in *Constitutional Commentary* 18 (2001): 295–99.

56. U.S. Const. art. VII, cl. 1.

57. Virginia's ratification came four days after New Hampshire became the ninth state to sign on. See Calvin H. Johnson, "Homage to Clio: The Historical Continuity from the Articles of Confederation into the Constitution," *Constitutional Commentary* 20 (2003–4): 464.

58. U.S. Const. art. I, § 2, cl. 2; § 3, cl. 3.

59. U.S. Const. art. VI, cl. 2.

60. Brest, "The Misconceived Quest," 221.

61. See, e.g., Barnett, *Restoring the Lost Constitution*, 89–93; Nelson, "Originalism and Interpretive Conventions," 553–54; Gary Lawson and Guy Seidman, "The First 'Establishment' Clause: Article VII and the Post-Constitutional Confederation," *Notre Dame Law Review* 78 (2002): 90.

62. See, e.g., Henry Paul Monaghan, "Stare Decisis and Constitutional Adjudication," *Columbia Law Review* 88 (1988): 723, 726.

63. See Stanley Fish, "Intention Is All There Is: A Critical Analysis of Aharon Barak's Purposive Interpretation in Law," *Cardozo Law Review* 29 (2008): 1110 ("The phrase 'original understanding'…is ambiguous. It could refer to what the original author or authors had in mind…or it could refer to how the words would be understood by literate and informed persons at the time of their utterance or publication").

64. At the explicit end of the spectrum are Lawson and Seidman, "The First 'Establishment' Clause," 90.

65. See E. Allan Farnsworth, *Contracts*, 3rd ed. (Aspen Law and Business, 1999), 473–74; *Restatement of the Law Second, Contracts* (American Law Institute Publishers, 1981), § 206.

66. Scalia, "Common-Law Courts," 17. In the passage Scalia is actually arguing in favor of "meaning" rather than "understanding," and we will turn below to that possibility. The point of the passage, however, seems to rest on the possibility of failure to understand, for which "understanding" would seem to be a better fit than "meaning."

67. "Recourse to intention is necessary because only certain people have the authority to make law." Whittington, *Constitutional Construction*, 94–95; see Nelson, "Originalism and Interpretive Conventions," 558–59.

68. See Barnett, *Restoring the Lost Constitution*, 94–100; Lawson and Seidman, "Originalism as a Legal Enterprise," 48–49 n. 11 (collecting adherents). This change in emphasis is often traced to Justice Scalia's 1988 William Howard Taft Lecture, subsequently published as Scalia, "Originalism: The Lesser Evil." See Randy E. Barnett, "Scalia's Infidelity: A Critique of 'Faint-Hearted' Originalism," 75 *University of Cincinnati Law Review* 75 (2006): 9. The trend was perhaps also fed by a 1985 article by H. Jefferson Powell arguing that the framers themselves did not believe that their subjective states of mind would or should be determinative of the meaning given to the Constitution's words. Powell, "The Original Understanding of Original Intent," *Harvard Law Review* 98 (1985): 885.

69. Gary Lawson, "On Reading Recipes…and Constitutions," *Georgetown Law Journal* 85 (1997):1834.

70. See Michael Stokes Paulsen, "Does the Constitution Prescribe Rules for Its Own Interpretation?" *Northwestern University Law Review* 103 (2009): 858.

71. Scalia, "Common-Law Courts," 17; see Randy E. Barnett, "The Original Meaning of the Commerce Clause," *University of Chicago Law Review* 68 (2001): 105; Vasan Kesavan and Michael Stokes Paulsen, "The Interpretive Force of the Constitution's Secret Drafting History," *Georgetown Law Journal* 91 (2003): 1118.

72. See generally Jonathan R. Siegel, "What Statutory Drafting Errors Teach Us about Statutory Interpretation," *George Washington Law Review* 69 (2001): 309–66.

73. Samuel Williston, *The Law of Contracts*, 1st ed., vol. 1 (New York: Baker, Voorhis, 1920), § 95.

74. *Restatement of the Law Second, Contracts* § 201(1).

75. Scalia, "Common-Law Courts," 23.

76. Ibid., 37–38. At another point he speaks of the "major purposes" of the confrontation clause in the process of giving it an entirely plausible reading but not one dictated in any straightforward way by its language. Ibid., 43–44.

77. Ibid., 38; compare Printz v. United States, 521 U.S. 898 (1997); see Dworkin, "Comment," 115–16.

78. See Robert W. Bennett, "Originalism: Lessons from Things That Go without Saying," *San Diego Law Review* 45 (2008): 645–72.

79. E.g., "Remarks of Suzanna Sherry, Panel on Originalism and Unenumerated Constitutional Rights," in Calabresi, *Originalism*, 113, 115.

80. U.S. Const. art. II, cl. 3.

81. See Robert W. Bennett, *Taming the Electoral College* (Stanford: Stanford University Press 2006), 14–17.

82. See United States v. Nixon, 418 U.S. 683 (1974).

83. U.S. Const. art. I, § 3, cl. 6.

84. U.S. Const. art. II, § 2, cl. 2.

85. See generally, Edward T. Swaine, "Hail, No: Changing the Chief Justice," *University of Pennsylvania Law Review* 154 (2006): 1709–28.

86. The Federalist Papers (New York: New American Library, 1961), no. 10 (James Madison).

87. Richard Hofstadter, *The Idea of a Party System* (Berkeley: University of California Press 1969), viii.

88. E.g., Fish, "Intention Is All There Is," 1112 ("Being focused on intention is not an approach to interpretation…it is interpretation"); Richard S. Kay, "Adherence to the Original Intentions in Constitutional Adjudication: Three Objections and Responses," *Northwestern University Law Review* 82 (1988): 226, 246 (1988); Stephen Smith, *Law's Quandary* (Cambridge, MA: Harvard University Press, 2004), 101; "Remarks of Charles Cooper, Debate on Radicals in Robes," in Calabresi, *Originalism*, 296, 298; cf. Nelson, "Originalism and Interpretive Conventions," 561, 563.

89. Whittington, *Constitutional Construction*, 194; see also ibid., 59 ("'interpretation' of writing means conveying…intent"); ibid., 94 ("Without an intentional agent behind the marks, the very concept of a text or of an interpretation becomes nonsensical").

90. In the case from which the example is drawn, it was actually a Federal Rule of Evidence, rather than a statute, that used the inappropriate expression. Green v. Bock Laundry Mach. Co., 490 U.S. 504 (1989).

91. See 490 U.S. at 528. For other originalists expressing a degree of sympathy with an absurd-results doctrine in constitutional law, see Vasan Kesavan and Michael Stokes Paulsen, "Is West Virginia Unconstitutional?" California Law Review 90 (2002): 336–37 n. 142, 344 n. 157; Lawson and Seidman, "Jeffersonian Treaty Clause," 7.

92. Scalia, "Common-Law Courts," 16, 21.

93. I am quite confident that Justice Scalia would similarly adopt a stance in favor of intention where, for example, the constitutional language was "intentionally" taken from international law. See Eugene Kontorovich, "The 'Define and Punish' Clause and the Limits of Universal Jurisdiction," *Northwestern University Law Review* 103 (2009): 158.

94. 490 U.S. at 529.

95. See Kontorovich, "The 'Define and Punish' Clause," 187–88.

96. See Lawson and Seidman, "Originalism as a Legal Enterprise," 54–55 nn. 24 and 25 (collecting authority).

97. See Kesavan and Paulsen, "Is West Virginia Unconstitutional?"

98. Lawson and Seidman, "The First 'Establishment' Clause," 90.

99. Many original-meaning originalists seem to want to deny the continued relevance of the summing problem. See, e.g., Barnett, "Scalia's Infidelity," 9.

100. See Kesavan and Paulsen, "Is West Virginia Unconstitutional?" 332–63; William W. Van Alstyne, "Second Amendment Commas," *Green Bag* 10 (2007): 469–81.

101. Compare Randy E. Barnett, "Underlying Principles," *Constitutional Commentary* 24 (2007): 413 (discussing Second Amendment), with ibid., 414 (discussing Fourteenth Amendment).

102. "The hard truth of the matter is that American courts have no intelligible, generally accepted, and consistently applied theory of statutory interpretation." Henry M. Hart, Jr., and Albert M. Sacks, *The Legal Process*, ed. William N. Eskridge, Jr., and Philip P. Frickey (New York: Foundation Press, 1994), 1169.

103. See, e.g., Akhil Reed Amar, "Foreword: The Document and the Doctrine," *Harvard Law Review* 114 (2000): 29 ("Textualism presupposes that the specific constitutional words ultimately enacted were generally chosen with care"); 133 ("The Constitution is wiser than the Court"); cf. Meese, "Speech before the American Bar Association," 53: see generally William Michael Treanor, "Taking Text Too Seriously: Modern Textualism, Original Meaning, and the Case of Amar's Bill of Rights," *Michigan Law Review* 106 (2007): 488 ("textualists stress precise word choice, placement of text in the document, and grammar").

104. Lawson and Seidman, "Jeffersonian Treaty Clause," 7 (emphasis in original). At another point in the same article, the authors refer to their hypothetical construct as "an ideal observer." Ibid., 34. In another article they characterize the fathomer of meaning as "a fully-informed public audience, in possession of all relevant information about the Constitution and the world around it." "The First 'Establishment' Clause," 90.

105. Lawson and Seidman also recognize the possibility of deploying a hypothetical character in the role of author. "Jeffersonian Treaty Clause," 56, 67.

106. Kesavan and Paulsen, "Is West Virginia Unconstitutional?" 398.

107. John F. Manning, "The Absurdity Doctrine," *Harvard Law Review* 116 (2003): 2392–93.

108. Randy E. Barnett, "The Original Meaning of the Commerce Clause," *University of Chicago Law Review* 68 (2001): 105.

109. See U.S. Const. art. I, § 8, cl. 18; Rakove, *Original Meanings*, 84.

110. Several originalists commentators—including Lawson and Seidman—at least recognize that the choice of role players is itself of little or no significance. See, e.g., Nelson, *Originalism and Interpretive Conventions*, 555; Lawson and Seidman, "Jeffersonian Treaty Clause," 56.

111. Lawson and Seidman, "Jeffersonian Treaty Clause," 26–48.

112. Ibid., 39; see David P. Currie, *The Constitution in Congress: The Federalist Period, 1789–1801* (Chicago: University of Chicago Press, 1997), 177; Curtis A. Bradley and Martin S. Flaherty, "Executive Power Essentialism and Foreign Affairs," *Michigan Law Review* 102 (2004): 553–54; see also Joseph J. Ellis, *American Creation: Triumphs and Tragedies at the Founding of the Republic* (New York: Knopf, 2007), 110 (depicting the members of the constitutional convention as "studiously avoiding any clear mandate for what…[the president] should do").

113. Lawson and Seidman, "Jeffersonian Treaty Clause," 39.

114. See, e.g., Fowler V. Harper, Fleming James, Jr., and Oscar S. Gray on Torts, 3rd ed., vol. 3 (New York: Aspen, 1966), 432, 439; Stephen G. Giles, "On Determining Negligence: Hand Formula Balancing, The Reasonable Person Standard and the Jury," *Vanderbilt Law Review* 54 (2001):818; Kenneth W. Simons, "The Hand Formula in the Draft Restatement (Third) of Torts: Encompassing Fairness As Well As Efficiency," *Vanderbilt Law Review* 54 (2001): 930–34.

115. Somewhat puzzlingly, Lawson and Seidman do recognize in one discussion the importance of "the characteristics and interpretive proclivities of…[their] imaginative yet crucial figure," "Jeffersonian Treaty Clause,", 49, but they then proceed as if those characteristics and proclivities can be defined in some obvious or objective fashion. These problems are not avoided by Kesavan and Paulsen's formulation, even though it does not use the word *reasonable*. They give no guidance on what is to be averaged or of what the reader is informed. Filling those gaps also requires normative judgments.

116. See, e.g., Michael Stokes Paulsen, "Is Bill Clinton Unconstitutional? The Case for President Strom Thurmond," *Constitutional Commentary* 13 (1996): 217–22.

117. 381 U.S. 479 (1965); see, e.g., Robert H. Bork, *The Tempting of America* (New York: Free Press 1990), 97–100; Steven Calabresi, "Critical Introduction," in Calabresi, *Originalism*, 10. Whittington writes of "general originalist agreement" on the disdain. *Constitutional Construction*, 37.

118. 381 U.S. at 484–85.

119. Scalia, "Common-Law Courts," 38; see also the discussion of Justice Rehnquist's dissenting opinion in *Nevada v. Hall*, 440 U.S. 410, 432 (1979), in Lawrence B. Solum, Originalism as Transformative Politics," *Tulane Law Review* 63 (1989): 1624–25. On Justice Scalia's embrace of originalism, see Antonin Scalia, Foreword to Calabresi, *Originalism*, 43, 44.

120. See, e.g., Michael J. Klarman, "An Interpretive History of Modern Equal Protection," *Michigan Law Review* 90 (1991): 252; Jed Rubenfeld, *Revolution by Judiciary* (Cambridge, MA: Harvard University Press, 2005), 7; Kermit Roosevelt III, *The Myth of Judicial Activism* (New Haven: Yale University Press, 2006), 68; Earl M. Maltz, "Originalism and the Desegregation Decisions—A Response to Professor McConnell," *Constitutional Commentary* 13 (1996): 223–31; but see Michael W. McConnell, "Originalism and the Desegregation Decisions," *University of Virginia Law Review* 81 (1995): 947–1140.

121. See generally, Erwin Chemerinsky, *Constitutional Law Principles and Policies*, 2nd ed.(Aspen Law and Business, 2002), 648–50.

122. See Solum, "Originalism as Transformative Politics," 1619.

123. Jack M. Balkin, "Abortion and Original Meaning," *Constitutional Commentary* 24 (2007): 293 (2007) (emphasis in original). And yet another "principle" associated with the clause is that "arbitrary and unreasonable distinctions between citizens or persons" was forbidden. See ibid., 315. See generally Robert W. Bennett, " 'Mere' Rationality in Constitutional Law: Judicial Review and Democratic Theory," *California Law Review* 67 (1979): 1049–1103.

124. U.S. Const. amends. V and XIV.

125. See U.S. Const. amend. V.

126. U.S. Const. amend. I.

127. See Reynolds v. Sims, 377 U.S. 533, 589, 590 (1964) (Harlan, J., dissenting).

128. See generally Stephen A. Siegel, "The Federal Government's Power to Enact Color-Conscious Laws: An Originalist Inquiry," *Northwestern University Law Review* 92 (1998): 477–590.

129. See, e.g., Brest, "The Misconceived Quest," 223.

130. See Ronald Dworkin, "The Forum of Principle," *New York University Law Review* 56 (1981): 490; see generally Terrance Sandalow, "Constitutional Interpretation," *Michigan Law Review* 79 (1981): 1035–36.

131. Compare, e.g., McCreary County v. ACLU of Kentucky, 545 U.S. 844, 885, 896–97 (2005) (Scalia, J., dissenting) and McIntyre v. Ohio Elections Comm'n, 514 U.S. 334, 358, 360 (1995) (Thomas, J., concurring) and O'Neill, *Originalism*, 178–79, with District of Columbia v. Heller, 554 U.S. 570 (2008) and Balkin, "Abortion."

132. See page 82.

133. See page 81.

134. See also Michael W. McConnell, "On Reading the Constitution," *Cornell Law Review* 73 (1988): 361–62; Frederick Schauer, "An Essay on Constitutional Language," *UCLA Law Review* 29 (1982): 806–12; Christopher R. Green, "Originalism and the Sense-Reference Distinction," *St. Louis University Law Review* 50 (2006): 555–627 (employing essentially the same distinction in terms of the "sense" of words and their "reference").

135. Balkin, "Abortion," 296; see Scalia, "Response," 149 (refusing to institute unisex toilets and women assault troops does not violate equal protection "because that is not what 'equal protection of the laws' ever meant").

136. E.g., Sandalow, "Constitutional Interpretation," 1046 ("Intentions do not exist in the abstract; they are forged in response to particular circumstances and in the collision of multiple

purposes which impose bounds upon one another"); Rehnquist, "The Notion of a Living Constitution," 699 ("[T]he Civil War Amendments…were enacted in response to practices that the lately seceded states engaged in to discriminate against and mistreat the newly emancipated freed men").

137. John O. McGinnis and Michael Rappaport, "Original Interpretive Principles as the Core of Originalism," *Constitutional Commentary* 24 (2007): 379.

138. Brest, "The Misconceived Quest," 217.

139. See Balkin, "Abortion," 320–21.

140. Sandalow, "Constitutional Interpretation," 1062; see Richard A. Primus, "When Should Original Meanings Matter?" *Michigan Law Review* 107 (2008): 206.

141. See Balkin, "Original Meaning and Constitutional Redemption," 433–34.

142. Ibid., 488; see also 493.

143. See, e.g., Berger, *Government by Judiciary*, 8.

144. See Oregon v. Mitchell, 400 U.S. 112, 152,203 (1970) (Harlan, J., concurring in part and dissenting in part); Nelson, "Originalism and Interpretive Conventions," 590 n. 289. Keith Whittington says, "I take it no originalist questions the validity of including specific practices directly analogous to practices considered by the founders." Whittington, *Constitutional Construction*, 288 n. 80; see Primus, "When Should Original Meanings Matter?" 208.

145. 463 U.S. 783 (1983).

146. U.S. Const. amend. I.

147. 463 U.S. at 789.

148. "It would be hard to count on the fingers of both hands and the toes of both feet, yea, even on the hairs of one's youthful head, the opinions that have in fact been rendered not on the basis of what the Constitution originally meant, but on the basis of what the judges currently thought it desirable for it to mean." Scalia, "Originalism," 852.

149. See, e.g., Gary Lawson, "Mostly Unconstitutional: The Case against Precedent Revisited," *Ave Maria Law Review* 5 (2007): 4.

150. See Whittington, *Constitutional Construction*, 169.

151. See "Remarks of Thomas W. Merrill, Panel on Originalism and Precedent," in Calabresi, *Originalism*, 223, 226.

152. See generally "Can Originalism Be Reconciled with Precedent? A Symposium on Stare Decisis," *Constitutional Commentary* 22 (2005): 257–348.

153. See, e.g., Lawson, "Mostly Unconstitutional"; Randy E. Barnett, "Trumping Precedent with Original Meaning: Not as Radical as It Sounds," *Constitutional Commentary* 22 (2005): 257–270; Michael Stokes Paulsen, "The Intrinsically Corrupting Influence of Precedent," *Constitutional Commentary* 22 (2005): 289–298.

154. See, e.g., Monaghan, "Stare Decisis"; McGinnis and Rappaport, "Original Interpretive Principles," 376; Bork, *The Tempting of America*, 158; Scalia, "Response," 138–39; Peter B. McCutcheon, *Mistakes, Precedent, and The Rise of the Administrative State:* "Toward a Constitutional Theory of the Second Best," *Cornell Law Review* 80 (1994): 18–20; Berger, *Government by Judiciary*, 412–13.

155. Scalia, "Response," 139.

156. Gary Lawson collects some proponents of this position in "Mostly Unconstitutional," 12 n. 39; cf. McGinnis and Rappaport, "Original Interpretive Principles," 375.

157. See Lawson, "On Reading Recipes." I have my doubts that Professor Lawson is able to fence his "factual" observations off from his normative judgments in the way he suggests. See, e.g., Lawson, 2007, 19 ("[T]here was never a golden age in which courts faithfully sought the original meaning of the Constitution through dispassionate application of a sound methodology").

158. See, e.g., Berger, *Government by Judiciary*, 413; Monaghan, "Stare Decisis," 758–59.

159. See Hans v. Louisiana, 134 U.S. 1 (1890); John F. Manning, "The Eleventh Amendment and the Reading of Precise Constitutional Texts," *Yale Law Journal* 113 (2004): 1666–71.

160. U.S. Const. amend. XIV, § 1, echoing language in U.S. Const. art. IV, § 2, cl. 1, and amend. V.

161. See Barnett, *Restoring the Lost Constitution*, 108; compare Whittington, *Constitutional Construction*, 35, with Balkin, "Original Meaning and Constitutional Redemption," 502.

162. Lawson and Seidman, "Originalism as a Legal Enterprise," 74–76.

163. See Daniel A. Farber, "The Originalism Debate: A Guide for the Perplexed," *Ohio State Law Journal* 49 (1989), 1097.

164. See U.S. Const. art. II, § 1, cl. 3. In the case of a tie between candidates commanding majorities, the House's choice was (and is) to be only from among those tied, whereas in the case of failure of any candidate to receive a majority, the choice was originally to be from among the top five.

165. See Bennett, *Taming the Electoral College*, 12–26. Whether the members of the House would have been bound by Burr's insistence that he was not a candidate for president is another question.

166. See Calabresi, *Originalism*, 33. Calabresi tells us that "original meaning textualists have never claimed that Congress understood what it was doing when it passed legal texts." Ibid., 35.

167. See Eric Schnapper, "Affirmative Action and the Legislative History of the Fourteenth Amendment," *Virginia Law Review* 71 (1985): 753–98; Stephen Siegel, "Federal Government's Power."

168. See FDA v. Brown & Williamson Tobacco Corp., 529 U.S. 120 (2000); Blanchard v. Bergeron, 489 U.S. 87, 97 (1989) (Scalia, J., concurring in part and concurring in the judgment).

169. 198 U.S. 45, 74, 76 (1905) (Holmes, J., dissenting); see Stephen M. Griffin, "Rebooting Originalism," *University of Illinois Law Review*, 2008, 1204.

170. See Leib, "Perpetual Anxiety."

171. See Stephen Siegel, "Federal Government's Power," 536 ("[O]riginalists insist that even though new application of old norms is appropriate, derivation of new norms is not").

172. U.S. Const. art. IV, § 4.

173. Pacific States Tel. & Tel. Co. v. Oregon, 223 U.S. 118 (1912); Luther v. Borden, 48 U.S. (7 How.) 1 (1849).

174. See *Federalist Papers*, no. 10; Rakove, *Original Meanings*, 41.

175. See Bennett, "Originalism," 657–61. I think of the republican form of government clause as vague constitutional language, where the historical record initially suggests two leading candidates for a more concrete understanding. Those two candidates suggest at least a surface ambiguity, but if the history is probed more deeply, the ambiguity can be resolved.

176. See pages 109, 111–13.

177. See Balkin, "Original Meaning and Constitutional Redemption," 487.

178. Ibid.; see Mitchell N. Berman, "Originalism and Its Discontents (Plus a Thought or Two about Abortion)," Constitutional Commentary 24 (2007): 384.

179. Mitchell Berman discusses the limited number of "expected applications" originalists, "Originalism and Its Discontents," 386–88, but the dividing lines are far from clear. See McGinnis and Rappaport, "Original Interpretive Principles."

180. O'Neill, *Originalism*.

181. See Sandalow, "Constitutional Interpretation," 1064.

182. See ibid., 1062; cf. Nelson, "Originalism and Interpretive Conventions," 590 n. 289.

183. Yick Wo v. Hopkins, 118 U.S. 356, 368, 374 (1886).

184. *Id.* at 373.

185. See Robert W. Bennett, "Objectivity in Constitutional Law," *University of Pennsylvania Law Review* 132 (1984): 468–72.

186. See Sandalow, "Constitutional Interpretation," 1067.

187. Youngstown Sheet & Tube Co. v. Sawyer, 343 U.S. 579, 634 (1952) (Jackson, J., concurring).

188. William J. Brennan, "Speech to the Text and Teaching Symposium," in Calabresi, *Originalism*, 58.

189. See Sandalow, "Constitutional Interpretation," 1039.

190. See Bennett, *Taming the Electoral College*, 14–17.

191. See Robert Bennett, "Originalist Theories of Constitutional Interpretation," *Cornell Law Review* 73 (1988): 355–58; Bennett, *Taming the Electoral College*, 105–114.

192. Scalia, "Common-Law Courts," 45.

193. Cf. Lawrence Lessig, "Fidelity in Translation," *Texas Law Review* 71 (1993): 1263; Nelson, "Originalism and Interpretive Conventions," 293.

194. Whittington, *Constitutional Construction*, 2.

195. See Edwin Meese, "The Law of the Constitution," speech delivered at Tulane University, October 21, 1986, in Calabresi, *Originalism*, 103.

196. 5 U.S. (Cranch 1) 137 (1803).

197. At one point Whittington seems to recognize the subsidiary role that interpretation plays in what the courts do. He acknowledges, for instance, that "interpretation is concerned with formalizing constitutional meaning in the interest of settling relatively narrow disputes." And at another point he says that "legal writing…occurs in a context of problem solving." *Constitutional Construction*, 6, 60.

198. See generally Bennett, *Taming the Electoral College*, 465–72.

199. Robert H. Bork, "Neutral Principles and Some First Amendment Problems," *Indiana Law Journal* 47 (1971): 13.

200. Bork, *The Tempting of America*, 82.

201. See generally Bennett, "'Mere' Rationality."

202. Bork, "Neutral Principles," 76, 77.

203. Ibid.; Bork, *The Tempting of America*, 81.

204. Pacific States Tel. & Tel. Co. v. Oregon, 223 U.S. 118 (1912).

205. See, e.g., U.S. Term Limits v. Thornton, 514 U.S. 779 (1995); Romer v. Evans, 517 U.S. 620 (1996).

206. See pages 87–91.

207. *Romer*, 517 U.S. at 636, 647 (Scalia, J, dissenting); *Thornton*, 514 U.S. at 845, 883 (Thomas, J, dissenting). For Justice Scalia's embrace of originalism, see "Common-Law Courts." For Justice Thomas's, see McIntyre v. Ohio Elections Comm'n, 514 U.S. 1511, 1525 (1995); see also Barnett, "Scalia's Infidelity," 14–15.

208. See Ellis, *American Creation*, 241; Whittington, *Constitutional Construction*, 125–26; but cf. Balkin, "Abortion," 306 (describing a "principle of democracy" as perhaps "the most frequently articulated principle in constitutional argument," even though it is not "specifically mentioned in the constitutional text").

209. See pages 104–8, 114–20.

210. 554 U.S. 570 (2008).

211. See Scalia, "Common-Law Courts," 43.

212. See page 98.

213. Commentary on *Heller* came fast and furiously, and much of it criticized the use of history in the majority opinion. See, e.g., Richard A. Posner, "In Defense of Looseness," *New Republic*, August 27, 2008; see generally Akhil Reed Amar, "*Heller, HLR*, and Holistic Legal Reasoning," *Harvard Law Review* 122 (2008): 174; Reva B. Siegel, "Dead or Alive: Originalism as Popular Constitutionalism in *Heller*," *Harvard Law Review* 122 (2008): 191–245; Cass R. Sunstein, "Second Amendment Minimalism: *Heller* as *Griswold*," *Harvard Law Review* 122 (2008): 255–57;

William G. Merkel, "*The District of Columbia v. Heller* and Antonin Scalia's Perverse Sense of Originalism," *Lewis and Clark Law Review* 13 (2009): 349–58.

214. Calabresi, Originalism, 22 ("[A]ll three branches of the federal government must have agreed that a matter is well settled for at least a generation").

215. Professor Solum once expressed his doubts as well. "Originalism as Transformative Politics," 1610; see David Couzens Hoy, "A Hermeneutical Critique of the Originalism/Nonoriginalism Distinction," *Northern Kentucky Law Review* 15 (1988): 479–98.

216. The Constitution set out an initial apportionment of the House of Representatives in which the state presumed to have the most population (Virginia) had ten representatives, while the least populous states had one. U.S. Const. art. I, § 2, cl. 3. Today the ratio is in excess of the 53 to one ratio in representation in the House of Representatives.

217. See Wesberry v. Sanders, 376 U.S. 1, 18 (1964); Reynolds v. Sims, 377 U.S. 533, 558 (1964), both quoting Gray v. Sanders, 372 U.S. 368, 381 (1963).

218. See Reynolds v. Sims, 377 U.S. 533, 574 (1964). Just what "population" is to be distributed equally is not entirely clear. See Robert W. Bennett, *Talking It Through: Puzzles of American Democracy* (Ithaca: Cornell University Press 2002), 66–84.

219. Compare Department of Commerce v. Montana, 503 U.S. 442 (1992).

220. U.S. Const. art. IV, § 3, cl. 1.

221. See Kesavan and Paulsen, "Is West Virginia Unconstitutional?" 297–301.

222. Ibid., 294, 300.

223. See pages 104–8.

224. See Kesavan and Paulsen, "Interpretive Force," 1132 (emphasis added).

225. See page 98.

226. U.S. Const. art. I, § 6, cl. 2.

227. An Internet piece reports that Michael Paulsen concludes that Senator Clinton is flatly ineligible, unless perhaps the use of the male pronoun *he* limits the reach of the constitutional provision to male members of Congress. Kriston Capps, "Hillary Clinton, the Saxbe Fix, and the Battle of Pelennor Fields," December 6, 2008, http://dcist.com. See Michael Stokes Paulsen, "Is Lloyd Bentsen Unconstitutional?," *Stanford Law Review* 46 (1994): 909–11. For an instance where the United States Supreme Court skirted the literal reach of a constitutional provision (the compact clause) in the name of "the object of the constitutional provision," see Virginia v. Tennessee, 148 U.S. 503, 518 (1893).

228. U.S. Const. art. I, § 2, cl. 3.

229. Const. art. II, § 1, cl. 1; art. I, § 3, cl. 1; art. I, § 2, cl. 1.

230. U.S. Const. art. I, § 2, cl. 5; art. I, § 3, cl. 6.

231. U.S. Const. art. I, § 3, cl. 6.

232. U.S. Const. art. V.

233. See, e.g., Mark V. Tushnet, *Taking the Constitution Away from the Courts* (Princeton: Princeton University Press, 2000), 154–76.

234. In a speech to the House of Commons on November 11, 1947, Churchill said, "Many forms of government have been tried, and will be tried in this world of sin and woe. No one pretends that democracy is perfect or all-wise. Indeed, it has been said that democracy is the worst form of government except all those other forms that have been tried from time to time." See *Oxford Dictionary of Quotations*, 3rd ed. (Oxford: Oxford University Press, 1980), 150.

235. Gordon S. Wood, "Comment" in Scalia, *A Matter of Interpretation*, 59.

236. See Balkin, "Abortion," 307, 310.

237. U.S. Const. art. II, § 2, cl. 2; art. I, § 9, cl. 7; art. III, § 2, cl. 2.

238. Mark A. Graber, "Foreword: From the Countermajoritarian Difficulty to Juristocracy and the Political Construction of Judicial Power," *Maryland Law Review* 65 (2006): 6.

239. Balkin, "Abortion," 303, 352.

240. Sandalow, "Constitutional Interpretation," 1061.

241. Calabresi, *Originalism*, 13. Brest makes the same point without the normative flavor in "The Misconceived Quest," 225. Lawson tells us that "there was never a golden age in which courts faithfully sought the original meaning of the Constitution, through dispassionate application of a sound methodology." Lawson, "Mostly Unconstitutional," 19. He also says that "[i]t is relatively rare that the justices even look for the Constitution's original meaning, much less look for it correctly." Ibid., 21.

242. Calabresi, *Originalism*, 40.

243. John O. McGinnis and Michael B. Rappaport, "A Pragmatic Defense of Originalism," *Northwestern University Law Review* 101 (2007): 393.

Living with Originalism

1. Friedrich Waismann, "Verifiability," *Proceedings of the Aristotelian Society* 19 (1945): 119–50.

2. Paul Brest, *Processes of Constitutional Decisionmaking* (New York: Little, Brown, 1975), 41–44.

3. Adam Samaha, "Dead Hand Arguments and Constitutional Interpretation," *Columbia Law Review* 108 (2008): 606–80.

4. Youngstown Sheet & Tube Co. v. Sawyer, 343 U.S. 579 (1952).

5. Fay v. New York, 332 U.S. 261, 332 U.S. 282-284 (1947).

6. Sanford Levinson, *Our Undemocratic Constitution: Where the Constitution Goes Wrong (And How We the People Can Correct It)* (New York: Oxford University Press 2006).

7. See Cass R. Sunstein, "Burkean Minimalism," *Michigan Law Review* 105 (2006): 353–408.

8. See Stephen M. Griffin, "Rebooting Originalism," *University of Illinois Law Review*, 2008, 1185–1223; Mitchell N. Berman, "Originalism Is Bunk," *New York University Law Review* 84 (2009): 35.

9. Paul Brest, "The Misconceived Quest for the Original Understanding," *Boston University Law Review* 60 (1980): 204–38.

Are We All Living Constitutionalists Now?

1. See pages 35, 71–73.

2. It is not clear, however, that all originalists who distinguish between interpretation and construction attach the same meaning to the latter notion. See Keith E. Whittington, *Constitutional Construction: Divided Powers and Constitutional Meaning* (Cambridge, MA: Harvard University Press, 1999) 513; Randy E. Barnett, *Restoring the Lost Constitution: The Presumption of Liberty* (Princeton: Princeton University Press, 2004), 121–130.

3. Raoul Berger is a plausible candidate for one who held that old originalist position. See Raoul Berger, *Government by Judiciary* (Cambridge, MA: Harvard University Press, 1977), 283–99.

4. I cannot resist the temptation to point out how natural it can be to use varying phraseology to express a single point and also how a reader might conceivably find nuances of difference in Solum's different formulations, even though in all likelihood he did not mean to imply any differences. One might think, for instance that exceptional circumstances would occur more frequently than extraordinary ones. Both phrases are vague, but that does not preclude the possibility that they are suggestive of different ranges. I am left to wonder whether Solum would prefer that we give the several phrases the kindred meanings he likely intended or the (multitude of) disparate meanings we might embrace. We will return below to related issues in constitutional interpretation.

5. 347 U.S. 483 (1954).

6. Randy E. Barnett, "Scalia's Infidelity: A Critique of Faint-Hearted Originalism," *University of Cincinnati Law Review* 75 (2006): 7–24.

7. District of Columbia v. Heller, 554 U.S. 570 (2008).

8. See page 84.

9. See also pp. 4, 16, 19, 23.

10. Randy Barnett may agree with Solum about this. See Barnett, "Trumping Precedent with Original Meaning: Not as Radical as It Sounds," *Constitutional Commentary* 22 (2005): 268 ("Most terms are not ambiguous in context"). So may other self-styled originalists. See Vasan Kesavan and Michael Stokes Paulsen, "Is West Virginia Constitutional?" *California Law Review* 90 (2002): 333 ("Article IV, Section 3 should lend itself to one best reading").

11. See page 53.

12. It is not at all hard to find other examples. In addition to the Second Amendment question discussed below, consider (1) the relationship between Article III's good behavior provision for judges and the "high crimes and misdemeanors" justification for impeachment found in Section 4 of Article II (see Saikrishna Prakash and Steven D. Smith, "How to Remove a Federal Judge," *Yale Law Journal* 116 (2006): 72–137; (2) whether in light of the Twelfth Amendment language and that of Article I, Section 3, Clause 4, the vice president has a vote in the Senate when there is an even split in the backup procedure for choosing a vice president necessitated by an indecisive (vice presidential) outcome in the electoral college (see William Josephson, "Senate Election of the Vice President and House of Representatives Election of the President," *University of Pennsylvania Journal of Constitutional Law* 11 (2009): 619); (3) whether the combination of Article III and the Sixth Amendment leaves room for a defendant to waive his right to a jury trial in criminal cases; (4) whether under the Twelfth Amendment, the House is to choose the president from among four or more candidates where no one has a majority of the electoral votes and two or more candidates are tied for third place in that count; (5) whether the ex post facto clauses of Sections 9 and 10 of Article I apply only to criminal laws or more generally (see Caleb Nelson, "Originalism and Interpretive Conventions," *University of Chicago Law Review* 70 (2003): 580 n. 246); and (6) an example to which I was alerted by my colleague Marty Redish: whether the due process clause of the Fifth Amendment qualifies the possibility introduced in Section 9 of Article I that the writ of habeas corpus might be suspended in contexts where the writ is sought not for collateral review of incarceration but to challenge incarceration when there has been no prior "process" to speak of. Regarding the last example, Professor Redish assumes that the later in time of the two provisions—the amendment—governs, and for that reason he finds no unresolvable ambiguity. But if the relationship between the original constitutional text and amendments is treated as looser than that, it is certainly possible to find ambiguity. See also Kesavan and Paulsen, "Is West Virginia Unconstitutional?" 371.

13. See Ethan J. Lieb, "Why Supermajoritarianism Does Not Illuminate the Interpretive Debate between Originalists and Non-Originalists," *Northwestern University Law Review* 101 (2007): 1915.

14. If one could confidently conclude that there were no significantly disparate authorial intentions, I would accede to any consensus view about meaning among the authors. I would, in other words, find the language had a definitive meaning, not because of some claimed objective linguistic fact of the matter but because of an authorial consensus. And note that a consensus about meaning could include ambiguity. It is even conceivable that Solum might agree that an authorial consensus should be dispositive about meaning, since that would seem to deal with one of his most important "success conditions" for "speaker's meaning." But I put that possibility aside to get to the crux of what divides us.

15. U.S. Const. art. I, § 8, cl. 11.

16. See U.S. Const. art. III, § 3, cl. 2.

17. U.S. Const. art. I, § 8, cls. 10, 11.

18. See Eugene Kontorovich, "The 'Define and Punish' Clause and the Limits of Universal Jurisdiction," *Northwestern University Law Review* 103 (2009): 149–203.

19. See Barnett, "Scalia's Infidelity," xx.

Suggested Readings

Key Works

There is a vast literature on originalism and living constitutionalism. The works that are listed in this section of the bibliography are among the most important to the development of these two approaches to constitutional interpretation.

Balkin, Jack M. "Abortion and Original Meaning." *Constitutional Commentary* 24 (2007): 291–352.

———. "Original Meaning and Constitutional Redemption." *Constitutional Commentary* 24 (2007): 427–532.

———. "An Originalism for Nonoriginalists." *Loyola Law Review* 45 (1999): 611–654.

Barnett, Randy E. *Restoring the Lost Constitution: The Presumption of Liberty*. Princeton: Princeton University Press, 2004.

Berger, Raoul. *Government by Judiciary*. Cambridge, Massachusetts: Harvard University Press, 1977.

Berman, Mitchell N. "Originalism Is Bunk." *New York University Law Review* 84 (2009): 1–96.

Bobbitt, Philip. *Constitutional Fate: Theory of the Constitution*. Oxford: Oxford University Press, 1982. A revised edition was published by Oxford University Press in 2006.

Bork, Robert H. "Neutral Principles and Some First Amendment Problems." *Indiana Law Journal* 47 (1971): 1–35.

Brennan, William J., Jr. "The Constitution of the United States: Contemporary Ratification." *South Texas Law Review* 27 (1986): 433–445.

Brest, Paul. "The Misconceived Quest for the Original Understanding." *Boston University Law Review* 60 (1980): 204–238.

Breyer, Stephen. *Active Liberty: Interpreting Our Democratic Constitution*. New York: Vintage, 2005.

Calabresi, Steven G., ed. *Originalism: A Quarter-Century of Debate*. Washington, DC: Regnery, 2007. Includes speeches by Attorney General Meese and Justice William Brennan and conference presentations by academics.

Farber, Daniel A. "The Originalism Debate: A Guide for the Perplexed." *Ohio State Law Journal* 49 (1989): 1085–1106.

Greenberg, Mark D., and Harry Litman. "The Meaning of Original Meaning." *Georgetown Law Journal* 86 (1998): 574–619.

Griffin, Stephen M. "Rebooting Originalism." *University of Illinois Law Review* 2008 (2008): 1185–1223.

Kay, Richard S. "Adherence to the Original Intentions in Constitutional Adjudication: Three Objections and Responses." *Northwestern University Law Review* 82 (1988): 226–292.

Kesavan, Vasan, and Michael Stokes Paulsen. "The Interpretive Force of the Constitution's Secret Drafting History." *Georgetown Law Journal* 91 (2003): 1113–1214.

Lawson, Gary. "On Reading Recipes...and Constitutions." *Georgetown University Law Journal* 85 (1997): 1823–1836.

McConnell, Michael W. "Originalism and the Desegregation Decisions." *Virginia Law Review* 81 (1995): 947–1140.

McGinnis, John O., and Michael B. Rappaport. "Original Methods Originalism: A New Theory of Interpretation and the Case against Construction." *Northwestern University Law Review* 103 (2009): 751–802.

Meese, Edwin III. "Toward a Jurisprudence of Original Intent." *Harvard Journal of Law and Public Policy* 11 (1988): 5–12.

Meyler, Bernadette. "Towards a Common Law Originalism." *Stanford Law Review* 59 (2006): 551–600.

Powell, H. Jefferson. "The Original Understanding of Original Intent." *Harvard Law Review* 98 (1985): 885–948.

Rehnquist, William. "The Notion of a Living Constitution." *Texas Law Review* 54 (1976): 693–706.

Scalia, Antonin. *A Matter of Interpretation: Federal Courts and the Law*. Princeton: Princeton University Press, 1997. Includes an essay by Justice Scalia and comments by Amy Gutmann, Gordon S. Wood, Laurence H. Tribe, Mary Ann Glendon, and Ronald Dworkin.

———. "Originalism: The Lesser Evil." *University of Cincinnati Law Review* 57 (1989): 849–866.

Strauss, David A. *The Living Constitution*. Oxford: Oxford University Press, 2010.

Whittington, Keith E. *Constitutional Construction: Divided Powers and Constitutional Meaning*. Cambridge, MA: Harvard University Press, 1999.

———. *Constitutional Interpretation: Textual Meaning, Original Intent, and Judicial Review*. Lawrence: University Press of Kansas, 1991.
———. "The New Originalism." *Georgetown Journal of Law and Public Policy* 2 (2004): 599–613.

Other Selected Works

There are literally thousands of books and articles that deal with the themes in constitutional theory raised by the debates between originalists and living constitutionalists. The works listed here provide a starting point for deeper research and reading.

Ackerman, Bruce. "The Living Constitution." *Harvard Law Review* 120 (2007): 1737–1812.
———. *We the People*. Vol. 1, *Foundations*. Cambridge, MA: Belknap Press, 1981.
———. *We the People*. Vol. 2, *Transformations*. Cambridge: Belknap Press, 1998.
Amar, Akhil Reed. *America's Constitution: A Biography*. New York: Random House, 2005.
———. "Rethinking Originalism: Original Intent for Liberals (and for Conservatives and Moderates, Too)." *Slate*, September 21, 2005. http://www.slate.com/id/2126680.
———. "The Supreme Court, 1999 Term—Foreword: The Document and the Doctrine." *Harvard Law Review* 114 (2000): 26–134.
Barber, Sotirios A., and James E. Fleming. *Constitutional Interpretation: The Basic Questions*. Oxford: Oxford University Press, 2007.
Barnett, Randy E. "The Original Meaning of the Commerce Clause." *University of Chicago Law Review* 68 (2001): 101–147.
———. "Scalia's Infidelity: A Critique of Faint-Hearted Originalism." *University of Cincinnati Law Review* 75 (2006): 7–24.
———. "Trumping Precedent with Original Meaning: Not as Radical as It Sounds." *Constitutional Commentary* 22 (2005): 257–270.
Beard, Charles. "The Living Constitution." *Annals of the American Academy of Political and Social Science* 185 (1936): 29–34.
Belz, Herman A. *Living Constitution or Fundamental Law? American Constitutionalism in Historical Perspective*. Lanham, MD: Rowman and Littlefield, 1998.
Bennett, Robert W. "Objectivity in Constitutional Law." *University of Pennsylvania Law Review* 132 (1984): 445–496.
———. "Originalism: Lessons from Things That Go without Saying." *San Diego Law Review* 45 (2008): 645–672.
———. "Originalist Theories of Constitutional Interpretation." *Cornell Law Review* 73 (1988): 355–358.
Berman, Mitchell N. "Originalism and Its Discontents (Plus a Thought or Two about Abortion)." *Constitutional Commentary* 24 (2007): 383–404.
BeVier, Lillian R. "The Integrity and Impersonality of Originalism." *Harvard Journal of Law and Public Policy* 19 (1996): 283–291.
Bickel, Alexander M. *The Least Dangerous Branch: Supreme Court at the Bar of Politics*. 2nd ed. New Haven: Yale University Press, 1986.
———. *The Morality of Consent*. New Haven: Yale University Press, 1977.
Brest, Paul. "The Fundamental Rights Controversy: The Essential Contradictions of Normative Constitutional Scholarship." *Yale Law Journal* 90 (1981): 1063–1109.

Bronaugh, Richard, Peter Barton, and Aileen Kavanagh. "The Idea of a Living Constitution." *Canadian Journal of Law and Jurisprudence* 16 (2003): 55–89.

Brown, Rebecca L. "History for the Non-Originalist." *Harvard Journal of Law and Public Policy* 26 (2003): 69–81.

Calabresi, Steven G. "The Originalist and Normative Case against Judicial Activism: A Reply to Professor Barnett." *Michigan Law Review* 103 (2005): 1081–1098.

Colby, Thomas B., and Peter J. Smith. "Living Originalism." *Duke Law Journal* 59 (2009): 239–307.

Dorf, Michael C. "Integrating Normative and Descriptive Constitutional Theory: The Case of Original Meaning." *Georgetown Law Journal* 85 (1997): 1765–1822.

Dworkin, Ronald. "The Arduous Virtue of Fidelity: Originalism, Scalia, Tribe, and Nerve." *Fordham Law Review* 65 (1997): 1249–1268.

———. *Law's Empire*. Cambridge, MA: Belknap Press, 1986.

———. *A Matter of Principle*. Cambridge, MA: Harvard University Press, 1985.

Ely, John Hart. *Democracy and Distrust: A Theory of Judicial Review*. Cambridge, MA: Harvard University Press, 1980.

Fallon, Richard H., Jr. "A Constructivist Coherence Theory of Constitutional Interpretation." *Harvard Law Review* 100 (1987): 1192–1286.

———. "How to Choose a Constitutional Theory." *California Law Review* 87 (1999): 535–579.

Fleming, James E. "The Balkanization of Originalism." *Maryland Law Review* 67 (2007): 10–13.

Friedman, Barry. *The Will of the People: How Public Opinion Has Influenced the Supreme Court and Shaped the Meaning of the Constitution*. New York: Farrar, Straus, and Giroux, 2009.

Gillman, Howard. "The Collapse of Constitutional Originalism and the Rise of the Notion of the 'Living Constitution' in the Course of American State-Building." *Studies in American Political Development* 11 (1997): 191–247.

Goldford, Dennis J. *The American Constitution and the Debate over Originalism*. Cambridge: Cambridge University Press, 2005.

Green, Christopher R. "Originalism and the Sense-Reference Distinction." *St. Louis University Law Journal* 50 (2006): 555–627.

Greene, Jamal. "Selling Originalism." *Georgetown Law Journal* 97 (2009): 657–721.

Harrison, John. "Forms of Originalism and the Study of History." *Harvard Journal of Law and Public Policy* 26 (2003): 83–94.

Kavanagh, Aileen. "Original Intention, Enacted Text, and Constitutional Interpretation." *American Journal of Jurisprudence* 47 (2002): 255–298.

Kramer, Larry. *The People Themselves: Popular Constitutionalism and Judicial Review*. Oxford: Oxford University Press, 2005.

Lash, Kurt. "Originalism, Popular Sovereignty, and Reverse Stare Decisis," *Virginia Law Review* 93 (2007): 1437–1481.

Lawson, Gary, and Guy Seidman. "Originalism as a Legal Enterprise." *Constitutional Commentary* 23 (2006): 47–80.

Leib, Ethan J. "The Perpetual Anxiety of Living Constitutionalism." *Constitutional Commentary* 24 (2007): 353–370.

Lessig, Lawrence. "Fidelity in Translation." *Texas Law Review* 71 (1993): 1165–1268.

McBain, Howard Lee. *The Living Constitution: A Consideration of the Realities and Legends of Our Fundamental Law.* New York: Macmillan, 1927.

McGinnis, John O., and Michael B. Rappaport. "A Pragmatic Defense of Originalism." *Northwestern University Law Review* 101 (2007): 383–396.

Miller, Charles A. *The Supreme Court and the Uses of History.* Cambridge, MA: Belknap Press, 1969.

Monaghan, Henry Paul. "Stare Decisis and Constitutional Adjudication." *Columbia Law Review* 88 (1988): 723–773.

Nelson, Caleb. "Originalism and Interpretive Conventions." *University of Chicago Law Review* 70 (2003): 519–598.

O'Neill, Johnathan. *Originalism in American Law and Politics: A Constitutional History.* Baltimore: John Hopkins University Press, 2005.

Paulsen, Michael Stokes. "The Intrinsically Corrupting Influence of Precedent." *Constitutional Commentary* 22 (2005): 289–298.

Post, Robert, and Reva Siegel. "Originalism as a Political Practice: The Right's Living Constitution." *Fordham Law Review* 75 (2006): 545–574.

Rakove, Jack. *Original Meanings: Politics and Ideas in the Making of the Constitution.* New York: Knopf, 1996.

Samaha, Adam. "Originalism's Expiration Date." *Cardozo Law Review* 30 (2008): 1295–1365.

Solum, Lawrence B. "*District of Columbia v. Heller* and Originalism." *Northwestern University Law Review* 103 (2009): 923–981.

———. "Incorporation and Originalist Theory." *Journal of Contemporary Legal Issues* 18 (2009): 409–446.

———. "Semantic Originalism." Illinois Public Law Research Paper No. 07-24 (November 22, 2008), http://ssrn.com/abstract=1120244.

———. "The Supreme Court in Bondage: Constitutional Stare Decisis, Legal Formalism, and the Future of Unenumerated Rights." *University of Pennsylvania Journal of Constitutional Law* 9 (2006): 155–208.

Strang, Lee J., "Originalism and the 'Challenge of Change': Abduced-Principle Originalism and Other Mechanisms by Which Originalism Sufficiently Accommodates Changed Social Conditions." *Hastings Law Journal* 60 (2009): 927–995.

Sunstein, Cass R. "Five Theses on Originalism." *Harvard Journal of Law and Public Policy* 19 (1996): 311–315.

Tushnet, Mark. "*Heller* and the New Originalism." *Ohio State Law Journal* 69 (2008): 609–624.

———. *Taking the Constitution Away from the Courts.* Princeton: Princeton University Press, 1999.

Winkler, Adam. "A Revolution Too Soon: Woman Suffragists and the 'Living Constitution.'" *New York University Law Review* 76 (2001): 1456–1525.

INDEX

CPSIA information can be obtained
at www.ICGtesting.com
Printed in the USA
LVHW091746020719
623008LV00004B/45/P

9 780801 447938